KOREAN
UNIFICATION

RELATED POTOMAC TITLES

Defiant Failed State: The North Korean Threat to International Security
by Bruce E. Bechtol Jr.

Red Rogue: The Persistent Challenge of North Korea
by Bruce E. Bechtol Jr.

Korea on the Brink: A Memoir of Political Intrigue and Military Crisis
by John A. Wickham

KOREAN UNIFICATION

Inevitable Challenges

JACQUES L. FUQUA JR.

Potomac Books
Washington, D.C.

Library of Congress Cataloging-in-Publication Data
Fuqua, Jacques L.
  Korean unification : inevitable challenges / Jacques L. Fuqua Jr. — 1st ed.
       p. cm.
  Includes bibliographical references and index.
  ISBN 978-1-59797-279-6 (hardcover)
  ISBN 978-1-61234-481-2 (electronic edition)
  1. Korean reunification question (1945–) 2. Korea
(South)—Relations—Korea (North) 3. Korea (North)—Relations—Korea
(South) I. Title.
  DS917.444.F87 2011
  327.519305195—dc23
                                                        2011023380

Potomac Books
22841 Quicksilver Drive
Dulles, Virginia 20166

First Edition

10 9 8 7 6 5 4 3 2 1

To a leading scholar of East Asian studies, Professor Richard Rubinger (Indiana University, Bloomington), who provided invaluable mentoring and guidance, but most importantly whose commitment to excellence in scholarship sparked in me a lifelong intellectual curiosity.

And to Dr. Patrick O'Meara (Indiana University, Bloomington), whose knowledge and wisdom, and patient willingness to share both, has contributed immeasurably to any success I might enjoy.

And finally, to my parents, Jacques and Barbara Fuqua, who have been a constant guiding light throughout my life.

Contents

KOREAN PENINSULA

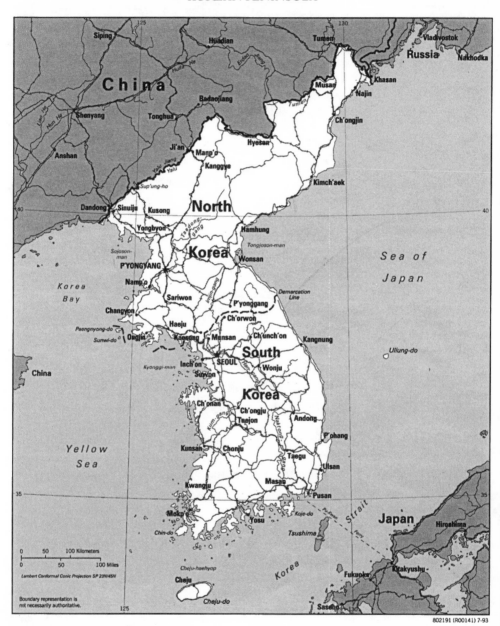

Abbreviations

CBM	confidence building measure
DMZ	Demilitarized Zone
DPRK	Democratic People's Republic of Korea (North Korea)
FDI	foreign direct investment
GDP	gross domestic product
KEDO	Korean Peninsula Energy Development Organization
MFN	most favored nation
NBLS	National Basic Livelihood Security
NGO	non-governmental organization
NHI	National Health Insurance
NLL	Northern Limit Line
OECD	Organization of Economic Cooperation and Development
PPP	purchasing power parity
PSI	Proliferation Security Initiative
ROK	Republic of Korea (South Korea)
WFP	World Food Program
WHO	World Health Organization
WMD	weapon of mass destruction

Chronology
of Korean History

Date	Dynasty/Activity
47 CE–562 CE	Kaya (also referred to as Mimana in Japanese)★
57 BCE–668 CE	Three Kingdoms Silla (57 BCE–668 CE) Koguryo (37 BCE–668 CE) Paekche (18 BCE–663 CE)
698–926	North–South States Period Unified Silla (668–935) Balhae (698–926)
892–936	Later Three Kingdoms
936–1392	Koryo Dynasty
1392–1910	Choson Dynasty Korean Empire established (1897–1910)
1910–1945	Japanese colonial rule
1945–1948	Occupation and division of peninsula
1948	Establishment of the Republic of Korea (South Korea) and Democratic People's Republic of Korea (North Korea)

★ Kaya was a confederacy comprising individual polities that developed strong trade relations with northern Kyushu (Japan) and served as a major purveyor of culture and technology. The area was ultimately absorbed by Silla.

Introduction

Webster's Unabridged Dictionary defines "reunite" as the act of "uniting again, as after separation." This, of course, is the concept that underlies "reunification" of the Korean peninsula—making whole again a land divided in the immediate aftermath of the Second World War, and that remains so to this day. Purportedly a long-standing goal shared by Korean people on both sides of the Demilitarized Zone (DMZ) and the governments that represent them, unification is still espoused as one of the top inter-Korean imperatives. Yet after over sixty years of division, unification appears as distant as it ever has, subject to the vagaries of inter-Korean polemics and North Korean miscreancy. Thus, bringing the halves of the peninsula together will be more than an exercise of the respective governments on the peninsula—the Republic of Korea (South Korea) and the Democratic People's Republic of Korea (North Korea)—declaring Korea to be a unified polity once again. Rather, it will be a complex, multi-staged and multi-dimensional process, buffeted by multiple variables. The concept and process of unification requires undertaking two broad tasks: creating a single Korean polity and constructing a unified Korean nation, which are two distinctly different undertakings. The former addresses the need to integrate disparate political and economic systems; the latter connotes a need to repatriate and assimilate people and cultures. While this book tangentially touches on the former in order to provide important context, its primary focus is addressing the tasks, challenges, and potential impediments associated with the latter.

Vast differences in political, economic, cultural, and social constructs that exist between the two Koreas must be addressed and resolved in order to successfully pursue unification. High among the priorities, of course, will be aligning or discarding incongruent political and economic systems: the North Korean regime's socialist system of governance and its command economy versus South Korea's democratic political system and capitalist construct. The task of creating a single polity embraces these integrative functions of unification. There are nearly innumerable challenges associated with integrating two such antithetical systems, but failure to successfully navigate them will undermine any unification effort. This, however, represents only half of the equation. The other half, perhaps fundamental and intrinsic to any other process associated with unification, is the task of nation-building. Within the context of this book, nation-building refers to the assimilation and integration of the Korean people themselves, the citizens of South and North Korea, who will come to compose any unified Korean state. The two Koreas have been socially and culturally divided for over sixty years and their citizens have evolved into two very different peoples—their respective values, cultures, languages, and socialization processes exist at opposite ends of a continuum. Thus, the twin tasks of creating a single Korean polity and building the Korean nation are mutually supportive and interdependent and must be undertaken simultaneously. Sequentially addressing them would at best exponentially complicate the unification process; in the worst-case scenario, it could derail any such efforts.

By most accounts, if and when unification is achieved, it will be on South Korea's terms as it has a stronger economy, a comparatively more vibrant society, and greater stability in the foundations of its political ideology. Yet such an outcome carries with it huge responsibilities and costs. Former North Korean citizens will need to be "de-programmed" as *Juche* citizens and required to learn how to live and function within a capitalist society, an outcome vehemently eschewed by most who subscribe to Juche ideology.[1] They will also need to learn the South Korean dialect of the "Korean" language, now nearly unintelligible to most North Koreans. With limited exposure to the technological and societal benefits most South Koreans take for granted in their daily lives, former North Korean citizens will also need to learn about banks, cell phones, computers, automated teller machines, modern kitchen appliances, and an array of other "foreign" things. Problems associated with health, education, employment, and other related issues will also require resolution if unification is to be successful. Failure to resolve fundamental issues like these in a post-unified Korea could create a debilitative two-class society similar to the political divisions that presently separate Koreans, except along cultural and social lines. In effect, unification will require that former North Korean citizens be re-made in order to fit within the South Korean social and cultural context.

Proponents of unification typically invoke the argument that as all Koreans are brothers and share a common history, current disparities in their respective ways of life are not potentially injuriously discordant and are consequently given rather short shrift. As a result, brotherhood justifies painting the ultimate unification of the peninsula with a brush of inevitability. Consider the comments of one scholar:

> The Korean peninsula has not seen a united and independent nation for the last eighty years (1919-1990). The Korean people are, however, determined to put an end to this unhappy chapter in their history before this century fades away and to welcome the twenty-first century as a proud and unified nation. When we add to the relatively long, historical continuity of Korea, the striking ethnic homogeneity of the Korean people, and their common language, the imperative of unification becomes more compelling.[2]

Yet a closer review of Korean history may not support such an optimistic analysis. While Korea was unified into a single polity as early as the Koryo period in 936, from the beginning of the fifteenth century the peninsula was divided de facto into northern and southern regions, resembling the peninsula's current division, only on a social and cultural basis, rather than a political one. During the Choson period, southern Korea was considered the advanced culture and served as the seat of power for the Yi Dynasty (1392–1910); northern Korea was considered culturally backward and its inhabitants as socially lesser beings, an outcome directly attributable to the policies put in place by the Choson court. Indeed, with the exception of the relatively brief period of time during which Korea was colonized by Japan (1910–1945) and made whole again, Korea's history since about the fifteenth century has been one of a divided nation, either de facto or de jure.[3]

This bit of historical irony has applicability to current discussions of unification because contemporary conditions mirror past peninsular circumstances. North Koreans, when compared to their southern brethren, are on whole considered bereft of any real culture save the political ideology they are required to absorb by the North Korean regime. Most of its citizens are indigent; lag educationally because pedagogy and content are ideologically derived; lack usable job skills; and generally, do not fit within the capitalist construct. Add to this the growing ambivalence many South Koreans feel toward North Korean migrants, and in some cases outright prejudice, and one finds that the necessary precursors are in place to again cast Koreans living on the northern half of the peninsula as the Korean "other," if and when unification is achieved.

South Korean government officials have been presented a unique opportunity to develop and test policies that might prove useful under a unification scenario. It comes in the form of North Korean migrants, roughly 20,000 of whom have successfully fled North Korea and presently live within South Korea's borders. While their official status is unclear outside South Korea—the North Korean government refers to them as defectors, the United States and United Nations label them as refugees, and China treats them as economic migrants who can rightfully be returned to North Korea. The South Korean government considers them to be citizens and "new settlers," or *saeteomin*. Despite their new citizenship, however, full assimilation is not coming easily as they are socially, culturally, and educationally ill equipped to effectively function in South Korean society. South Korean government officials are, as they become more conversant in the challenges confronted by saeteomin, developing new policies to help facilitate their assimilation, but progress is slow and costly. Consequently, models developed to date do not show any real promise for broader application when potentially millions of northern Koreans must be ministered under unification.

This book focuses primarily on the challenges officials of a unified Korean government will face in repatriating millions of former North Korean citizens and assimilating them into broader Korean society based on a South Korean model of governance. Predicting what will occur under unification, or for that matter when it will occur, is a nearly impossible task; there are too many potential variables. By examining the challenges saeteomin must presently negotiate, however, it is possible to at least identify major issues requiring resolution if there is to be any hope of achieving full and successful unification.

The first half of this book offers historical background that helps provide context for the Korean cultural and social experience while identifying important "through lines" that have a potential impact on contemporary discussions of unification. The second half addresses key issues associated with the repatriation of former North Korean citizens under a unification scenario—assimilation, employability, and education numbering chief among them. The experiences of saeteomin also figure prominently as important inferences and "lessons learned" can be drawn from how they have assimilated or, in some cases, have failed to assimilate into broader South Korean society.

What this book does not presume to address is whether or not peninsular unification should be pursued. This is a question that can only be answered by the governments of South and North Korea and their respective citizens. Rather, the scope is limited to identifying what repatriation factors should be considered and addressed to help ensure the greatest potential for success if indeed peninsular unification is to be pursued.

PART I

1

Deconstructing the Unification Issue

Since the foundation of the South Korean state in 1948, the rhetoric of unification has occupied a prominent place in its official vocabulary. Unification with the North was always presented as the great national goal, which any government should pursue at any cost.

—*Andrei Lankov*[1]

Despite endless prognostications to the contrary, the decades-long status quo on the Korean peninsula remains intact, one of the final clinging vestiges of the Cold War (the other, of course, being Cuba), defined by an arbitrarily imposed dividing line between the two Koreas. Since the peninsula's bifurcation at the end of World War II, first into U.S. and Soviet occupation zones and then as two sovereign nations in 1948, Korean leaders and people alike, on both sides of the DMZ, have contemplated some form of peninsular unification. Belief in its inevitability has in fact achieved near dogmatic following among many Koreans. Andrei Lankov notes, "For decades, the myth of unification as Korea's supreme goal has been enshrined in the official mythology of both nations. The lip service to this myth is still paid by virtually all political forces in both Koreas."[2]

Thus, while some amount of shared agreement exists in both South and North Korea as to the inescapability of unification, such agreement suffers, as one might suspect, from notable variance and discord over the form and process any amalgamation might ultimately take. The root of such differences is fairly straightforward and has depended on two factors: 1) which side of the peninsula proffers a unification formula, and 2) the period during which any national unification formula has been articulated. For example, in the case of South Korea, discussion of unification during the mid-twentieth century was more apt to be accompanied by the well-worn vituperative rhetoric of the Cold War era rather than the approach of pursuing broader engagement initiatives characteristic of the country's policies during the Kim Dae-jung and Roh Moo-hyun administrations from 1998 to 2008. Emblematic of earlier postwar strategies is the unwavering commitment of South Korea's first president, Syngman Rhee (July 1948–April 1960), to peninsular unification under his policy of "March north and unify Korea."

North Korea's case, on the other hand, is replete with historical examples of its overtly combative approach to unification and inter-Korean engagement, among which, of course, the Korean War stands as the most prominent manifestation. Other examples of equal audacity abound, if not in scope then certainly in concept and spirit. The two assassination attempts on the life of South Korean president Park Chung-hee on January 21, 1968, and August 15, 1974, respectively; the 1983 attempted assassination of former president Chun Doo-hwan in Yangon (Rangoon), Myanmar (Burma) in which twenty-one people were killed and another forty-six injured; and the 1987 bombing of Korean Airlines flight 858 stand in particular notoriety among the North Korean regime's long list of misdeeds.[3] Presently, North Korea concerns itself more with geopolitical issues and regime survival than with issues of national unification, although lip service continues to be paid to this end.

Emphasis on the various approaches to unification and the models to which they have given rise on either side of the DMZ has led to unidimensional treatment of the topic and tends to mask the true enormity of the task. Discussions usually advance no further than how South and North Korean unification formulae, confederal or federal, respectively might contribute to or hinder political and economic integration processes leading to complete unification. For example, Ambassador Jack Pritchard, one of the leading American Koreanists who served as U.S. ambassador and special envoy to North Korea (2001–2003) and currently serves as president of the Korea Economic Institute, highlights the major challenges of unification in the following manner:

> In the best-case scenario the government of South Korea would have allocated many hundreds of billions of dollars for social and infrastructure investment in North Korea in preparation for reunification.

Seoul would have "on-the-shelf" an actionable plan for all aspects of government services from transportation, power generation, communications, medical, commerce and industry, as well as a demilitarization and reintegration plan for the extraordinarily bloated North Korean military apparatus.[4]

Ambassador Pritchard's observations are indeed on point. While giving the proverbial nod to "social" investment, however, his observations also focus primarily on issues of integration, following the basic paradigm of most discussions related to unification.

The problem of Korean unification, however, is no longer one of merely integrating existing infrastructure and ameliorating ideological differences as might have once been the case during the Occupation, when the United States and former Soviet Union functioned under the terms of the Moscow Agreement (December 1945) to make whole again a Korean peninsula the two nations had divided for military and political expediencies in August 1945.[5] Rather, the problem that confronts both Koreas is how best to integrate two quite different nations that have emerged over the ensuing decades with very little in common and that are indeed polar opposites. South Korea's people have created a culturally vibrant society with a strong economy, the twelfth largest globally (2010), and make notable contributions to global advances in the sciences, arts, literature, and other areas.[6] North Korea, conversely, exists as a displaced enigma time-warped from another decade into the contemporary global community of nations. It is ideologically bereft; economically destitute; and, geopolitically, remains the final soldier in a cold war long abandoned by the rest of the world, looking for a battle to fight.

These differences are further exacerbated by other factors seldom discussed in association with unification such as Korea's own history, often cited as the source of "common heritage" shared between citizens of the two Koreas and the basis for unification's inevitability. While a common history and heritage do exist between the two Koreas, their circumstances were hardly equal. In fact, with the exception of the Japanese colonial period during which all Koreans were treated equally poorly, political, social, economic, and cultural inequality between southern and northern Korea most accurately describes the history of the Korean experience. Indeed, one might reasonably argue, as is done in this book, that two distinct Koreas existed throughout the Choson period.

From the establishment of the Yi Dynasty in 1392 until the onset of the Japanese colonial period, northern Koreans were viewed quite contemptuously as an underclass of people, the proverbial "Korean other," and northern Korea as an outland. These historical differences remain germane to contemporary discussions of peninsular unification because similar perceptions and patterns of behavior could well re-emerge under a unification scenario characterized by the joining of two such unequal economic, antithetic political, and incongruent cultural entities. For example, consider the starkness of the two countries' economic disparity. In 2007, South Korea's annual per capita gross national income, according to the South Korean Unification Ministry, was $20,045 (U.S.), while North Korea achieved an unimpressive $1,152 (U.S.).[7] Gross domestic product (GDP) growth rates for the same year highlight similar disparities: while South Korea enjoyed a 5 percent growth rate, North Korea suffered 2.3 percent negative growth.[8]

Consequently, this book is premised on five fundamental ideas. First, while national unification will geographically rejoin the halves of the Korean peninsula, after more than sixty years of political division and centuries of discordant cultural, social, and economic policies and practices that created de facto peninsular bifurcation, what will actually be integrated under a unification scenario are not halves of the same whole, but rather two distinct sovereign entities. (For this reason, I use the term "unification" to describe the amalgamation of the peninsula in lieu of "reunification.") Second, that Korean unification will be achieved via a "soft" landing: a planned and orderly road to unification. Another possible course does exist, typically referred to as a "hard" landing, characterized by a sudden, unplanned, and unexpected catastrophic failure of the North Korean regime, either the result of implosion or conflict; this scenario would require South Korea and the rest of the world to undertake immediate and extensive mitigative measures to ensure maintenance of peace and stability on the peninsula and in the region. Third, that Korea's history offers a predictive glimpse into the true complexities of unification, offering important insights into its cultural and social dimensions. Fourth, that the multifarious challenges confronting South Korean government officials with regard to North Korean migrants presently living in South Korea offer a valuable primer of potential problems attendant to unification. Finally, that national unification is in fact a multidimensional undertaking that should be regarded as two subsets of issues that include the "integration" of political and economic systems, or institutional factors, on the one hand and "repatriation" of citizens, or cultural and social factors, on the other. Integration and repatriation must be addressed in parallel to ensure the overall success of Korean national unification.

There is no dearth of literature addressing the various issues associated with political and economic integration of the two Koreas. There has, however, been less treatment of the social and cultural issues attendant to the unification scenario, leaving the false impression that if integration is achieved repatriation will follow as a matter of course. The dimensions of repatriation are broad and run through the entirety of any unification effort though. They could, in some regard, be considered even more complex than integration issues because they are dependent on the human factor—emotions, perceptions, prejudices and fears—and they spill over into and are inextricably linked with integration issues.

Following is a brief discussion of representative integration and repatriation issues attendant to unification in order to provide some perspective on the enormity of any effort to unite the two Koreas.

ISSUES OF INTEGRATION

Herculean efforts will be needed to successfully integrate the political and economic systems of an amalgamated Korea. For example, beyond the basic argument of which unification model will prove most efficacious, one must also consider other fundamental issues such as what the ultimate fate will be of the current North Korean leadership under a unified Korea. Will North Korean leaders have a role in government, and if so, what will that role be? It is difficult to envision a scenario under which the North Korean leadership would willingly abdicate positions of power in favor of non-governing roles, yet given the huge economic advantage South Korea enjoys over its northern neighbor and the barrenness of the North Korean regime's *Juche* ideology, it has become a foregone conclusion that the South will, in some manner, subsume the North. Unlike circumstances that existed during the mid-twentieth century, little credence is given to the notion that the peninsula might somehow be organized under the North Korean government.

If former North Korean leaders are given a role in governance, how will former North Korean citizens view them and, in turn, the legitimacy of the new government itself given the decades of human rights abuses that have been perpetrated against the North Korean citizenry? More fundamentally, can a newly unified government turn a blind eye to the decades of human rights abuses suffered by North Korean citizens? Should North Korean leaders be tried in international court for crimes against humanity as defined by the Rome Statute of the International Criminal Court, or for the sake of advancing unification goals should they be absolved of all past crimes?[9] In the end, it is highly unlikely that any unification accord could ever be struck that does not in some way hold harmless North Korean leaders responsible for past acts of persecution against their citizens. Yet doing so might well strain the credibility of a unified government.

Under a democratic form of government, what kind of representation can former citizens of the Democratic People's Republic of Korea (DPRK) anticipate—proportional or equal? Or indeed should there be any official representation of former North Korea? Any course offers challenges to both North and South Korea and will be impacted by various factors—relative population densities, relative economic strengths, and other considerations. Another substantive issue to be considered is what the ultimate disposition of the North Korean military will be. How, when, and under what circumstances it is disbanded, as the United States learned in the war against Iraq, could be key to subsequent issues of governance.

Factors of economic integration will prove equally confounding given the tremendous disparity between the Koreas' respective economies. As noted earlier, the per-capita GDP between the two countries is measurable by a factor of 17.5. Other economic indicators point to equally stark contrasts. While the South Korean economy now numbers among the world's largest, North Korea continues to rank among its most needy. For the period 1988 to 2008, the regime ranked third among all nations receiving international food assistance (11.9 million tons), eclipsed only by Ethiopia (18.1 million tons) and Bangladesh (14.1 million tons).[10] And projections for its chronic food shortage remain bleak for the foreseeable future. For example, World Food Program (WFP) officials in Pyongyang have reported that international "donor fatigue" stemming from massive relief efforts in response to the 2010 earthquakes in Haiti and Chile, and providing decades of support to North Korea, has caused a precipitous drop in international assistance for North Koreans. Consequently, in spring 2011 WFP officials were forced to launch emergency food operations in an attempt to provide assistance to the nation's most vulnerable segment of the population—women, children, and the elderly, 3.5 million in total—and stem the negative effects of malnutrition.[11]

Finally, and perhaps serving as the exclamation point on an already ill-boding message, during summer 2011 South Korean government officials discovered North Korean police reports citing cases of cannibalism, the result of growing severe food shortages.[12]

These kinds of economic disparities require resolution of a host of factors, some inextricably linked to and potentially impacting political integration. For example, what will become of the North Korean population under a unification scenario? This question must be considered within the context of the ordinary North Korean citizen's freedom of mobility within a new democratic society. With growing knowledge of the chasm in lifestyle that exists between themselves and their southern neighbors, what incentive will there be for North Korean citizens to remain within the boundaries of what had been North Korea once its oppressive regime is dissolved?[13] Most areas of northern Korea are mountainous, offer lands ill suited for agriculture, and are rampantly destitute. Thus, the potential for mass diasporic movement into South Korea presents a major challenge. The specter of millions of North Koreans streaming southward in search of jobs and food represents a potentially dangerous destabilizing factor for South Korea. But the very act of forcibly trying to keep the population in place would be reminiscent of the regime that was displaced, likely impacting perceptions of the newly unified government. Nor is the threat of a North Korean diaspora limited to the Korean peninsula; it looms as a potential regional destabilizing factor as well. China has raised concerns over increasing numbers of North Korean refugees fleeing across its borders on numerous occasions.

One possible means of stemming the potential flow of North Korean refugees in either direction would be to undertake massive industrialization projects that could help employ many North Koreans, thus providing the means for them to earn a living wage. Implicit in such a notion, however, is the idea that the North Korean workforce possesses the requisite skill sets to allow its members to be employed. However, it appears woefully undertrained to meet such demands. Lankov notes,

> Imagine a North Korean engineer who will aspire to keep his job in a unified country. This is a natural aspiration, to be sure, but a typical North Korean engineer has never used a computer—unless he or she worked in the military industry or some other privileged companies. Can such a person be employed by a modern factory? Obviously, not. Can he or she be re-educated? Perhaps, yes, but it will take years and cost a large amount of money which will be in short supply in post-unification Korea.[14]

This is borne out through South Korean government statistics on saeteo-min. Kim and Jang cite in their article, "Aliens among Brothers?: The Status and Perception of North Korean Refugees in South Korea," several examples of such conditions. According to Ministry of Unification findings, by 2005 only two of 128 professional saeteomin were employed in their professions in South Korea after leaving the North during 2000–2004.[15] They also offer an anecdotal account of a former North Korean chemistry teacher who immigrated to South Korea and took a job as a waitress, but her difficulty in understanding the South Korean dialect led her to ultimately abandon the job and seek factory employment making bags.[16] If such is the case, a re-education program of epic dimensions is demanded to prepare North Koreans to become functional citizens in a twenty-first-century unified Korea. Consider, for example, that the population of North Korea, which totals 22.6 million citizens, is roughly about half the size of South Korea's, at 48.5 million.[17] (This topic will be treated in greater detail in chapter 9).

Consider as well the massive infrastructural assistance that will be required to build roads, schools, hospitals, adequate housing, and factories in northern Korea, all basic projects but long permitted to languish under the North Korean regime. The large infusion of financial capital required to undertake such an expansive program only to achieve basic "livability" standards is staggering. The differences between the two nations' GDP purchasing power parity (PPP) helps to illustrate this point. North Korea's GDP (PPP) achieved a laggardly $40 billion (U.S.), while South Korea's topped $1.3 trillion (U.S.).[18]

Different dimensions of the North Korean military issue must also be considered. What is to become of a North Korean military, nearly 1.1 million strong? If it is immediately dissolved, how then will its members be absorbed into the new economy? What will they be trained to do in a civil democratic society? Yet keeping them in place undermines the entire premise of unification: a peaceful and integrated Korea devoid of lingering Cold War threats.

Establishing a social safety net for North Korea's impoverished and most vulnerable citizens will be yet another concern. In the wake of the 1997 Asian financial crisis, the South Korean government undertook social security reform (in the year 2000) through a program called National Basic Livelihood Security (NBLS), which now guarantees South Korean citizens a minimum standard of living. Are North Koreans to be extended the same benefits under this program? Given the rampant poverty of the North, how would its nearly twenty-three million citizens be absorbed into the existing social security program structure and at what cost? Failure to do so potentially puts in place a system recognizing two classes of Korean citizens. That newly integrated citizens will require a helping hand from their new government is obvious. The challenge confronting a unified government, however, will be how best to fulfill such needs and expectations with the appearance of equity.

ISSUES OF REPATRIATION

Despite the many complexities presented by integration issues, those introduced previously being only a representative sample, inclusion of repatriation factors further complicates the unification discussion because they span nebulous, and in some cases unquantifiable, factors—cultural, social, and educational—all of which will require full resolution to ensure successful assimilation of former North Korean citizens.

Issues of repatriation can generally be distilled to one critical point: ensuring mechanisms are established that facilitate assimilation of the North Korean citizenry into a unified Korea while avoiding creation of a new underclass of Koreans. Very few, if any, will have had a meaningful context for living in a democratic society, yet will be expected in very short order, to function in a free and capitalist society. The North Korean experience is one in which individualism and initiative is stifled, indeed quite actively discouraged, but success in a capitalist society demands the honing of these very skills. Authors Ko, Chung, and Oh elaborate as they describe the economic and social circumstances for the individual North Korean as being fully controlled from "cradle to grave," pointing out that the social system

> organizes the lives of all people. . . . Every person is organized into one or more social organizations such as Boy Scouts, the Kim Il Sung Socialist Youth League, Labor Party, Workers' League, and Women's League. Education, medical services, and even daily necessities, including food, have been provided virtually free of charge.[19]

Fending for themselves will require North Korean citizens to develop entirely new skill sets, the success of which will rest on an important common denominator—language—no longer so common given the decades of sovereign separation on the peninsula. According to a 2005 Ministry of Unification report,

"Report of Saeteomin Employment Situation," South Korean employers noted that saeteomin inability to comprehend the South Korean language served as the greatest obstacle to their employment, a condition compounded by the increasing use of English loan words.[20] Another 2003 study conducted by the Korea Institute for National Unification found that a majority of saeteomin responding to a survey, 52.3 percent, required longer than three years to attain functional levels of the South Korean language.[21] As one looks toward full assimilation then, the experience of saeteomin, while microcosmic, serves as quiet warning of the challenges that lie ahead when a unified Korea attempts to integrate North Korea's 22.6 million residents.

This represents only the very beginning of repatriation tasks. North Koreans will also need to be taught about the basic technologies on which many South Koreans have come to rely in their daily lives and now take for granted: kitchen appliances, cell phones, computers, mass transit, and others. And technology is not the only challenge. Most North Koreans have not shopped in large, bustling shopping areas like those prevalent in urban areas of the south. They have no familiarity with the concept of credit cards, nor have they had exposure to the broad range of choices of goods that confront shoppers daily. Cognizant of such challenges, the South Korean government established Hanawon in July 1999, a resettlement and training center located about one hour south of Seoul, designed to teach saeteomin skills necessary to survive in South Korea's capitalist society. Undertaking similar initiatives for the whole of North Korea's population will be resource, labor, and time intensive.

An ancillary problem that will also require attention is the government stipends presently paid to Hanawon residents. Will the South Korean government continue its policy of providing stipends to North Koreans who become South Korean citizens, in order to facilitate unification? If so, it could add substantially to unification's bottom line. And if not, how might this comport with the expectations of former North Koreans, and would such a policy hinder assimilation?

Education will present yet another area of challenge. The question of assimilation must address how North Korean youth, given the great variance in pedagogy and subject matter that exists between the two educational systems, can be brought to the academic level of their South Korean counterparts among whom education is a prime consideration. Again, the experience of saeteomin schoolchildren could serve as a national primer on potential issues that will need to be navigated for purposes of unification. Statistics compiled by the Ministry of

Education in 2005 cited school attendance among saeteomin high school–aged youth was a mere 10.4 percent, while the drop-out rate among saeteomin middle school– and high school–aged children was 13.7 percent, nearly 10 times the national average.[22] Failure to resolve issues surrounding education potentially lays the foundation for the creation of an underclass of northern Korean citizens.

Despite these challenges, the problems with education are at least tangible. There is a subset of related hurdles, tangential and less visible, but perhaps even more difficult to surmount because of their strong cultural roots. Not necessarily unique to Korean culture, as other Asian cultures share similar practices, they are presented here in the Korean context: *hakyeon*, or the system of informal relationships based on university ties and relationships, and *jiyeon*, a system of relationships based on regional ties. Such systems are, by their nature, exclusionary of outsiders as they function to recognize and insulate members who share common attributes from those who do not possess them. Under unification North Koreans would fall into the excluded group as they possess neither the regional nor academic affiliations required to maneuver within the hakyeon or jiyeon systems. Given the additional challenges posed by integration and repatriation factors discussed to this point, there is little cause for optimism that such institutionalized practices can be overcome in the near-term. In fact, Korean history points toward the likelihood that these kinds of attitudes could well become further entrenched, potentially relegating northern Koreans to cycles of poor education, few job opportunities, exclusion, and second-class citizen status from which escape would be difficult.

Another intangible consideration is patriotism, i.e., those feelings of allegiance toward the respective Koreas rather than a unified one. Old feelings of allegiance will likely color perceptions of a unified Korea, less so perhaps for South Koreans because any unified permutation will likely have a democratic foundation. The potential problem of residual patriotism is effectively captured in the documentary film, *Repatriation*, directed by Kim Dong-won and winner of the 2004 Sundance Film Festival in the Freedom of Expression category.[23] The film chronicles the lives of former North Korean spies captured and imprisoned in South Korea during the Cold War and now living in South Korea as its citizens. An emergent theme among some former North Koreans, despite having lived in South Korea for years, is their belief that unification should, and in some instances must, take place under a North Korean model. Thus, any notion that North Koreans will somehow embrace their southern cousins and a newly unified government as saviors simply because the current North Korean regime might no longer be in power may amount to wishful thinking, particularly if former North Korean citizens are not properly assimilated into the broader society.

2

In the Beginning

When it comes to reunification, we need to emphasize that Korean people share the same blood.

—*Kim Yoon-ki, researcher, Ministry of Education, Science and Technology*[1]

A review of Korean history renders three important findings that potentially bear on the question of unification. First, since the inception of the Choson period, with the brief exception of its colonization by Japan, Korea has existed in one form or another as a divided state—either formally or de facto. The concept of nationalism and the spirit of Korean racial and ethnic homogeneity are rather recent phenomena, finding their genesis in the foreign incursions onto the peninsula beginning in the latter half of the nineteenth century. These concepts flourished in the lexicon of Korean political thought during the early twentieth century, spurred by the onset of the colonization of Korea by Japan. Although the Japanese colonial period proved to be a powerful unifying force on the peninsula, it was rather short-lived, having been followed almost immediately by Korea's formal division during the Occupation period.

Second, the combination of Choson period policies, such as the *samin* policy of the fifteenth and sixteenth centuries, discussed later in this chapter, coupled with the existing rigid social stratification of Choson society, helped to promote an underclass of Koreans living in northern Korea, which in effect created two Koreas: the aristocracy of southern Korea and those considered to be of a lower social status, or cultural outliers, in northern Korea. These policies and cultural practices manifested themselves in blatant discriminatory practices against northerners, the result of which led to the emergence of two very distinct cultures in northern and southern Korea.

Finally, migration patterns of peoples on the peninsula and Asian mainland from as early as the fourth century BCE, continuing well into the Choson period, militate against the argument of Korean racial and ethnic homogeneity, an argument often proffered as the basis for the inevitability of peninsular unification. Existing borders in northern Korea were very porous and resulted in the intermingling of ethnic groups, for example, Koreans and the Jurchen, a Tungusic people who inhabited Manchuria in northeast China until the seventeenth century.

At the heart of the unification issue rests the common notion that Koreans are homogeneous—ethnically, racially, and culturally—and have been so for many centuries. The argument follows then that "reunification" is the inevitable end state for the two Koreas. The history of the Korean peninsula, however, does not necessarily support the popular supposition of homogeneity. Long-held beliefs regarding Korean racial and ethnic homogeneity are now, in fact, being questioned among the Korean people themselves, no longer enjoying a protected status of dogma. Indeed, a growing number of Korean scholars have begun calling for the South Korean government to divest itself, and in the process the Korean people, of the commonly held notion of racial and ethnic homogeneity. For example, Lee O-young, honorary chair professor of Ewha Academy for Advanced Studies and former culture minister indicates that

> we were originally a mix of marine people and equestrians because Korea is a peninsula. They coexisted and this is the power of Korea. . . . The perception of "ethnic" actually didn't exist for 19 centuries. However, under Japanese rule, we needed a strong national identity and started to stress that we are homogeneous people. The division of the two Koreas has also driven us to emphasize we are analogous people.[2]

Such sentiments are echoed by Professor Chun Kyung-soo of Seoul National University:

It is crazy to say Koreans are a homogeneous people. You are mixed, so am I, all Koreans are mixed. The term "homogeneous people" should disappear. It is a superficial term.[3]

Similarly, a recent national public opinion survey revealed that of 1,000 respondents, only 26.7 percent considered ethnic homogeneity "a proud legacy that we should hand down to our descendants."[4]

The following two chapters will highlight: 1) the creation of a unified Korean polity, 2) the impact Choson court policies had in culturally dividing the peninsula, and 3) how the influence of external powers beginning in the nineteenth century ignited for the first time a peninsula-wide populist recognition of Korean "oneness."

BIRTH OF A NATION[5]

Creation of a single unified polity on the Korean peninsula was a long and arduous undertaking beginning during the second century BCE with the emergence of the Confederated Kingdoms, and not fully achieved until the ascendancy of the Koryo dynasty (918) and its unification of the peninsula in 936. This dynasty too would be supplanted nearly five hundred years later as the process of political consolidation on the peninsula continued, which in the end gave advent to the Yi (Choson) Dynasty in 1392.

The creation of Korea was characterized by a combination of dynamic factors that included internal instability and internecine fighting among existing groups on the peninsula, territorial aggrandizement perpetrated by neighboring groups against one another, and wars of territorial expansion undertaken by peninsular factions against neighboring powers on the Asian continent.

The kingdoms of Koguryo, Silla, and Paekche, the three political entities of the Three Kingdoms period (57 BCE–668 CE), emerged as a result of successful political consolidation among the various groups located on the peninsula. These groups ultimately drove out the commanderies the Chinese Han Dynasty had established in the second century BCE to maintain control over the area. Silla and Paekche bisected that portion of the peninsula south of the Han River, while Koguryo occupied the vast area north of the Han River to the Chinese border.

During this period, Koguryo proved the most intent among the three political entities in pursuing policies of territorial aggrandizement, primarily through attacks on the Chinese Sui Dynasty in 598 (589–618). While unsuccessful, Koguryo's military incursions invited four retaliatory attacks during the remaining years of the Sui Dynasty in 598, 612, 613, and 614, none of which proved successful. As a result of the costly failed campaigns against Koguryo, however, the Sui Dynasty collapsed in 618, replaced by the T'ang, which beginning in 645 continued the earlier Sui policy of launching attacks against Koguryo. Meeting a fate similar to that of earlier Sui efforts, the T'ang subsequently formed an alliance with Silla and in 660 attacked both Paekche and Koguryo, defeating the former but failing against the latter. In 667 T'ang and Silla again aligned forces against Koguryo, which this time proved successful. As a result, the T'ang moved to assert dominance in Paekche and Koguryo while simultaneously attempting to exercise dominion over Silla, ultimately leading to dissolution of the Silla-T'ang alliance. Abrogation of the alliance led to an eventual battle between Silla and the T'ang with Silla emerging victorious and recovering both the former Paekche and Koguryo territories. The T'ang retreated from the peninsula, providing the circumstances necessary for the first real exercise in political consolidation on the peninsula and for an indigenous political culture to begin taking root.

Silla's unification of the peninsula extended as far north as modern-day Pyongyang. The territory north of this area, settled by former Koguryo leaders and people, became a successor state to Koguryo known as Balhae, which in its entirety comprised the northern portion of the Korean peninsula, southern Manchuria, and what is presently the Russian Maritime Province. This period during which unified Silla and Balhae existed is known as the North–South States Period (698–926).

Two important results emerge from this period in Korean history. The first was one of Balhae's most notable characteristics: its multi-ethnicity owing to the various ethnic tribes brought under the control of Balhae rulers. Second, and perhaps more importantly for the future development of the Korean peninsula, was the haven afforded by unified Silla for the development of the political, social, and cultural framework from which a unified Korean polity and culture would subsequently arise.

The Later Three Kingdoms period emerged in 892 (892–936) as another transitional period. Balhae was attacked and defeated by the Khitan, a nomadic people who dominated the Mongolia and Manchuria regions until ultimately defeated by the Mongols in 1218. Balhae fell in 926 and its territory split, its northern areas absorbed by the Liao Dynasty, while Balhae's southern territories would ultimately become part of Koryo. Unified Silla, on the other hand, fell prey to internal disgruntlement among its citizenry—both the aristocracy and commoner—the sources of which centered on political and economic discord. Among the aristocrats, growing resentment at the increased authority exercised from the center served as the basis for discontent. But as they banded together to oppose the growing authority of the king, the aristocrats found that the lack of the very authority they opposed led to growing discord among themselves, a trend that manifested itself in the proliferation of personal armies created by the gentry. Consequently, ascension to the throne became a function of the number of alliances any one contender could muster and thus how much military support upon which he could rely. Under such circumstances, of course, factional warfare and politics were unavoidable as was the partisan governance to which they gave rise.

The growing instability among the aristocracy was exacerbated by the increasingly untenable economic conditions being imposed on commoners, which in the end led to peasant rebellions that served to further weaken the governing center. The strengthening of the aristocracy led to the rise of strong and autonomous families in the countryside able to exercise control over the commoners in their respective areas. As the power of the local gentry extended, so too did their economic control in the regions over which they exercised dominion. The commoners living under their control were forced to pay taxes directly to them at the expense of the central government. As one might expect, such an economic arrangement amounted to a zero-sum game between the central government and local authorities and negatively impacted the central government's coffers.

In order to reverse this trend, in the latter half of the ninth century, the central government devised a tax system under which peasants were required to pay taxes to the government in addition to those exacted by the local gentry. The additional tax burden resulted in increased discontent among the peasants, leading them to join together in uprisings throughout the Silla territory against government authorities. Ultimately two of the leaders of these bands of peasants became powerful enough to challenge the rule of a weakened Silla government, subsequently establishing two competing states that vied for power on the peninsula along with Silla: Paekche and Koryo. Their leaders claimed that the states they created were successors to the fallen Paekche and Koguryo (Koryo) states of the earlier Three Kingdoms period, hence this period's moniker of the "Later Three Kingdoms." While called such, Silla was now quite powerless against potential claimants to its kingdom, as it had all but ceased to exercise any meaningful control on the peninsula. Thus battle for control of the peninsula was effectively a two-way contest between later Paekche and Koryo. By 935 the issue was no longer in doubt as Koryo defeated Paekche in decisive battle, Silla surrendered, and by the following year Koryo had successfully unified the peninsula.

Koryo and the Khitan maintained an uneasy truce until about 1010 when the Khitan launched an unsuccessful attack against the former, an act repeated in 1018 with largely similar results. The Jurchen, however, another group to emerge out of Manchuria, and founders of the Jin Dynasty in China (1115–1234), enjoyed greater success at subjugating Koryo and compelling its leaders to accept Jin suzerainty over its territory, once the Jurchen had successfully overrun the Khitan. Given the tumult that characterized this period of history on the Asian mainland, it comes as no surprise that the Jurchen themselves ultimately succumbed to the Mongols and their leader, Genghis Khan, by 1215. By 1273, the entirety of Koryo had fallen under Mongol suzerainty where it remained until 1388.

The decline of the Koryo Dynasty was closely linked to other geopolitical events on the Asian mainland, namely the eroding power of the Mongols and the rise of the Ming Dynasty in China (1368–1644), circumstances that ultimately divided the Koryo court and its loyalties between the Ming and Mongols and that, in the end, led to its downfall. The circumstances that contributed significantly to the political chasm of Koryo's divided loyalties, however, originated not from the Asian mainland but from the Japanese archipelago in the form of Japanese pirates or *wakou* (*waegu* in Korean).

The wakou ravaged the Korean coastline at will beginning in the thirteenth century, but their activities became particularly devastating from the mid-fourteenth century. Wakou raids drove farmers from the fertile lands they tended along the coastal areas and impeded maritime trade, activities that had a pernicious impact on tax revenues paid to the aristocracy in Koryo's capital city of Kaesong. Koryo dispatched military forces to counter the wakou raids, and two of its commanders, Ch'oe Yong and Yi Song-gye, rose to prominence as a result of their success against the pirates. Ironically, one of these two prominent commanders who helped to reduce the wakou threat would, in the end, prove instrumental in the downfall of the Koryo Dynasty itself.

Ch'oe Yong and Yi Song-gye occupied opposite ends of a continuum with regard to Koryo's foreign policy toward the emerging Ming dynasty, with the former strongly aligned against the Ming and the latter more amenable to them. These differences became more acute when in 1388 the Ming announced plans to subsume the northeastern territories that composed Koryo. Ch'oe Yong and Yi Song-gye were dispatched with the king's forces to militarily engage the Ming. At some point during the expedition, however, pro-Ming Yi Song-gye doubled back with his troops, returned to the capital, and undertook an almost unopposed coup, deposing the king and usurping power for himself. He then undertook a series of actions, such as land redistribution, that consolidated his power and by 1392 had created the Choson Dynasty and moved the capital from Kaesong to its new location in Hanyang or present-day Seoul. This dynasty would remain in place for over five hundred years until the presence and activities of Western nations on the Korean peninsula fomented the requisite instability to bring about its demise.

A WORD ABOUT CHOSON SOCIETY

Although an exhaustive discussion of Choson society lies beyond the scope of this book, some treatment of its composition merits attention to more fully understand the impact of later Choson court policies with regard to the Korean population. Choson society was divided into four distinct social classes: the *yangban*, *chung-in*, *yangmin*, and *ch'onmin*, but was for all intents and purposes a yangban society. The yangban class, which constituted less than 10 percent of the population, comprised scholar-gentry and thus represented the privileged ruling class.[6] Yangban, which means "two branches," themselves were divided into the civil and military branches, although they were not considered to be of equal status; the civil branch was treated as more prestigious. Many became government officials and were responsible for creating policies that developed Choson society and its citizens in accordance with Confucian precepts. The yangban were the purveyors of social morality and ethics, controlled the society's wealth, and concentrated on creating the ideal Confucian state. They were unconcerned with matters of commerce, agriculture, or technical work; this was left to lower level functionaries. As one might expect, the yangban class sought to protect its privileged position within Choson society in any number of ways. For example, the creation of a civil service examination system limited the number of yangban who could be appointed as officials to civil service posts. The yangban were also prohibited from marrying into other classes and segregated themselves, living apart from others within the city limits of the capital.

The chung-in, or "middle people," occupied the next rung of the social ladder beneath the yangban and comprised petty central and local officials. While they were educated, chung-in were less educated than yangban in the study of Confucianism. Rather, they were technically adept at functions such as medicine, translation, astronomy, and other pursuits.

By far the largest group in Choson society was the yangmin class, or "good people." Comprising some 80 percent of the population, farmers, craftsmen and merchants filled their ranks.[7] Finally, occupying the bottom rung of the Choson social ladder were the ch'onmin, or "inferior people." Members of this class included those whose occupations dealt with death—butchers, tanners, leather-workers, grave diggers—as well as entertainers. Also included among the ch'onmin were both public and private slaves, whose numbers were not insignificant. During the early years of the Choson Dynasty it is estimated that there were as many as 400,000 publicly and privately owned slaves.[8] As a point of reference, the total mid-seventeenth-century population of Choson Korea is estimated to have been approximately 2.3 million. (Population counts during the Choson period have, however, proven to be notoriously inaccurate because of poor record-keeping, leading to wide disparities in population estimates. For example, while one source estimates the population of mid-seventeenth-century Choson to have been 2.3 million, another source cites a much lower number for the same time period, 1.5 million; consequently the number of publicly and privately owned slaves may have been greater or lesser. Although exact figures may be difficult to ascertain, some scholars estimate that as much as 30 percent of the population may have been held in slavery, thus the total population count may have been closer to the estimate of 1.5 million, which accords more closely with the estimate of 400,000 slaves.[9])

Given a social order under which the yangban was the dominant class, distribution of wealth and political power in Choson society mirrored these circumstances and were the inverse of the population distribution. Thus, while the yangban constituted a small percentage of the total population of the Choson kingdom, they owned the preponderant wealth. Conversely, the yangmin, who were the largest of all the classes, owned little, if any, of the wealth. Most farmers, in fact, despite the Confucian belief that they were to be respected as the backbone of the nation, were landless peasants working private or public lands in servitude.

Such was the state of Choson society as the court and its civil servants began enacting and implementing policies during the fifteenth century that de facto would create two Koreas: southern Korea, dominated by the yangban class, and northern Korea, which through action and edict came to be populated with many of Choson society's outcasts.

THE MAKING OF TWO KOREAS

The successful transformation of Korea into a long-lasting single polity did not translate into the emergence of a society without social upheaval. There was, of course, the need for the Choson Dynasty's founder, Yi Song-gye, to secure his power base, a task accomplished by conducting cadastral surveys, land redistribution, and implementation of other means of wealth and political consolidation and transfer. Even after these new policies had been implemented and some consolidation accomplished, there remained continued internal upheaval, none perhaps more emblematic of the divided society outlined in the previous section than the *samin* policies instituted beginning in the fifteenth century, a topic discussed more fully in the next section.

That Korean society was stratified primarily among four social groups wasn't unique to the peninsula; such practices find their roots in the principles of Confucianism. Japan as well had a similar social structure known as *shi-no-ko-sho*, although the social groups and their ordering were slightly different: *shi* comprised the "bushi" or warrior class; *no* were the "hyakusho" or farmers; *ko* were the craftsmen; and *sho,* the merchants. Japan also had a social group akin to the ch'onmin called the *eta* (presently known as *burakumin*) who too were socially shunned because of their occupations. While they performed necessary functions for the larger society, theirs were occupations associated with death and thus they were not only looked down upon but actively ostracized and socially demeaned as inferior. The eta of Japan, however, existed outside the formal shi-no-ko-sho system rather than as a part of it. What was unique to the Korean case, however, were the additional institutional practices put in place that de facto led to the creation of two Koreas on the peninsula. Put differently, there were those Koreans who occupied the "center" of Choson society (Koreans living in southern Korea) and those who were outlanders (those living in northern Korea).

De facto bifurcation of the peninsula found its origins in one primary source: the exclusion of northerners from the hereditary system that favored the yangban and upon which appointment to the civil service bureaucracy relied. Such practices had two negative effects. First, they facilitated the promulgation of policies that reinforced the status quo and helped institutionalize practices affecting the political, economic, and cultural well-being of Koreans living in northern Korea. The second effect carries with it derivations of Newtonian law—the law of reciprocal action. Just as the center imposed policies oppressive to other classes of citizens throughout the Choson period, but particularly to those in northern Korea, there was retaliation from the masses in the form of rebellions, several of which became historically significant, including the 1812 Hong Kyongnae and the 1894 Donghak (Tonghak) rebellions.[10]

Indeed, discrimination based on hereditary exclusion, according to Kyung Moon Hwang, was first instituted by the Choson Dynasty's founder, Yi Song-gye, who would ultimately assume the name and title of King T'aejo, the first dynastic ruler of the Choson period.[11] Interestingly, Yi Song-gye, himself a northerner, espoused open discrimination against other northerners. According to the eighteenth-century cultural almanac, *T'aengniji*, the origins of this practice can be traced back to the Choson period's inception:

> T'aejo was a general who assumed the mantle of the throne from the Wang family . . . and his subordinates and merit subjects included many illustrious military commanders from the northern territories. When he took over, however, T'aejo ordered that people from the north not be widely appointed to government posts, and therefore for three hundred years no one from the two provinces of P'yongan and Hamgyong has served in a high bureaucratic office. . . . The northern people thus have not been able to stand as equals with the aristocracy . . . for aristocrats have not gone to live in those regions.[12]

Thus, the basis of the Choson Dynasty's bifurcation policy was laid.

While the preceding offers a plausible explanation as to the practice's origins, it does not address two important points: 1) the rationale for the policy's creation, or 2) the policy's continued observance under subsequent rulers. Recall that Yi Song-gye had been a military general prior to assuming the mantle of power; the successful overthrow of the reigning Koryo monarch was owed in some measure to the fact that he commanded a sizeable military force that was brought to bear against a faltering dynasty. Perhaps some recognition on his part that a yangban class populated with potential claimants for the throne who had been former rivals or who could potentially rally enough support among the aristocracy to pose a threat to his plans for consolidation lay at the heart of Yi Song-gye's actions. Or understanding the potential of the military to bring down a government, he sought to limit access to his base of power. In any case, the historical evidence appears to point to the edict of King T'aejo as the starting point of the less-than-equal policies under which northern Koreans would suffer during the Choson period.

The Dynasty's continued adherence to this exclusionary policy was the manifest result of its successful institutionalization of the Korean "other" linked particularly to the central government's mass migration policies of the fifteenth and sixteenth centuries, which forced many of the country's social undesirables to move northward. This then became later justification for the southern aristocracy to argue that northerners were the product of society's lower echelons, thus rendering them inferior.

Indeed, records indicate that as the Choson dynastic period wore on, the institutionalization of the "northern other" became such a matter of course that nearly all elements of southern Korean society came to look upon northerners with disdain, aristocracy and commoners alike. For example, Sun Joo Kim, in her work, *Marginality and Subversion in Korea*, cites the rebel manifesto of the 1812 Hong Kyongnae rebellion in which they put forth their grievances, which in part read:

> The central government abandoned P'yongan Province as one abandons rotten earth. Even when the slaves of powerful families saw men from P'yongan Province, they always called them "the common rabble from P'yongan." How unfair and what a source of resentment this is for the people of P'yongan Province![13]

Such perceptions, while generally held among those Koreans living in the country's southern provinces, were rooted within the aristocracy. For example, during the early fifteenth century, dynastic officials openly, and as a matter of public record, described northerners as "suspicious and fawning" and therefore "untrustworthy."[14] Such denigrations continued, serving only to reinforce these perceptions; subsequent "official" references included designations of being "stupid" as well as the dynastic ruler pointing to the tendency of northerners to be "foolish and naïve."[15]

If the practice of hereditary exclusion formed the rationale for discriminating against northerners, what then facilitated the successful institutionalization of political and economic policies that ostensibly divided the peninsula into two halves? The success of these policies can be traced to several factors. First was the northern region's long history, beginning in the fourteenth century, serving as the nation's first line of defense against overland invasion by external "barbarians." Consequently, northerners' proximity to the barbarians and their distance from the "center of governance" would cast them in such a pall.

Recall that toward the end of the Koryo period Mongol suzerainty had begun to wane, which in turn left unclaimed northern territories in the Yalu and Tumen river basin areas. Because of the regional power vacuum that ensued, Choson officials laid claim to these areas as sovereign Korean territories. Claiming them, however, turned out to be an easier task than defending them. The indigenous peoples, primarily the Jurchen, had to be reckoned with; some were absorbed into sovereign Korea while other groups were expelled. As the Jurchen were a nomadic culture, those who were expelled would return to what they considered to be their homelands, sometimes forcibly, thus requiring Choson officials to fortify the area through the creation of various military installations. In an effort to protect Koreans and the nation's sovereign rights in the area, Choson officials had the Four Outposts constructed in the Yalu River area and the Six Forts along the Tumen River, which would also come to serve as administrative centers in their respective areas (see map).

Second, as is often the case, the realities of daily life trump political considerations and such was the case among those Koreans living along the border areas. They often interacted with the Jurchen who also occupied border areas. Despite the efforts of Choson officials to defend the area and keep Jurchen tribes out, the borders were impossible to close completely and as a result there was a good amount of border-crossing that occurred in both directions. Indeed, Kyung Moon Hwang cites the fact that many Jurchen tribe members were readily absorbed into communities in northern Korea.[16] These circumstances could well have fostered some amount of intermarriage, further reinforcing perceptions of northern Koreans as having been more barbarous than their southern brethren. Hwang notes that

> accounts from visitors to the north reported that Jurchen and Koreans were living in peaceful coexistence and might have been intermarrying.[17]

Another factor contributing to the institutionalization of practices supporting bifurcation can be attributed to the Choson Dynasty's samin policy—its efforts to effect forced mass migration of the society's undesirables northward in an attempt to populate the border areas.

THE CHOSON DYNASTY SAMIN POLICY

Choson Dynasty security concerns served as the original impetus for creation of a policy that would move Korean citizens into the upper reaches of northern Ko-

KOREA

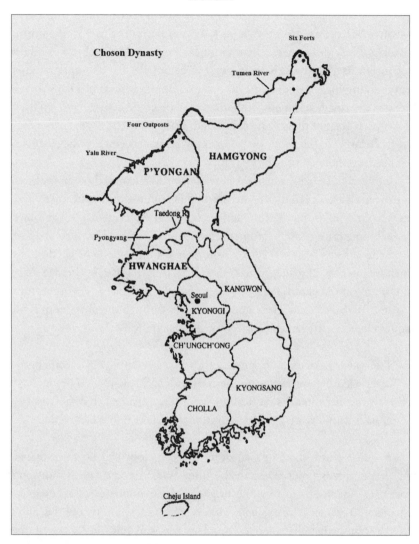

rea. Despite the Choson government's efforts to strengthen its defenses within the northern border provinces of P'yongan and Hamgyong, officials ultimately concluded that because of the porous nature of its borders the most effective means of securing them was to populate the area with Korean citizenry.

These areas were plagued by perennial famine, poor agricultural conditions, military skirmishes, and inhospitable weather, thus keeping settlements populated had been at best problematic owing to the large numbers who fled toward the southern regions of these two provinces. In the mid-fifteenth century Choson officials enacted a policy of extensive resettlement to "move tens of thousands of Koreans from throughout the southern provinces to the northern territories."[18] At the outset, execution doesn't appear to have been as robust as the concept itself, as most Koreans who were initially forced to migrate under this program wound up coming from the southern regions of Hamgyong and P'yongan provinces and many of them, as had been the case earlier, fled back to the southern areas of these two provinces. It wasn't until the latter half of the fifteenth century that the policy began to enjoy greater success, a policy that would continue into the mid-sixteenth century.

Under samin, from which the aristocracy was exempt, thousands of southern Koreans were forced to migrate north. Those constituting the preponderant element of the effort were of the lower strata of Choson Korea's social hierarchy, including criminals, government slaves, and commoners, which had several deleterious effects: 1) it served to reinforce existing notions of northerners as somehow inferior, 2) it helped to create de facto two separate cultures and social systems on the peninsula, and 3) it provided the fodder necessary to further institutionalize political and economic practices through the nineteenth century that disfavored northern Koreans. Hwang concludes,

> The *samin* migrations imported a glut of low-level social elements that sealed the north's fate as the country's backwater. . . . The rigidity of Korea's social stratification system . . . ensured that the *samin* project would work as a kind of internal colonization scheme.[19]

A quick word on the social order that developed in northern Korea is appropriate at this point. Despite the unfavorable circumstances confronting northern residents, there was one bright spot—the absence of an established aristocracy. This allowed northern culture and society to develop outside the rigid constraints that characterized southern yangban culture. As a result, what emerged was a heterogeneous society that afforded greater opportunity for social mobility. Despite northerners' inauspicious origins, their new fortunes were limited largely by either a lack of ingenuity or innovation. To be sure, a hierarchical society did ultimately emerge, spawning a local aristocracy, many of whom came to constitute the merchant class.

Merchant success was linked directly to the various commercial opportunities that presented themselves through the many tribute missions that traveled between the Chinese and Korean courts. While substantial numbers of northerners found success as merchants, some of whom emerged as quite prominent and wealthy during the Choson period and came to comprise a "northern aristocracy," the Confucian social order did not accord to merchants the social recognition or status their success might have otherwise warranted; under Confucian precepts the handling of money was considered a plebeian and unclean pursuit. This northern aristocracy would, however, ultimately become committed to joining the ranks of the ruling aristocracy and by the end of the nineteenth century actually outperform some southerners on the civil service examinations used to seat bureaucratic officials. Despite this, northerners would remain the target of contempt.

POLICY MANIFESTATIONS AGAINST THE KOREAN "OTHER"

Two important examples, one political and the other economic, help to illustrate the impact of Korea's divided society and its implications for Korean citizens living in the northern regions of the peninsula. Politically, northerners were actively denied entry into the Choson bureaucracy through yangban refusal to recognize their achievements on the rigorous civil service examination that any aspirant seeking entry into the Choson bureaucracy or higher office was required to successfully complete. In the process not only did the yangban safeguard their own prerogatives, but they also perpetuated the false notion that northerners were incapable of passing the necessary examinations and those who did pass somehow failed to demonstrate the requisite "merit" for appointment. As will be discussed, northerners not only passed the tests successfully, they also outperformed many of their southern brethren by the time the tests were discontinued at the end of the nineteenth century. Economically, it was a tale of exploitation, using the resources of the northern regions, through taxation, pilferage, and other means, for enrichment of the central government and aristocracy. In the end, it was such practices that fomented discontent among northerners, ultimately leading to open and violent manifestation of their growing resentment.

Conceptually, the civil service examination system was meritocratic, designed in principle to allow anyone, including commoners, to sit for the examinations and, if successful, ultimately to be appointed to the bureaucracy. In practice, however, the system was heavily weighted in favor of the aristocracy and thus became a tool to exclude those not of yangban pedigree. The means through which bureaucratic appointments would become most effectively limited was the system of appointments used to place successful examination takers. Sun Joo Kim notes,

The elite in the northwestern region, whose successful performance at the *munkwa* outnumbered that of their southern counterparts in the late Choson period, shared social and political concerns deriving from this regional discrimination by the center, which provided a focal point for collective discontent.[20]

The development of a contingent of local northern elites, despite the emergence of institutionalized discriminatory practices, attests not only to northerners' commitment to assimilate into the southern yangban social hierarchy but also to the vibrancy of northern culture and society. For example, from 1392 to 1450 P'yongan province produced only five successful munkwa examination passers—a mere 0.58 percent of all munkwa passers. By the end of the nineteenth century, P'yongan province reached a pinnacle producing 353 successful munkwa, which amounted to just over 16 percent of all munkwa passers. Despite this success, there was no commensurate increase in the number of appointments to higher office.[21]

As difficult as passing the civil service examinations was, it proved to be the easier task when compared with overcoming entrenched yangban attitudes toward northerners. The institutional discrimination that came to characterize Choson yangban society proved much more difficult to surmount. Many successful examination passers found themselves essentially sequestered into areas of the bureaucracy that typically did not afford opportunity for advancement, thus denying northerners access to what they most sought—entry into the upper levels of the bureaucracy and yangban society. For example, Kim points out that only those from the most prestigious backgrounds were appointed to entry-level positions in the Office of Diplomatic Correspondence, which facilitated future advancement for those who demonstrated the requisite capacity. Those of lesser pedigree, particularly from the north, may have wound up posted at the less prestigious Royal Academy, which did not afford similar advancement opportunities.[22]

The appointment system for those taking the military examination was similarly weighted toward those of higher pedigree. Only those with the proper yangban background might have been assigned to the Office of Transmission thus allowing for possible future advancement. Those without an acceptable background, again northerners numbering heavily among them, would find themselves in the Office of Patrol or some other similarly lower-ranked office.

Other safeguards were instituted that at once ensured the integrity of yangban prerogatives were maintained while denying northerners entry into the upper echelons of yangban society. For example, once incumbents were posted to the various offices of the bureaucracy, irrespective of civil or military branch postings, their backgrounds were further closely scrutinized via additional screening processes before being considered for any promotion.

Thus, the civil service system, which in principle was designed to function as a meritocracy, by mid-Choson was reduced to a vehicle through which the yangban systemically excluded northerners from attaining advancement while simultaneously further institutionalizing discrimination against them.

THE ECONOMICS OF DISCRIMINATION

The economic discrimination attendant to Choson-period policy against northerners came about gradually, not in the form of deprivation, but rather through exploitation of the region. The circumstances precipitating such practices began to evolve during the mid-Choson period; at the outset of the period, northern Korea suffered from perceptions of being an economic outland as well.

By the mid-Choson period, however, several factors were working in tandem to change the economic circumstances of the north. First, as noted earlier, there emerged in northern Korea a distinct class of wealthy merchants due in large measure to the many tribute missions to and from China requiring various forms of logistical support, which enterprising northerners were only quite willing to provide. Second, rice paid as tribute to the central government remained in the region rather than being shipped elsewhere, the normal practice, in order to support tribute missions to and from China and the military units stationed in the area. As the turmoil associated with the Chinese dynastic transition from Ming to Qing settled and the number of tribute missions precipitated by the Qing's emergence decreased, a surplus of tribute rice in the area grew. (The pattern of undertaking a greater number of tribute missions to China at the outset of a dynastic change was a typical practice. One of the purposes of such missions was to communicate continued fealty to the suzerain–vassal state relationship shared by China and its tributary states. Once loyalty was reaffirmed, the number of tribute missions in both directions tended to decrease.)

Finally, earlier discussions pointed to the frequent raids undertaken by Jurchen tribes along Korea's northern borders. There were also increased military raids perpetrated by Ming military against northern Korea prior to the end of the Ming Dynasty. But the Jurchen raids significantly decreased in number as they were subdued and coexisted with northern Koreans, which also contributed to a grain surplus. This surplus gave rise to numerous exploitative practices, an example of which was the grain loan system.

The grain loan system was designed to serve two main functions: provide subsistence to military units in the region and grain loans to farmers during those times of the year when they most typically experienced food shortages. At the outset, a nominal rate of interest was affixed to such loans, but over time government officials instituted measures that afforded the opportunity to compel commoners not only to pay higher rates but also to force them to take loans they did not require or to pay interest on non-existent loans. Rich merchant households were particularly susceptible to being forced to pay interest on loans that existed only on paper.[23]

Such economic exploitation, along with the political, social, and cultural discrimination practiced by the center helps to complete the picture of the northern region's de facto treatment as an entity separate and distinct from "Korea" itself. There existed no basis for the discrimination other than safeguarding yangban status and prerogatives for a select few. That undesirable social elements were removed from the country's center to its northern regions during early Choson Korea served as a convenient rationale for such practices. Yet these discriminatory practices flourished and became institutionalized to the extent that Choson officials essentially divided the country in half, southern and northern Korea, which ironically is how the country has remained, albeit with slightly different boundaries, since 1392, with the brief historical exception of the Japanese colonial period.

The purpose of this historical treatment is neither to make a case against long-standing claims of Korean homogeneity nor to argue against future unification of the Korean peninsula. It is, however, designed to point out that there were pervasive factors at play throughout Korea's history that worked against the development of cultural and social traditions for the whole of the peninsula, in essence fomenting the emergence of two Koreas. These conditions have led to long periods of de facto and de jure division that ultimately impact the issue of Korean unification, making it far more complex than a cursory review of the peninsula's present-day political and economic differences might reveal.

3

A Shrimp Among Whales

Gorae ssaum ae saewoodung tuhjinda. (In a fight between whales, the back of a shrimp bursts.)

—*Korean saying*[1]

Geopolitically, the script for Korea's fate was being written as early as the mid-nineteenth century, in which two factors figured dominantly: the arrival of Western nations in East Asia, and the Sino-Japanese rivalry that ensued in the wake of Western encroachment. While Korea's direct contact with Western nations occurred slightly later than China's and Japan's, because its own fate was inextricably linked to these two countries, it consequently began experiencing the ill effects of Western encroachment as early as the mid-nineteenth century. Sino-Japanese competition on the Korean peninsula was the result of an emergent regional power vacuum that resulted as China fell prey to Western activities within its borders yet attempted to maintain the viability of its traditional relationship with Korea. China's efforts ran afoul of Japan's national commitment to establish itself as a co-equal colonial power to Western nations at the expense of other East Asian countries after being forcibly opened to trade with the West itself.

One factor that contributed significantly to the deleterious effect of Western encroachment and regional rivalries over Korea was its own weakened position vis-à-vis other East Asian nations, resulting from the centuries-long suzerain-vassal relationship it shared with China; most of Korea's foreign relations had in fact been conducted through China. Such circumstances exacerbated an already atrophied, or perhaps more accurately nonexistent, regional geopolitical power-base, rendering Korea incapable of warding off Japanese and Chinese aggression during the regional instability that followed the spread of Western activity. This became particularly evident during the two decades preceding the Japanese colonial period.

Three watershed periods in Korean history present themselves as relevant to the present discussion. The first is the fifty years preceding the colonial period, because it was during this time the critical foundations were laid that proved necessary to Japan's success in colonizing the peninsula. The second is the colonization of Korea itself, because it represented one of the few times in Korean history when the country functioned as a unified entity against an external power. Finally, the Occupation period proved critical because, rather than returning sovereignty to an expectant Korea, the United States and former Soviet Union essentially reimposed the de facto peninsular bifurcation that had existed during the Choson period. The joint failure to execute their mandate to reunify the peninsula led to a formalized division, the repercussions of which the world continues to work to resolve.

THE FALL OF QING CHINA

The decline of China's Qing Dynasty during the nineteenth century is chronicled by the treaties it was compelled to conclude with various Western nations and the detrimental impact those treaties had on domestic stability. These agreements, often referred to as China's "unequal treaties," share certain commonalities that in the aggregate were, from the Chinese perspective, both intrusive and an infringement on Chinese sovereignty. First, the unequal treaties forced open numerous ports to Western trade and provided for a permanent Western presence within China. Second, they granted to citizens of Western nations rights to purchase property within newly established treaty ports while extending to them the benefits of extraterritoriality. Third, parties to the treaties were granted most favored nation (MFN) status. And finally, in the case of some treaties, China was forced to cede its theretofore sovereign territory to Western powers. Examples of such treaties include the Treaties of Nanjing (August 1842), the Bogue (October 1843), Wangxia (July 1844), and Tianjin (June 1858).

The Treaty of Nanjing ended the Qing Dynasty's First Opium War with Great Britain. The terms required that five treaty ports be opened to trade with the West (Amoy, Canton, Foochow, Ningpo, and Shanghai), that the Qing pay the British war reparations and reimburse them for the cost of lost opium, and that Hong Kong island be ceded to Great Britain in perpetuity. The Treaty of the Bogue was concluded as supplemental to the Treaty of Nanjing. On a whole, it gave British citizens residing in China the protections afforded under extraterritoriality, granted to the British government MFN status, and generally provided the modalities for Sino-British trade. The Treaty of Wangxia, concluded with the United States, was patterned after the two preceding British treaties with the Qing. Its purpose was to secure U.S. trade rights in the region vis-à-vis Great Britain's expanding presence. Specifically, it provided for extraterritoriality, the right for U.S. citizens to purchase land in treaty ports, and the right to learn the Chinese language, something previously forbidden by the Qing. The Treaty of Tianjin, which ended the first part of the Second Opium War, opened eleven additional ports to foreign trade and permitted the United States, France, and Great Britain to open diplomatic missions in Beijing, foreign vessels to navigate the Yangtze River without restriction, and Westerners to travel into the interior of China for trade and missionary work.

The Western experience with China, which had to that point been considered the preeminent East Asian power, helped to lay the foundations for broader Western expansion into Japan and Korea. In turn, Western expansion into Japan helped to facilitate Korea's future subjugation by Japan.

THE FALL OF TOKUGAWA JAPAN

The nineteenth century was a period of decline for the Tokugawa shogunate in the capital city of Edo (Tokyo), beset by numerous problems: economic malaise, social upheaval, domestic political unrest, and geopolitical uncertainty. Emblematic of Japan's economic problems was the Tempo famine, precipitated by poor rice harvests, lasting from 1833 to 1836. The famine impacted nearly the whole of Japan, but was particularly severe in the northeast.[2]

Social upheaval also plagued the Tokugawa shogunate. The official class system, shi-no-ko-sho, established in the mid-seventeenth century, began breaking down as merchants, who occupied the lowest position in the official class system, became more powerful through their money-lending activities, particularly to the samurai class. The Edo economy was rice-based, but many of the cultural and entertainment pursuits enjoyed by the samurai class—teahouses, kabuki theaters, and other social diversions—required money, especially in Edo. Growing numbers of merchants were in a position to advance such funds to samurai.[3] (Under the shogunate's policy of *sankin kotai*, alternate year-long attendance in Edo by the *daimyo,* or "domanial lords," and their retinue of samurai was required by edict.) In times of poor rice harvest, however, samurai who had been advanced money on the strength of their annual rice stipends were unable to repay such debts, yet they borrowed more to sustain their lifestyles. By the nineteenth century, the increasing weight of samurai indebtedness led to rather unprecedented practices such as the selling of samurai rank to merchants, allowing them to use surnames or permitting them to wear swords. Thus, the lowest class, as dictated by Confucian precepts, came to enjoy the privileges of the highest.

The relationship of domestic political and geopolitical circumstances were inextricably linked and, when considered alongside the economic and social upheaval of the nineteenth century, precipitated the fall of the Tokugawa shogunate. One such example was the significantly increased traffic of foreign ships off Japan's coasts. The shogunate's policy of *sakoku* (self-isolation) forbade entry of foreign ships into the country's territory. However, the Morrison Incident brought the Tokugawa shogunate's policy of self-isolation and increasing Western curiosity into stark confrontation.

In 1837 the *Morrison,* a U.S. merchant ship approaching Japan in order to repatriate shipwrecked Japanese sailors, was fired upon by the shogunate's shore batteries, which forced the ship to retire. The incident, however, served as impetus for compelling Japan to repeal its policy of sakoku. By July 1853, the United States was making official requests of Japan to open its doors to the world as Commodore Matthew Calbraith Perry sailed into Edo Bay at Uraga Harbor and presented demands to establish formal U.S.-Japan relations. On March 31, 1854, representatives of the shogunate, divided internally over what to do about Western incursions in general, signed the Treaty of Kanagawa. The treaty called for Japan, among other things, to open two ports (Shimoda and Hakodate) to American ships for purposes of resupply and to grant the United States MFN status and the right to post a consular official in Shimoda.

By August 1856 Townsend Harris had been dispatched to Shimoda as the first U.S. consul general to Japan, with the expressed task of concluding a full commercial treaty. Despite the efforts of the shogunate to thwart his mission, Harris was ultimately successful in concluding the U.S.-Japan Treaty of Amity and Commerce in July 1858, calling for the opening of several more ports as well as Edo and Osaka, the right of American citizens to reside in those ports, extraterritoriality, fixed import and export duties, and the exchange of diplomats.

Concluding the treaty with the Americans would set into motion a number of events that changed the course of Japan's history and, in the process, Korea's history as well. First, it forced Japan, in very short order, to conclude similar treaties with other Western powers—Great Britain, Russia, France, and the Netherlands, collectively known as the Ansei commercial treaties; informally they are referred to as Japan's unequal treaties. Second, because the shogunate had sought the opinion of the daimyo in resolving the problem of increased foreign incursions, a practice theretofore unheard of, the shogunate telegraphed a growing weakness in Japan's governing center. This resulted in greater internal destabilization as there were those within the shogunate, and among the daimyo, who felt Japan's security had been compromised and the emperor shown disrespect by not first seeking imperial consent to conclude the treaties. Open opposition—to the shogunate's policy of engaging Western nations diplomatically and commercially—followed. In an attempt to reassert its authority, the shogunate undertook what is now known as the Ansei Purge (1858–1860), which in reality sought to remove from power those opposed to the Tokugawa shogunate's new policy toward the West. Any gain achieved through the purge was short-lived as by 1868 the *Meiji Ishin* (the Meiji Restoration, ostensibly restoration of imperial rule) was underway and the Tokugawa shogunate relegated to Japan's historical annals.[4]

The new governing leaders of the Meiji oligarchy were mindful of the fate befalling China—Western powers were dividing that country into spheres of influence—and they were determined not to allow Japan to follow a similar course. Consequently, Japan's policy pursuits during the latter half of the nineteenth century focused on three primary areas: modernization along Western lines, abrogation of its unequal treaties, and regional expansion at the expense of both Korea and China. All were with one goal in mind: to stand as a co-equal with Western nations. Japan undertook a number of pursuits in support of the first two policy objectives. One such example was its dispatch of the Iwakura Mission in 1871, an eighteen-month-long endeavor led by Iwakura Tomomi, which had two key objectives. First, to investigate firsthand the extent of Western modernization, assessing how far behind Japan had fallen technologically and what measures would be required to bridge any gaps. (The mission found huge gulfs.) Second, to assess the willingness of Western powers to abrogate the unequal treaties into which Japan had been forced to enter, something none was prepared to do at that time. Understanding the enormity of the task confronting Japan, the Meiji oligarchy rallied the country and its resources around a new national slogan—*fukoku kyohei* (enrich the country, strengthen the military). This policy would ultimately prove fatal to Korean sovereignty.

KOREA—"A DAGGER POINTED AT THE HEART OF JAPAN"

China and Korea became the focal point of Japan's regional expansion efforts during the Meiji period for several reasons. In the case of China, it proved an obstacle to Japan's emerging policies. During the last half of the nineteenth century the Korean court became divided: there were those who sought to remain ensconced in earlier traditions and continue Korea's subservience vis-à-vis China, while others preferred a different course that at varying times saw alignment with Japan or Western nations as a superior strategy. In any case, the Meiji government regarded a Korea that continued to observe the past suzerain-vassal relationship with China as weak and thus potentially hazardous to Japan's own national security interests. From a Japanese perspective, China needed to be supplanted.

Korea, on the other hand, became an attractive target primarily for two reasons. First, as noted above, Japan regarded Korea's continued relationship with China as a security threat. Second, Korea also offered a unique opportunity. Given Meiji Japan's commitment to modernizing along Western lines and abrogating its unequal treaties with the West, a weak Korea under Japan's control afforded Meiji leaders the opportunity to recast Japan as a colonial power, much like Western powers, and to exist as their co-equal. This is precisely the course Japan followed.

In 1875 the Meiji government dispatched several ships off the coast of Korea near the island of Kanghwa under the ruse of conducting water surveys. It was in actuality an attempt to engineer an "incident" with the Korean government. When Korean shore batteries fired upon the Japanese vessels, they retired and Japan dispatched six war vessels ultimately forcing Korea to capitulate and conclude the Treaty of Kanghwa (Korea-Japan Treaty of Amity) in February 1876, the first unequal treaty imposed by one East Asian nation on another and the first unequal treaty to be imposed on Korea. The treaty was designed to accomplish two major ends: to recognize Korea's sovereign independence from China in order to break traditional Sino-Korean ties, and to open trade between Japan and Korea. Its terms were similar to earlier unequal treaties imposed on Japan, the major points of which included opening three new treaty ports to trade with Japan, securing the right to post consuls in new treaty ports, and extending the right of extraterritoriality to Japanese citizens.

Events of the 1880s and 1890s had even further measurable negative impacts on Korea's sovereignty. First, Korea was obliged to enter into its own unequal treaties with Western nations, such as the Treaty of Chemulpo (also known as the Shufeldt Treaty), which it signed in 1882 with the United States (see appendix A). The period also witnessed heightened tensions between Japan and China over the question of Korea's future as each country tried to exert its influence on the peninsula, culminating in the Sino-Japanese War (1894–1895), a war Japan won handily, as evidenced by the 1895 Treaty of Shimonoseki (see appendix B). The treaty again required Korea's independence from China, this time fully and without equivocation, opened several Chinese ports to Japanese trade, granted Japan MFN status, and ceded Taiwan (then Formosa) to Japanese control. The Sino-Japanese War had even greater significance beyond the immediacy of the victory itself or the treaty to which it gave rise. It identified Japan as the preeminent power of East Asia in the eyes of Western nations, supplanting China. What the treaty failed to deliver to Japan, however, was greater immediate access to Korea because of a growing Western influence and interest in Korea and Manchuria. Japan's access would await a conclusive military confrontation with Russia, the nation posing the greatest challenge to its supremacy within Korea.

As the Chinese and Japanese continued to grapple for control of the peninsula during the last half of the nineteenth century, both fell into increasing disfavor among Koreans, the result of which was that the Korean court pursued relations with the Russians to provide a counterbalance to their activities. Consequently, the Russians gained not only the diplomatic upper hand on the peninsula but also a commercial dominance as well. Additionally, following the pattern established during the mid-1800s, as Russia began deriving greater benefit from its presence on the peninsula, so too did other Western nations, and as the influence of Western nations grew there was a commensurate decrease in Japanese influence: Japan was being isolated.

The onset of the twentieth century found Japan's appetite for regional expansion unsatiated, particularly on the Korean peninsula, and this continued desire to expand ran headlong into Russian interests. The mutual exclusivity of Russian and Japanese interests ultimately erupted into military conflict, the Russo-Japanese War (1904–1905), which Japan won decisively, marking the first defeat of a Western power by an East Asian nation. The end result of the conflict was that Japan achieved, in a meteoric thirty-seven-year rise, its Meiji period–inspired goal of standing on equal footing with Western nations.

The Russo-Japanese conflict finds its genesis in three factors that ultimately combined to ignite the military conflagration. First were the conflicting territorial designs of both countries on the Asian mainland, primarily Korea and China. In addition to its expanding influence on the Korean peninsula, Russia gained rights from China during the 1890s to build the Chinese Eastern Railway in Manchuria and lease ports in Dalian and Port Arthur. The second factor was the growing fervor of Japanese nationalism resulting from what Japan considered a national affront in the wake of its victory against China in the Sino-Japanese War. Among the various terms of the Treaty of Shimonoseki was one that ceded the Liaotung Peninsula to Japan. Seen as a threat to Western interests, this prompted the "Tripartite Intervention," which included Russia, France, and Germany intervening to block the hand-over of the peninsula to Japan. In return Japan received a greater indemnity from China, but it was considered a national humiliation among the Japanese that their nation was unable to stand against these three Western powers, the resentment of which would linger. This led directly to the *gashin shōtan* movement that called for a redoubling of Japan's efforts at strengthening its industrial capacity and military capabilities, particularly its naval power.

The third precipitating factor of the Russo-Japanese War was the ever-weakening center of Korean government brought about by domestic instability as a result of an increased foreign presence and dissatisfaction with the ruling class. Recall that the United States also contributed to a growing Western presence on the peninsula. U.S. policy interests on the peninsula included gaining access to Korea's rich natural resources, like gold; extracting monopoly rights in the areas of electricity, railways, waterways, and street cars; and obtaining trade concessions. Thus, the conclusion of the Treaty of Chemulpo on May 22, 1882, can, from the U.S. standpoint, be regarded as a success of its foreign policy pursuits on the peninsula. This increasing presence of external powers, however, led to greater internal destabilization, which manifested itself in events like the Donghak Rebellion of 1894.

The Treaty of Portsmouth, signed on September 5, 1905, formally ended the Russo-Japanese War. It provided that both nations would return sovereign control of Manchuria to China. Japan, however, was leased the Liaotung Peninsula, the prize lost through the Tripartite Intervention, which included both Port Arthur and Dalian. Japan was also leased the Russian rail system in southern Manchuria, providing greater access to strategic resources. Finally, Japan received the southern half of Sakhalin Island, a part of the Kuril archipelago. Russia claimed the islands as its own sovereign territory.

One of the most important prizes Japan took away from its victory against Russia, however, regarded Korea. Often overlooked and not stipulated in the Treaty of Portsmouth, it came at the hands of the United States via the Taft-Katsura Agreement concluded in July 1905. Japan continued to seek official recognition that Korea remained a threat to its security; permitting the issue to languish might invite another incident similar to the Russo-Japanese War. The United States, on the other hand, had placed primacy on its control of the Philippine Islands, regarding them as a strategic stronghold that would help ensure maintenance of an open door policy in China. Thus, the two countries agreed that each would recognize the preponderant interests of the other in their respectively self-designated strategic areas of importance in Asia: the United States recognized Japan's rights in Korea and would not oppose establishment of a Korean protectorate, while reciprocally Japan recognized U.S. supremacy in the Philippines. It was through the aggregate weight of events that Japan achieved a goal that had eluded it for decades—control over the Korean peninsula. The Taft-Katsura Agreement represented the final piece of the puzzle that ensured the demise of Korean sovereignty.[5]

4

Korea Under the
Japanese Colonial Model

Japanese assimilation policy did not simply attempt to eradicate any
notion of Korean identity: it attempted to create a new one.

—*Gi-wook Shin*[1]

The transition from "sovereign nation" to protectorate and colony was
brief but definitive. Japan consolidated control over Korea during 1904–
1907 through the enactment of three conventions, the first of which was
signed in 1904 and extended to Japan the right to install diplomatic and financial
advisors within the Korean government, required Korean officials to seek Japan's
approval on all important diplomatic dealings, and allowed Japan to move military
units onto the peninsula.

The second convention, known as the Eulsa Treaty (Japan-Korea Protectorate Treaty), signed in November 1905 in the wake of the Taft-Katsura agreement (July 1905), gave Japan full administrative control over Korea's foreign
affairs. It also placed all trade activity taking place within Korean ports under
Japanese control and provided for the establishment of the Office of Resident
General, the office responsible for overseeing all Japanese activity on the peninsula. In toto, the Eulsa Treaty transformed Korea into a protectorate.

After the second convention was concluded, the Korean monarch secretly
approached the Second Hague Convention on World Peace, held in June–
October 1907, to entreat the assistance of Western nations in setting aside the
Eulsa Treaty. Korea was not permitted to participate in convention proceedings

nor were the powers interested in interceding on its behalf, consequently leaving the treaty intact. In reaction to the monarch's actions, however, yet a third convention was signed in July 1907 that extended Japan's administrative powers to now include Korea's domestic affairs. The king was also forced to abdicate and the Korean army disbanded.

Full annexation followed on August 22, 1910, via consummation of the Japan-Korea Annexation Treaty (see appendix C). In addition to appointing its first governor-general to administer the new colony, the treaty stipulated the following, among other things:

> Article 1: His Majesty the Emperor of Korea concedes completely and definitely his entire sovereignty over the whole Korean territory to His Majesty the Emperor of Japan.

> Article 2: His Majesty the Emperor of Japan accepts the concession stated in the previous article and consents to the annexation of Korea to the Empire of Japan.

Three major points are to be made with regard to Japan's colonial policy in Korea. First, it was anything but static; it evolved in support of and in response to Japan's broader regional initiatives. Generally, the colonial period, which ran from August 1910 to August 1945, can be divided into four subsets: subjugation of the Koreans, appeasement of the population, supplantation of Korean culture with Japanese culture, and finally, full assimilation.[2] Second, and a point alluded to earlier, as harsh and oppressive as Japan's colonial rule came to be, it represented for the Korean citizenry a point around which to rally. For the first time since the onset of the Choson period, Korea existed as a single and unified polity, both de facto and de jure, sans any internally imposed arbitrary political, cultural, or social divisions. This common focus against an external threat, in turn, led to the growth of Korean nationalism, an awareness of the collective Korean self—political, cultural, and social—vis-à-vis external others, that manifested itself in popular independence movements. Concomitantly, and purely through pursuit of its own self-interests, Japan's colonial administration also brought the halves of the peninsula together economically, creating mutually supportive northern and southern regions on the peninsula to provide necessary resources for the Japanese islands and its later military conquests.

CHARACTER OF JAPANESE OCCUPATION

With full colonization of the peninsula achieved, the character of Japanese administration changed as well. Gone was the post of resident-general, which had been occupied by civilians; it was replaced by the post of governor-general, a position held largely by active-duty military officers. (Japanese colonial authorities were, however, compelled to make one exception to this practice in subsequent years.) Generally, the period of subjugation, which ran roughly from 1910 to 1920, was characterized by the efforts of colonial authorities to promulgate laws extending Japanese control over Korean society and eliminating potential outlets for anti-Japanese sentiment. Thus, all Korean political organizations were abolished and citizens were denied the right to assemble, being forbidden to engage in any meetings, debates, or public speeches. They were also prohibited from owning firearms, swords, knives, and other weapons. Korean newspapers were dissolved, being replaced by government newspapers, one each in Japanese, Korean, and English.[3] Additionally, the *Kyoiku Rei* (Education Law) of August 1911 made Japanese the primary language in Korean schools.[4]

A period of appeasement followed the subjugation period, running from approximately 1920 to 1931, a response to growing Korean demands for independence and general rebellion against harsh colonial rule. Emblematic of such events was the Samil Independence Movement or March 1 Movement, explained in greater detail in a later section. Segueing into a more conciliatory period, the Japanese emperor issued an imperial rescript calling for reconciliation and cultural sensitivity and, as a placatory measure, posted retired Admiral Saito Makoto as governor-general to the Korean colony. Along with reinstatement of other rights, citizens were also permitted to form community organizations and the right to publish newspapers and magazines. This largesse of governance, such as it was, was finite both in scope and duration. For example, while five Korean language newspapers emerged from 1920 to 1931, their content remained closely controlled and censored.

By 1931, colonial policy in Korea had undergone yet another shift, away from appeasement and toward supplanting Korean culture with Japanese culture, based on the idea of unifying Koreans behind the Japanese war effort. This shift, which covered the period 1931–1942, coincided with Japan's more active expansion on the Asian continent, initially into Manchuria, the advent of which can be traced to the Mukden Incident of September 18, 1931.[5] Designed to "engineer" an incident that would warrant a military response, Japan used the incident as a pretext for occupying Manchuria. Colonial policy in Korea sought to support such efforts of expansion: new textbooks were ordered and new curricula developed in addition to mandating classroom instruction in the Japanese language, ethics, and history.

By the time of the second Sino-Japanese War in 1937, the Japanese need to mobilize the Korean people had grown, as had the tenor and speed of supplantation. Colonial administrative authorities sought to mobilize the Korean population in Japan's war effort by inculcating such ideology as *kyouzon kyouhei* (co-existence and co-prosperity) and *naisen yuuwa* (reconciliation between Japan and Korea). Consequently, authorities formed the Korean Association for General National Spiritual Mobilization and initiated anti-Christian campaigns requiring all Christians to participate in Japanese Shinto rituals. They also established national labor camps requiring hundreds of thousands of Korean youth to work in mines and factories. Finally, the Rise Asia Service Day was also created, a program under which Koreans were required to perform certain tasks on the first day of each month for the sake of developing a new Asia. Such policies were in keeping with Japan's concept of the "Greater East Asia Co-Prosperity Sphere," formally announced in 1940 but which had existed under other iterations since 1938.

Full assimilation, which occurred from 1942 to 1945 with the onset of hostilities in the Pacific after the attack on Pearl Harbor on December 7, 1941, represented less of a radical change in policy than it did promulgation of similar "supplantation" policies in greater degrees, in an effort to have Korea render ever-greater service to Japan's war effort. For example, through thorough moral training of the Korean population, colonial authorities hoped to achieve "thought control." Under the Korean Temporary Security Ordinance (December 26, 1941), an increasing number of Koreans were arrested as "thought criminals," with 5,600 arrested during the period 1940–1944.[6] By the close of 1941, education had also felt the hand of Japan's new focus on the war in the Pacific. Classroom instruction was halved and children given other duties such as visiting Shinto shrines to display loyalty to the Japanese emperor, seeing off Japanese troops at the railways, participating in street parades to celebrate battlefield victories, and working at construction sites, such as railroads and airfields.

It was amid implementation of these colonial policies that Korea and its citizens found their solidarity in being "Korean" and nationalism strengthened. The roots of nationalism, however, can be traced back to the latter half of the nineteenth century.

THE BIRTH OF KOREAN NATIONALISM

The rise of Korean nationalism is commonly attributed to the advent of Japanese colonialism. Although Japan's colonial activities on the peninsula fanned nationalism's flames, it was the open competition between China and Japan at the nineteenth century's close, as well as the increased presence of Western nations on the peninsula, that provided the necessary seedlings for its growth. The Donghak Rebellion, emblematic of these trends, chronicles nationalism's embryonic stirrings.

The Donghak Rebellion (1894) was fundamentally a peasant backlash. The rebellion's first phase, carried out January–May 1894, was characterized by its anti-yangban sentiment; the second phase was focused more against the foreign presence on the peninsula. While the preponderant participants in the rebellion were peasants, their number did include disenfranchised and disaffected yangban and scholars as well. Its anti-foreign element, from the perspective of the peasants, was not necessarily focused against any single group but rather opposed all foreign incursions onto the peninsula as a manifestation of festering discontent. For example, anti-Chinese sentiment reached its zenith in 1888–1889 as China continued to attempt to exercise ever-greater control on the peninsula. Korean resentment manifested itself in anti-Chinese riots, resulting in many Chinese shops being looted and burned.

Resentment against the Japanese was twofold, the first source of which derived from Japan's open competition with China to wrest control of the peninsula, effectively symbolized by the Tientsin Convention.[7] Secondly, peasants were reeling from increased taxes imposed upon them by the yangban; many in fact had to sell ancestral lands in order to meet the tax burdens levied on them by landlords. As the yangban profited, their consumption became more conspicuous, examples of which included traveling to Japan or sending their children to attend school there. Such anti-Japanese sentiment crested during the second phase of the Donghak Rebellion (October–November 1894), which was directed against the Japanese and the pro-Japanese government that had been installed in Seoul. The aggregate weight of Chinese and Japanese activity, along with Western incursion into Korea discussed earlier, undergirded growing popular anti-foreign sentiment.

The response to the increased foreign presence on the peninsula was by no means monolithic: there were factions among the ruling class in support of forging stronger alliances with foreign powers and those against following such a course. What is significant, however, irrespective of any single position in the argument for or against a foreign presence, was the emerging recognition among Koreans of Korea's national identity juxtaposed against the cultural kaleido-scope of nations with a presence on the peninsula: Japan, China, Russia, Great Britain, United States, and France. Expanded contact and interaction with other nations then allowed Korean citizens to develop a sense of the "Korean self," a distinct and unique political, cultural, and historical entity, a phenomenon that more fully took root during the colonial period.

Japan's colonial policy was at its core an attempt to supplant Korean cultural identity with an ethos of subordinate Japanese "subject" embraced in the concept of *chosenjin*, which was at once defining and disparaging. As Henry Em points out, the term "applied to all Koreans regardless of gender, regional origin, or class."[8] Implementation of the chosenjin concept led to such practices as forcing Koreans to adopt Japanese names while at the same time distinguishing them as being somehow inferior to the Japanese.[9] Ironically, that Japanese colonial authorities pursued policies treating all Koreans with equal disdain, former yangban and commoners alike, fortified the growth of nationalism by helping unite Koreans against political and cultural emasculation wrought by an external power.[10]

Recall that the four phases of Japan's colonial policy are distinguishable only in terms of degree and the impact external events had on the evolution of these policies. Policy pursuits of this nature led to increasing anti-colonial resentment among Koreans, one of the best examples of which was the March 1 Movement (1919), which was essentially an expression of the Korean self against an external "other," the first of its kind in Korean history.

While Gi-wook Shin and other scholars of similar thought argue that there exists a more complex and nuanced linkage between Japanese colonialism and the emergence of a respondent Korean nationalism, an identifiable and credible relationship nonetheless does exist between the two.[11] Fundamentally, without the external systematic attempts of the Japanese colonial administration to subjugate and eradicate Korean culture as it existed and assimilate "Korean" subjects into the Japanese empire, there would have been little impetus for uniting theretofore politically and culturally disparate halves of the peninsula. There simply was no historical context for doing so.

As the close of World War II approached, new hope emerged among Koreans that sovereignty and the right to self-determination would be returned to them, as was put forth in the Cairo Declaration (November 1943).[12] The fate that awaited Korea, however, was vastly different and would represent a return to the past—a peninsula divided—except this time formal and de jure.

THE OCCUPATION—A FAILED MANDATE

The Allied decision to divide and ultimately occupy the peninsula was one of strategic expediency for the United States. The Soviets formally declared war on Japan on August 8, 1945, and within two days had moved onto the Korean peninsula and into the northeastern cities of Chongjin and Nanam. Concerned that the Soviets were building momentum to sweep farther south, U.S. planners devised a scheme that would essentially divide the peninsula between the United States and Soviet Union. The plan called for dividing Korea roughly equidistantly along the 38th parallel, a location that recognized U.S. interests— as the southern part included the capital city of Seoul as well as Kaesong, the ancient capital and important cultural site—while also recognizing Soviet interests farther north—natural resources and ice-free ports.[13] The division left the preponderant natural resources and land mass in the Soviet half, while much of the population (twenty-one of thirty million) and twelve of Korea's twenty major cities remained in the southern half to be administered by the United States.

Soviet and U.S. occupation authorities had four mandates: 1) accept surrender of Japanese military forces and colonial officials and facilitate demobilization, 2) disassemble the colonial administrative apparatus, 3) replace the colonial administration with a functional governing apparatus, and 4) establish an intermediate trusteeship on the peninsula that would facilitate restoration of Korea's sovereignty sans any occupation authority. It was with the fourth and final mandate that U.S. and Soviet occupation authorities fell short and, in the process, set into motion events that would leave Korea formally divided.

The concept of creating a trusteeship on the peninsula resulted from the Foreign Ministers' Conference of December 1945 held in Moscow and attended by the Soviet Union, United States, and Great Britain. It was agreed during this summit that the line bisecting the peninsula into its then two occupation zones should be removed at the earliest practicable opportunity. To assist in working through the modalities of such an undertaking, a joint commission was established, consisting of American and Soviet representatives. While the commission did enjoy some amount of success in working through lesser issues such as establishing guidelines for conducting transborder ground and water transportation, mail exchange, and radio frequencies, U.S.-Soviet relations were, on the whole, marred by distrust and acrimony, as discussions of the peninsula's future were taking place within the broader context of an emerging Cold War. Consequently, returning sovereignty to a unified Korea became a secondary objective, supplanted by activities that ensured the respective occupation zones aligned themselves politically with their occupation overseers.

Ultimately, failure of the Soviets and Americans to reconcile political differences led U.S. authorities to seek redress through the United Nations, which on November 14, 1947, created the architecture for moving forward with Korean self-determination, including the formulation of the UN Temporary Commission on Korea, mandated to hold free elections on the peninsula. The Soviets vehemently opposed these measures, refusing to permit elections in the northern zone. Elections were held in the southern occupation zone, and on August 15, 1948, the National Assembly created the Republic of Korea (South Korea). By contrast, no free elections were held in the Soviet zone, however, the Supreme People's Assembly ratified a constitution in September 1948 and elected Kim Il-sung as its premier. By the following month the Soviet Union and other communist bloc nations officially recognized the Democratic People's Republic of Korea (North Korea). With this, Korea's fortunes had come full circle—a nation that had existed as a de facto bifurcated nation since the onset of the Choson period was now divided de jure.

5

A Post–World War II
Overview

Fewer than one in five South Koreans believe reunification will occur
within the next 10 years.

—Gallup News[1]

U ntil about the late 1980s, both South and North Korea, refusing to recognize the legitimacy of the other's sovereignty, staunchly held that
Korean unification could only occur through absorption under their respective governments, the tools for which included some combination of force
and fomentation of internal strife and instability. The resultant nadir of this approach manifested itself in the Korean War, commencing on June 25, 1950, with
a pre-dawn attack by North Korea on its southern neighbor, and ending July 27,
1953, with the signing of the Korean Armistice Agreement by U.S., Chinese,
and North Korean representatives. Conspicuous through absence was any South
Korean signatory to the armistice as then president Syngman Rhee refused to
take part in the negotiations or signing. The armistice did little, however, toward
bringing about the cessation of peninsular polemics between the two Koreas
during the ensuing decades. Rather, the continued enmity provided grist for the
continuation of "war" through other means: vitriolic propaganda, subterfuge,
acts of terrorism, and political assassination.

CHANGE IN THE SOUTH

Although mutual animus best describes conditions on the peninsula through the
mid-1980s, 1988 witnessed the beginnings of a fundamental shift on both sides

of the DMZ with regard to inter-Korean relations and attendant unification policies. Under the administration of then president Roh Tae-woo (1988–1993), Seoul pursued a new policy of *Nordpolitik* under which it achieved rapprochement with various socialist nations through targeted economic and diplomatic outreach, resulting in the successful geopolitical isolation of the North Korean regime. Among those nations with which South Korea achieved rapprochement were China and the former Soviet Union, North Korea's primary socialist guarantors during most of the Cold War.

At the core of this newly established détente was Chinese and Soviet abandonment of the maligned "command economy" model that had to that point characterized socialist economies. This resulted in ever-reduced levels of economic and military support to the North Korean regime. As a result of Seoul's successful engagement of past socialist adversaries, and the accompanying isolation of the North Korean regime, its own previously hard-line approach to national unification began softening. This ultimately spawned a series of South Korean engagement policies espousing pursuit of more robust economic, cultural, and diplomatic relations with its northern neighbor, while simultaneously seeking to reduce military and nuclear tensions, that would provide the precursors necessary for more serious consideration of, and consultation on, the unification issue.

The most familiar of these engagement policies, and arguably among the most forward leaning, was late former president Kim Dae-jung's (1998–2003) Sunshine Policy, although the genesis for such engagement can be traced to a point some ten years earlier under the Roh administration. Under his Han People's Commonwealth Unification Plan formula, first proposed in September 1989, Roh posited that unification required: 1) the two Koreas pursue unification independently of the world's then superpowers, 2) peaceful pursuit of unification rather than the incessant threat of hostile absorption that had come to characterize their respective unification policies, and 3) pursuit of unification through democratic means that recognized the will of the Korean people.[2] Roh, in his July 4, 1988, Special Presidential Declaration for National Self-Esteem, Unification and Prosperity, also called for the two Koreas to work for the peninsula's common prosperity, and to that end supported mutual exchanges and open trade. Finally, Roh laid the groundwork for future cross-border economic cooperation by promulgating the 1990 Law of Inter-Korean Exchanges and Cooperation, which came to form the basis for later inter-Korean commercial activity. Thus, the Roh administration represents a key transitional period with respect to South Korea's more recent northern engagement policies.[3]

With the exception of former president Kim Young-sam (1993–1998) whose approach to inter-Korean relations was more hard-line, South Korean presidential administrations since the late 1980s have followed various models of comparatively broader engagement of the North Korean regime espoused by Roh Tae-woo's approach and his Han People's Commonwealth Unification Plan.

Kim Dae-jung's Sunshine Policy represented the next major step forward in the evolution of the nation's engagement policy of the North Korean regime. Kim's program sought to advance inter-Korean relations based on two fundamental principles: 1) purposely setting aside contentious political issues in favor of economic and cultural pursuits that were more easily agreed upon, and 2) requiring reciprocity from the North Korean regime. Kim subscribed to the idea that compromise would help to stabilize the relationship and, in turn, the situation on the Korean peninsula.

In retrospect, the policy has received mixed reviews with regard to its effectiveness. On the one hand, Kim was instrumental in laying the groundwork for several major initiatives such as the Kaesong (Gaesong) Industrial Complex, several reunions of family members separated by the DMZ, creation of the Mount Kumgang tourist region that until June 2008 permitted over one million South Korean tourists to visit the North Korean coastal resort area each year, and the historic summit between the countries' respective leaders in June 2000.[4] On the other hand, criticism runs deep that the Kim administration was long on concessions but short on demanding reciprocal actions from the North that could be considered meaningful confidence-building measures. Detractors also point to the cost of undertaking some of the initiatives under the rubric of the Sunshine Policy. For example, during Kim's administration nearly $1.2 billion (U.S.) was provided to North Korea in the form of food, fertilizer, and other aid; investments associated with the Mount Kumgang project were in excess of $1.5 billion (U.S.); and $79 million (U.S.) was spent to construct the new railroad from Munsan in South Korea into the DMZ.[5] Yet the North Korean regime provided little in the way of substantive reciprocal confidence-building measures and indeed continued to pursue its nuclear and ballistic missile programs during the period.

An important historical point, however, should be borne in mind. Both the *Nordpolitik* of Roh Tae-woo and the *Ostpolitik* of Willy Brandt, chancellor of West Germany (October 1969–May 1974), took time to develop. Nordpolitik,

having the advantage of confluent destabilizing economic and social circumstances occurring within socialist bloc nations by the late 1980s, took a far shorter time to yield results; Ostpolitik took several decades to facilitate the demise
of socialism. In the end, however, each was successful. Thus, the final chapter of
the Sunshine Policy may not yet have been written.

Late former president Roh Moo-hyun's (2003–2008) Peace Prosperity
Policy represented a continuation of Kim's Sunshine Policy, which expressly
stated,

> The policy of reconciliation and cooperation promoted by the previ-
> ous government has paved the way for the dismantling of the Cold
> War structure on the Korean peninsula and produced substantial im-
> provements in inter-Korean relations. The new government's Policy
> for Peace and Prosperity is intended to build on the progress achieved
> through the policy of reconciliation and cooperation.[6]

The policy's stated goals included promotion of peace on the peninsula,
pursuit of shared prosperity, resolution of issues through dialogue, mutual trust
and mutuality, promotion of international cooperation based on the principle of
"parties directly concerned," and expansion of public participation.[7] By far the
most visible materialization of this policy was the completion of the Kaesong
Industrial Complex, the planning for which appropriately began under Kim's
administration in 2000. Despite its associated problems and the North Korean
regime's tendency to use the complex against the South Korean government as
leverage, it stands as South Korea's single greatest testament to its commitment
to further inter-Korean cooperation.

Current president Lee Myung-bak's "Vision 3000: Denuclearization and
Openness" policy seeks to infuse greater pragmatism into, and demands more
reciprocity from, the relationship with North Korea than did the policies of his
two predecessors. Conceptually, the policy calls for the North Korean regime to
abandon its nuclear weapons program in exchange for massive economic aid, to
include ultimately increasing the average per capita annual income in North Korea to a level of $3,000 (U.S.) within one decade nearly three times the current
per capita gross national income. Lankov points to the improbability of this policy ever succeeding, however, because of its problematic wording. Specifically,
he cites the Korean word used for openness, *kaebang*, which has always had negative connotations within the peninsular geopolitical context for North Korean

officials. As Lankov notes, "North Korean ideologues have repeatedly described [openness] as a cunning imperialist trick aimed at destroying the North's socialist system."[8] Another point that clearly militates against the success of this policy—and an idea central to my earlier book, *Nuclear Endgame: The Need for Engagement with North Korea*—is that the regime will be highly unlikely to voluntarily relinquish what it sees as its only, and very effective, geopolitical bargaining chip against the rest of the world—its nuclear weapons program.[9] Directly linking denuclearization to unification relegates such policy discussions to the same moribundity the Six Party Talks currently suffer, for largely the same reasons.

Thus, what can be gleaned from the preceding review of engagement overtures is that Seoul's successive policies since the late 1980s have been predicated on two fundamental principles. First, that setting aside immediate discussion of sensitive political matters (this does not, however, include denuclearization discussions) in favor of pursuing expanded economic, cultural, and diplomatic relations with the North Korean regime would: 1) ameliorate relations with its vitriolic northern neighbor in the near term; 2) facilitate reduction of military and nuclear tensions on the peninsula; and 3) help promote North Korea's stabilization, particularly its economy, so as to minimize the possibility of major disruption of the South Korean economy, in the event of unification. The second principle upon which these policies have been predicated, and intrinsic to the first, is the notion that unification will occur through circumstances favorable to South Korea, either through creation of a confederation or absorption of the North. In short, the premise of Seoul's northern policy since the late 1980s is based on the belief that expanded economic and cultural engagement with the North will facilitate an evolutionary, non-violent, non-antagonistic approach to unification.

CHANGE IN THE NORTH

Pyongyang too has undergone a metamorphosis over the decades in regard to its relationship with Seoul and its own unification formula. The impetus for this transformative change was brought about not by any successful policy implementation but rather by begrudgingly pragmatic responses to a series of long-term miscalculations, failures, and changing external factors, which in the end isolated the regime at a critical juncture of confluent events.

First, the timing and success of South Korea's Nordpolitik policy proved a major blow to the regime. Seoul's economic outreach to socialist bloc nations began netting results early on as rapprochement was achieved with Hungary, Poland, and Yugoslavia by the end of 1989; Bulgaria, Czechoslovakia, Romania, Algeria, Mongolia, and the Soviet Union joined their ranks by the close of the following year. Equally significant during 1990, of course, was German reunification, and by 1992 Seoul had achieved rapprochement with Beijing as well. The common denominator in each of these cases was an underperforming command economy that plagued socialist nations and inhibited their ability to sustain themselves or the societies they had been designed to support. Thus, as economic pragmatism replaced socialist ideology, Seoul's willingness and ability to provide expanded trade opportunities and other forms of economic remedies, along with diplomatic engagement, proved to be a strong attraction to socialist bloc nations. While the aggregate weight of the abandonment of socialist ideals proved devastating to the North Korean regime, in the end nothing had a greater impact than the loss of its Cold War guarantors, China and the former Soviet Union.

Under the leadership of Deng Xiaoping, China committed to market reforms and extricating itself from the weight of an ineffective command economy model as early as 1978 and continued along that trajectory into the 1990s. Deng's vision was one of a new "socialist market economy" model that introduced a measure of openness toward global markets and key elements of capitalism.[10] Similarly, an economically beleaguered Soviet Union, under the tenets of Mikhail Gorbachev's policies of perestroika (economic reforms and restructuring) and *novoe myshlenie* ("New Thinking" with regard to Soviet foreign policy pursuits), began to demand a more pragmatic relationship with the North Korean regime. Gone were the days of providing extensive economic and military support based solely on shared ideological principles. The Soviets began requiring cash payments for support, a demand the North Korean regime was in no position to satisfy.[11] Consequently, economic relations between the two countries cooled quite rapidly. For example, whereas, until 1990, trade with the Soviet Union had represented 50 percent of North Korea's trade volume, that level dropped precipitously to an inconsequential 3 percent in the post-1990 period.[12] Other examples were equally stark. According to Soviet sources, by October 1986, the Soviet Union was responsible for either reconstructing or newly constructing sixty industrial plants in North Korea, accounting for some 28 percent of North Korean steel, 66 percent of total electricity production, and 50 percent of petroleum products.[13] Soviet unwillingness to continue such policies of largesse thus had a debilitating impact on the regime.

Another regime miscalculation came in the form of its own domestic economic policies, both agricultural and industrial. By the early 1960s the regime had set about modernizing the country's agricultural base, a goal it pursued with little regard for long-term consequences. Pyongyang's agricultural policies called for indiscriminant use of chemical fertilizers and increased mechanization, both of which in the short term led to desired higher crop yields, but in the long term resulted in overuse of the soil and depletion of its nutrients, ultimately drastically reducing crop yields. To compensate for this, farmers were forced to look for new agricultural lands, in short supply in the mountainous North. The immediate response was to denude more and more hillsides of natural vegetation and put them to agricultural use. The long-term consequence of having done so was to amplify the impact of natural disasters. Hillsides denuded of natural vegetation were more susceptible to soil run-off during heavy rains, which deposited rocks and dirt into streams and rivers making them more shallow and liable to greater flooding. This, in turn, magnified the impact of drought. The 1990s bore witness to both devastating floods and drought in North Korea, leading to massive starvation.[14]

Industrial policy proved equally deficient. Despite the industrial comparative advantage North Korea enjoyed over its southern neighbor at the time the peninsula was divided in 1948—a by-product of Japanese colonial policy that sought to build a robust industrial base in northern Korea to help sustain its war effort in the Pacific—by the end of the 1950s the regime had begun to put in place programs and policies that would ultimately squander this advantage. For example, in 1958, as part of its five-year plan (1957–1961), the regime implemented a program called *Chollima Undong* (Flying Horse Movement) designed to spur rapid industrialization and economic growth. Its objectives and execution were remarkably similar to Mao's Great Leap Forward, also launched in 1958.[15] The long-term results of the Chollima movement were as unimpressive as the model upon which it was based largely because: 1) industrialization depended more heavily on ever-increasing inputs of human capital rather than refining processes or improving associated technologies, and 2) the program was substantially based on maintaining industrial symbiosis—the success of any single industry hinged on the ability of others to sustain it.

By 1959, however, this symbiotic relationship had begun to break down primarily because managers within the various sectors of the economy were being pressured to over-produce in order to exceed targets spelled out in the five-year plan. Over-production in one sector required over-production in the other sectors to maintain a critical balance, which did not happen. Consequently, mounting inequities developed, leading to rivalries between and among the various ministries in charge of production.[16] B. C. Koh notes that the regime's efforts at industrialization had gone even further afield by 1977 as the North Korean economy was plagued by interrelated problems in five areas: logistics, electric power production, mining, agriculture, and management.[17] Because transportation assets were inadequate, sufficient raw material, such as iron, could not be transported to production facilities to keep them operating at full capacity. This condition was further exacerbated by the mining industry, itself functioning at less than optimal levels. Drought impacted operation of hydroelectric plants, which together provided two-thirds of the country's power requirements.[18] Finally, the nation's cadre of management proved generally incapable of properly handling the regime's factors of production: machinery was improperly maintained, human capital was ill employed, and managers lacked the requisite skill sets to effectively bring about the increased levels of industrialization the regime pursued.

There were other clear signals during the mid-1970s that the North Korean economy was beset by trouble. By 1976 the full extent of North Korea's inability to repay its debts to Japanese firms became known: Tokyo banks estimated that the regime was in arrears $62 million (U.S.) to various Japanese commercial activities.[19] Additionally, the Japan External Trade Organization estimated that North Korea's trade deficit for the years 1973 to 1975 totaled nearly $1.4 billion (U.S.).[20] By 1984 the regime was compelled, because of deteriorating domestic economic conditions, to reassess its long-standing policy of isolation from the rest of the world, which manifested itself in the promulgation of a special joint-venture law in September of that year. The goal of this legislation was to create opportunities to establish economic ties with other countries irrespective of their ideological leanings provided they respected North Korean sovereignty. Not surprisingly, the regime's long and well-documented history of defaulting on debts and its unpredictability undercut any potential success this program might have offered, as world governments and corporate interests were not keen to engage it.

Such reassessment, nonetheless, stood in stark contrast to the regime's bellicosity of earlier decades and continued throughout the 1980s into the 1990s, in the wake of North Korea's increased isolation, decreased support from former socialist partners, and pursuit of its nuclear weapons and ballistic missile programs. What I refer to as North Korea's "belligerent survival period," which prioritizes regime survival over national unification, continues presently and is most accurately characterized by adherence to two seemingly antithetical policies: its continued vituperative posture toward South Korea (and the United States) on the one hand, while demonstrating a willingness to accept humanitarian assistance from South Korea, China, and the world on the other. Consider North Korea's continued lambasting of President Lee Myung-bak's administration since it came to power in February 2008 for what the regime regards as its hostile posture against the North.[21] This was underscored by the expulsion of South Korean officials from the jointly operated Kaesong Industrial Complex in December 2008 and the unilateral closing of the overland border between the two countries in March 2009.[22] Yet the regime relies on South Korean firms at the complex to employ over 40,000 North Korean workers.[23] The regime also profits directly from complex operations as it takes in a total of USD\$33.5 million annually.[24]

Since 1995, the South Korean government and non-governmental organizations (NGO) have also supplied a total of 3.032 trillion won (over \$2.21 billion) worth of humanitarian assistance in the form of food and fertilizer.[25] North Korea remains among the world's largest recipients of humanitarian assistance through the United Nations World Food Program. Recall that for the period 1988–2008, the regime ranks third among all nations receiving food assistance globally. When one considers only the ten-year period from 1999 to 2008, North Korea climbs to number two on the list having received 9.1 million tons of food assistance; Ethiopia received 10 million tons during the same period.[26] Despite this massive infusion of aid, need for external assistance continues unabated as underscored by emergency relief operations undertaken by the WFP in spring 2011. Additionally, an international NGO, Good Friends, reported that from January to February 2010, 300 deaths were recorded in the Sinuiju area, a western region bordering China. Another 1,000 were reportedly "on the verge of starving to death."[27]

Given the regime's nearly insatiable need for external assistance, its open antagonism toward South Korea and the United States seems incongruent. It is this dichotomous approach the regime pursues in regard to inter-Korean relations and its geopolitical engagement policies that complicates the unification process geometrically.

PART II

6

The Roads toward Unification

Korea is like an organism that can live only as one and which cannot live if divided into two. . . . It is important for us to always work with the question of unification in mind. We should think of unification when we awake in the morning and when we go to bed at night. All our thinking should be linked to unification.

—*Kim Jong-il*[1]

The leaders of the two Koreas must contemplate what they can do to make the lives of all 70 million Koreans happy and how each side can respect the other and open the door to unification.

—*President Lee Myung-bak, South Korea*[2]

It is against this kaleidoscopic backdrop of geopolitical, economic, and diplomatic events and circumstances that both North and South Korea have publicly (and often) pronounced their individual or joint support for building a framework that promotes peaceful coexistence and unifies the Korean peninsula. In fact, since the year 1972, both have articulated, in various forms and through numerous official forums and media, mutual support of efforts to move toward unification. For example, the South-North Joint Communiqué (July 4, 1972), to which both nations were signatories, stipulated the following points:

Firstly, reunification should be achieved independently, without reliance upon outside force or its interference;

Secondly, reunification should be achieved by peaceful means, without recourse to the use of arms against the other side;
Thirdly, great national unity should be promoted first of all as one nation, transcending the differences of ideology, ideal and system.[3]

Thus, a formally articulated concept for peaceful peninsular unification has
existed for decades, since reiterated in various forms. The Joint Statement issued
June 15, 2000, in the wake of the historic meeting between then South Korean
president Kim Dae-jung and North Korean leader Kim Jong-il, continued in
the tradition established three decades earlier:

The North and the South agreed to solve the question of the country's reunification independently by the concerted efforts of the
Korean nation responsible for it. . . . The North and the South, recognizing that the low-level federation proposed by the North and the
commonwealth system proposed by the South for the reunification of
the country have similarity, agreed to work together for the reunification in this direction in the future.[4]

This commitment was again reinforced on October 4, 2007, when then
president Roh Moo-hyun and chairman Kim Jong-il concluded the Declaration
for Inter-Korean Development, Peace and Prosperity:

The South and the North [will] resolve the problem of unification
through "the spirit of our own initiative," and through the primacy
of Korean people's dignity and interests. . . . The South and the North
[will] develop inter-Korean relations toward the direction of unification and adjust necessary legal institutional apparatus respectively.[5]

But what do such official proclamations really mean? And what are their
foundational elements?

Despite these periodic official expressions of mutual support for unification, peninsular amalgamation is anything but a foregone conclusion for two
important reasons. First, just as the two nations have developed diametrically
over the decades in the political, cultural, and economic sense, so too have their
respective visions for how best to unify the peninsula come to diverge. Second,
any unification formula leaving in place the current unpredictable, belligerent,

and militant North Korean regime in fact would not achieve true unification, but rather some permutation of present conditions.

North and South Korea have, over the years, proffered differing formulas for achieving unification, each evolving through various iterations, the end result of which yielded a South Korean unification formula based on principles of "confederation" and a North Korean model based on "federation" principles. (Evolution of the models may well continue. For example, during the 2000 Summit, Kim Jong-il described the North Korean federation model as a "loose" form of federation. The aim here, however, is not to dissect each model and explain their respective permutations, but rather to give the reader a sense of the general divergence that exists between the two countries on the issue of unification.) Despite the variance in the two visions, however, both are undergirded by one important similarity: each model seeks to play to respective strengths while mitigating weaknesses to ensure one Korea maintains dominance over the other, hence decreasing the likelihood that either represents a bona fide workable solution for peninsular unification under a scenario in which both existing governments remain intact.

Fundamentally, unification can broadly occur under one of two conditions: peacefully or through conflict. This book assumes any unification efforts will follow a peaceful course for three reasons. First, North Korea has demonstrated no appetite for large-scale conflict despite its long history of geopolitical histrionics; indeed, its best interests are protected through maintenance of peace. Conflict puts the regime itself at risk, and regime survival has been the prime motivator for much of North Korean behavior since the 1990s. Conflict also portends grave economic consequences. For example, regime leadership reaps direct benefits from the Kaesong Industrial Complex, all of which are placed in certain jeopardy in a conflict scenario. In addition to taking a percentage of each worker's salary, the regime derives benefits through foreign currency earnings, corporate taxes, and the sale of raw materials and other industrial goods, the potential total earnings of which could reach over $1 billion (U.S.).[6] Other inter-Korean economic linkages would also be jeopardized, such as the various joint venture initiatives between South and North Korean commercial firms.[7]

Second, with the Korean War standing as testament to the waste that could result on both sides of the DMZ, the South Korean people have no interest in pursuing unification through conflict. Late former president Roh Moo-hyun effectively captured such sentiment in comments offered during a speech delivered to the Foreign Affairs Council of Los Angeles in November 2004, when he noted, "Koreans, who haven't gotten over the trauma of the Korean War half a century ago, do not want another war on the peninsula."[8] One must also consider the American public's lack of appetite for additional conflict given the nation's protracted involvement in Afghanistan and Iraq. The mutual security arrangement outlined in the 1953 U.S.-R.O.K. Mutual Defense Treaty would, however, require such involvement. Finally, conflict is economically unviable. The South Korean economy is among the largest and most robust global economies; conflict could devastate not only South Korea's economy but many larger economies in the world to which it is connected. For example, South Korea is the seventh largest trading partner to the United States, with total 2010 annual trade figures reaching nearly $49 billion in imports and $39 billion in exports.[9]

Peaceful unification presents several possible scenarios, first among them being a sudden and cataclysmic implosion of the regime followed by North Korea's absorption. Since as far back as the 1980s, when true conditions of the North Korean economy began to emerge, prognosticators have offered a hopeful yet chimerical assessment of conditions in North Korea that would lead to regime demise; while it ranks among the world's most needy nations, North Korea continues to defy the odds of its own implosion. One must also consider the possibility of unification based on the formulas proffered by the two Koreas themselves through which some accommodative middle ground would be reached, allowing for the continued existence of both governments. While outwardly they may represent the least controversial approach because neither Korea is absorbed into the other, both the federal and confederal formulas lack the basis for true unification absent a massive and fundamental shift in the regime's inter-Korean policies and the antagonistic manner in which they are pursued. Peninsular amalgamation cannot be achieved with the continued existence of the North Korean regime. Finally, I envision another possible scenario: absorption through economic attrition—the purposeful and gradual wearing down of the North Korean economy with a commensurate increase in its dependency on external sources of economic assistance, to the point that it can no longer stand on its own. At the heart of such a scenario lies the concept of Asymmetric Economic Statecraft introduced in an earlier book, *Nuclear Endgame: The Need for Engagement with North Korea.*[10]

In the end, the path toward unification remains murky and unpredictable. Many major geopolitical events often occur with little warning and are based on various sets of uncontrollable circumstances. Peninsular unification will likely number among them. Consequently, the discussion that follows, in this chapter and the next, does not attempt to predict how unification will unfold but rather examines each of three roads toward unification in terms of viability—both the South and North Korean formulas, and the possibility of absorption.

SOUTH KOREAN MODEL OF CONFEDERATION

Although variances have existed in the policies crafted by successive South Korean presidential administrations that would put into place the necessary precursors for unification—for example the pragmatic Vision 3000 policy versus the more forward leaning and accommodating Sunshine Policy—the ultimate goal of achieving a unified Korean state based on the principles of a confederal model has remained fairly constant. (While the current Lee administration has not expressly abandoned this formula, there are indications that it may be moving in another direction, a topic discussed in the following chapter.) The South Korean unification model provides a two-tiered transition into unification, the second of which calls for the creation of a Korean commonwealth based on confederal principles, a concept known formally as the National Commonwealth Unification formula, first introduced by the Roh Tae-woo administration in 1989. It should be noted, however, that while general agreement exists among South Korean political leaders on the broad formulaic construct of a confederal model, universal agreement has not necessarily extended to its detailed application.

Generally, the first tier of the South Korean plan, functioning as the foundation for the entire process and facilitating advancement to the second tier, is predicated upon instituting a host of cross-border confidence-building measures that assist in establishing mutual trust, dispelling decades-long animus, and extending cooperative ventures across a broad field of exchanges and other activities. Thus, rapprochement achieved during this initial period, it is argued, will help to advance the unification process to the next tier, establishing the National Commonwealth based on the principle of "one nation, two states, two governments, and two systems." Basically, this concept provides for the following:

1. Creation of a central government under which two separate, sovereign, and autonomous states would exist and over which any central government would exercise no real control. Thus, each state would maintain and pursue its own foreign policy and diplomatic activities. This, of course, would not necessarily preclude joint pursuit of common goals, but it is not mandated either. Further, both countries

would maintain their respective military force structures; the confederation as an entity would have no military.

2. While a constitution for the confederation would be jointly developed by South and North Korea, each would maintain its own constitution and any legislation enacted by the central government would lack force of law until it was ratified by each state.

3. Under such a model the question of nationality is not broached until the third phase (full unification) as citizens of each nation would maintain their current citizenship.[11]

The single greatest advantage this model affords is that the existing South Korean governmental structure remains intact with little or no authority vested in the central government. This allows the South Korean government to function much as it does presently with little involvement by the North Korean government.

DEMOCRATIC CONFEDERAL REPUBLIC OF KORYO

Alternatively, North Korea has adhered to and promoted a federation model for unification under the moniker *Democratic Confederal Republic of Koryo*, a plan first introduced by the late Kim Sung-il in October 1980 during proceedings of the sixth plenary session of the Korean Workers' Party, and predicated upon the principle of "one nation, one unified state, two local governments, and two systems." At its core, the federation model is based on the following principles:

1. That both states create a central national government to exercise control over the nation's diplomatic and political functions and military force structure. The two local governments would be officially recognized and permitted to create their own policies and adhere to their individual ideologies.

2. That the central government would have equal representation from both North and South Korea through creation of a Supreme National Confederal Assembly.

3. That some amount of representation for emigrant Koreans would also be permitted.

4. That a fundamental overhaul of the South Korean government take place to ensure its "full democratization," which would allow the Koreas to independently pursue unification.[12]

One intriguing feature of this model is that it allows for no gradual phasing of its proposed federal state and offers no working solutions as to how such an end state might be achieved given the diametrically opposed political ideologies of the two Koreas, which raises some basic questions as to its viability. For example, given the fundamental disparities in the ideologies of the two nations, how would issues related to stark differences in military or diplomatic postures be reconciled to the point that a unified position could be put forward? There is nothing in the history of inter-Korean relations that provides context for this; consider the geopolitical wrangling over North Korea's ballistic missile and nuclear weapons programs since the 1990s.

The fourth point cited earlier also provides grist for additional consideration. North Korean officials have typically used the term "independently pursue" in regard to the Koreas' efforts to unify, meaning no interference from outside powers, which has historically been directed at U.S. involvement and the need to eliminate the presence of U.S. forces on the peninsula.

One of the primary advantages this model affords the North Korean regime is that it dismisses inherent imbalances that exist between the two nations with regard to their respective populations, economies, per capita income, and other metrics. Under North Korea's Democratic Confederal Republic of Koryo plan, proportionality is given short shrift in favor of a governmental structure that allows for equal representation and voice between the two Koreas. Another advantage, of course, is that under this model the South Korean government would be required to abrogate its decades-long security relationship with the United States and fundamentally discard the democratic basis of its government.

REAL WORLD CONDITIONS

Analysis of the two competing unification formulas proffered by South and North Korea amounts to a hollow exercise unless juxtaposed against possible real-world scenarios. This section examines these concepts in regard to several real-world cases in order to offer an instructive glimpse into the challenges that potentially lie ahead under a transition into unification.

As discussed earlier, the confederal and federal unification models present their respective conceptual challenges as each is designed either to capitalize on existing strengths, mitigate weaknesses, or perhaps neutralize the other's perceived advantages. South Korea's confederal model keeps at arm's length the specter of any real North Korean influence within South Korea's structure of governance and reduces unification to a process of establishing a loose central governing structure that is essentially secondary to the two autonomous states. It also reduces the prospect of regime influence in South Korean domestic affairs by leaving untouched constitutional and legislative prerogatives, thus providing no mechanism for equal representation. With no legislative leverage, the North Korean regime would have no substantive means of "democratizing" the South Korean governance structure. Similarly, the North Korean model seeks an equal voice in what can only be described as a largely unequal relationship, at once eliminating all existing inequities between the two countries.

From the South Korean perspective, the expediencies of the confederal model appear perfectly logical given the inconsistent and brinkmanship-like behaviors that have become the hallmark of North Korean geopolitics, which represents a huge variable in the unification equation. Thus, the larger question becomes, what does North Korean intransigence portend for successful implementation of either model? Given the sixty-three-year history of inter-Korean politics, it is difficult to envision any short-term successful implementation of either the federal or confederal unification concepts as efforts would undoubtedly become mired in the usual peninsular polemics.

The tumultuous state of inter-Korean relations since the inauguration of President Lee Myung-bak on February 25, 2008, presents a set of circumstances that would challenge either model. The Lee administration has followed a policy of pragmatism that demands some measure of reciprocity with regard to South Korea's relationship with the North Korean regime, a clear departure from the policies of his predecessors, and one that has elicited unyielding North Korean intransigence and vituperation.[13] Reciprocity is usually defined in terms of the North Korean regime's denuclearization. In return for the regime's willingness to provide such a "de-weaponizing" confidence-building measure, Lee has proposed his "Grand Bargain," a package of security assurances and economic incentives, conceptually not unlike past assurances offered through the Six Party Talks but larger in scope. As a part of this package of inducements the South Korean presidential administration has put forth its Vision 3000: Denuclearization and Openness, which in addition to other inducements promises to increase the average North Korean per capita annual income by three times its current level, from $1,152 (U.S.) to $3,000 (U.S.) within a decade. (The entire Vision 3000 proposal envisions assistance across five sectors: industry, education, welfare, infrastructure, and finance, all of which would be underwritten by a $40 billion [U.S.] international development fund.[14]) Predictably, the North Korean response to these overtures has been characteristically truculent. The regime's

May 27, 2009, announcement that it was abrogating the 1953 cease-fire agreement concluded in the wake of the Korean War as a result of South Korea's participation in the Proliferation Security Initiative (PSI) serves as just one example.[15]

In the recent past, the northern regime has, by any account, been provocative in its actions. For example, in March 2008, the regime unilaterally and unexpectedly expelled eleven South Korean officials from the Kaesong Industrial Complex liaison office in retaliation for umbrage taken from a comment made by South Korean unification minister Kim Ha-joong, linking expansion of the complex to denuclearization talks.[16] In March 2009, as a response to joint U.S.-South Korean military exercises, the regime closed the border between North and South Korea without notice, stranding more than 700 South Korean workers, twice within one week's time, and cut the military telephone hotline between the two Koreas.[17] Along the way, the regime also triggered worldwide concern by conducting a long-range ballistic missile test in April 2009, followed a month later by the test of a nuclear device. Additionally, as of spring 2011, the Six Party Talks, designed to negotiate a settlement with the North Korean regime over its nuclear program, remained largely moribund.

Of course, one must also include among the regime's misdeeds its taking and holding of hostages. In two separate incidents North Korea held two American journalists, Laura Ling and Euna Lee, and a South Korean Hyundai-Asan worker, Yu Seong-jin, who worked at the Kaesong Industrial Complex. The former were found guilty of illegally entering North Korea and undertaking "hostile acts" against the regime, for which they received a sentence of twelve years in a forced labor camp. They were, however, freed in August 2009 after former president Bill Clinton made a trip to Pyongyang and met with Kim Jong-il. Worker Yu Seong-jin, accused of trying to persuade a North Korean female to defect to South Korea, was also ultimately freed after 136 days in captivity.[18]

The representative string of events highlighted above makes it difficult to conceive how a unification scenario under either a federation or confederation formula might be successful. That in most cases regime miscreance actually functions as a means for leverage, rather than open incitement to hostilities, hardly serves as a source of solace. Consider North Korea's history of unilateral ballistic missile testing and nuclear detonations begun in July 2006 and October 2006, respectively, and resumed in 2009. Under the South's confederation model, given the inherent weakness of any central government under this conceptual rubric, how might such provocative scenarios play themselves out? Would South

Korea be as supportive of global sanctions against North Korea as it has in the past? And if so, how would this differ materially from the current state of inter-Korean affairs? Perhaps more troubling is considering this scenario under the regime's federation model because this could potentially lead to debilitating civil discord, particularly given the shared governance within the central government and the combined legislature under the concept of a Supreme National Confederal Assembly. Such a scenario is not without precedence. Yemeni unification, which saw the integration of the Yemen Arab Republic and the People's Democratic Republic of Yemen, followed just such a course. An amicable, but rushed, unification process, concluded in May 1990, was followed by civil war only four years later, the result of deep political and economic inequities left unaddressed at the time of integration.

Examination of less extreme examples renders similarly unoptimistic prognoses. For example, how would the South Korean government respond to global demands for official censure of the North Korean regime for continued perpetration of human rights violations against its citizens? Would South Korean officials openly support such efforts to improve human rights inside its northern neighbor, something that has historically angered the regime, or should it remain mute on the issue for the sake of maintaining a unified Korea? Turning a blind eye to rampant human rights abuses would be tantamount to tacitly condoning such actions against citizens of a unified Korea, casting any post-unification government in a very negative pall. Yet neither formula offers any real promise that a unified Korea could successfully address such issues.

To be sure, the Lee administration has reversed course on the human rights issue pursued by its more liberal predecessors by voting in favor of a 2008 U.N. resolution denouncing the regime's alleged human rights abuses.[19] Lee also agreed, during a 2008 summit held in Seoul with former president George W. Bush, to jointly push for human rights reforms in North Korea.[20] The northern regime, however, staunchly contends that such demands are an intrusion into its sovereign prerogatives, thus potentially jeopardizing inter-Korean relations.[21] While it is difficult to predict how such a scenario might play out under either unification formula, perhaps the course of inter-Korean relations since Lee's inauguration and implementation of his administration's more pragmatic strategy offer a glimpse of what might be anticipated.

Another consideration is the degree of independence the respective Koreas would exercise under either unification model. Given the regime's propensity for histrionics and one-upmanship, how would the day-to-day relationship evolve if regime officials acted unilaterally for the sake of gaining leverage over the South much as they did in January 2010 when, without warning, the North Korean Army fired a barrage of field artillery shells into the Western Sea just north of the Northern Limit Line (NLL), the functional sea border between the two countries?

In summary, one fundamental factor weighs heavily in any assessment of the overall potential for success with regard to implementation of the two competing roadmaps for unification proffered by the two Koreas: North Korean intransigence and vituperative behavior. This, coupled with the inherent weaknesses of the envisioned confederal and federal models, increases the complexity of the unification task to the point that neither model presents itself as a viable solution for facilitating unification. Indeed, one might reasonably argue that the situation under such a unified Korea would not differ materially from the present status quo. There does exist, however, a third model for unification: absorption. Because of the multidimensional issues surrounding this outcome, it is treated separately in the following chapter.

7

The Absorption Scenario

The collapse-and-absorption argument has been marred by free-wheeling conceptualization, by right-leaning bias and inattention to the evidence of the many obstacles and barriers to peaceful Korean reunification that are evident in the harsh realities on the ground.

—*Professor Samuel Kim, Columbia University*[1]

Absorption is a rather straightforward concept, the precedent of which would be, of course, the collapse of one Korea, either through unexpected and cataclysmic or premeditated circumstances, which is then subsumed by the other. As discussed earlier, given the relative inequities of the two Koreas, the most likely outcome is South Korea's absorption of North Korea. This model enjoys two important advantages that neither the confederation nor federation model offers. First, it does not allow for the continued existence of the North Korean regime, which would in the end undermine genuine unification efforts. Second, it is not reliant on self-serving unification models presently proffered by the two Koreas, which do not accord with the spirit and intent of unification as articulated in official pronouncements issued by North and South Korean leaders since agreement was reached on the July 1972 South-North Joint Communiqué. Thus, absorption appears to be the most likely means through which full unification could be undertaken, although this model is not without its own shortcomings.

Some form of absorption may be the course favored by the current South Korean presidential administration as well. When President Lee met with U.S.

president Barack Obama in June 2009, they unveiled a comprehensive vision for a strategic alliance that also addressed the issue of unification, which specifically articulates a "peaceful reunification on the principles of free democracy and market economy."[2] Such an outcome, highly desirable from the South Korean perspective, is hardly achievable unless absorption is the applied method for unification preceded by some sort of regime collapse. Reinforcing this idea is President Lee's proposal to develop a "unification tax," announced in August 2010, to help defray the enormous anticipated costs of unification. The subtext of this idea is also predicated on the concept of absorption.[3] Nothing in the present context of inter-Korean relations, however, would lead to the conclusion that the North Korean regime is prepared to willingly embrace such principles.

The notion of a free democracy or market economy taking root in North Korea sans any external impetus was again dispelled in a report issued by the UN special rapporteur for North Korea, Vitit Muntarbhorn, in which he noted the existence of extensive "ongoing" and "abysmal" human rights violations inside North Korea to include torture, public executions, and women's rights violations.[4] The report also noted that despite the regime's export activities and joint ventures through which it brings in billions of dollars in revenue, such as its partnership with Egyptian conglomerate Orascom Telecom, the Middle East's largest wireless firm, nine million people still suffer from food shortages. Neither of these continuing conditions points to a regime committed to democratizing or embracing the principles of a market economy anytime in the near future.

Notwithstanding Lee's apparent "wink and nod" toward the absorption model, there are inherent disadvantages associated with the concept and its execution. First, as can be surmised from the preceding, the road toward unification is subject not only to the vagaries of inter-Korean relations but to those of South Korean politics as well: each administration has pursued, and will continue to pursue, unification based on a philosophy that may or may not accord with those of previous administrations, thus introducing elements of incongruence in unification policies between and among South Korean presidential administrations. Juxtaposing the approaches of the four most recent presidential administrations offers a meaningful comparison. The hard-line approach of former president Kim Young-sam differed markedly from the more liberal approaches of late former presidents Kim Dae-jung and Roh Moo-hyun, which in turn diverged considerably from current president Lee Myung-bak's pragmatic approach, providing some indication of the complexities associated with the domestic politics of unification. Additionally, if the Lee administration's new comprehensive vision for unification based on "free democracy and market economy" doesn't necessarily preclude consideration of absorption, a concept eschewed by the more liberal policies of Kim and Roh, then this, too, represents an antithetical shift in policy from those of his predecessors.

Second, achieving the conditions necessary for absorption are inconceivable at this point—it is difficult to envisage a scenario under which the North Korean regime would voluntarily submit to its own dismantlement. Thus, time and awaiting the requisite circumstances for unification are key detractors of this model although quick results are not necessarily assured under the other models. Samuel S. Kim, prominent Korea scholar and Columbia University political scientist, notes that

> the argument/advocacy for imminent unification via collapse and absorption depends on a set of unrealistic assumptions: first, that North Korea would collapse or succumb to a peaceful reunification by absorption, without a big fight and without triggering another war; second, that North Korea's one-million-strong troops would somehow disappear; third, that South Korea has both the will and the capacity to absorb a collapsing North Korea politically, militarily, economically, socially and culturally.[5]

The idea of a forced takeover of North Korea involving armed conflict, given long-standing memories of the Korean War, has little credibility among South Koreans: the cost to human life, economic prosperity, and regional instability would be nearly incalculable. Kim's question regarding the disposition of the North Korean military is also a valid one; the absorption model can only reasonably suggest what might need to be done with a 1.1-million-man military after it has stood down, but not necessarily how to ensure that it does stand down. Similarly, the spectrum of challenges Kim puts forth—political, economic, military, social, and cultural—are central to any discourse on unification. To be sure, definitive answers are in short supply in all quarters, but thoughtful examination of key repatriation factors related to unification can contribute to the development of a workable construct, assuming other precedents have been satisfied.

Third are the staggering economic costs associated with absorption. German reunification offers a hint at what awaits South Korea, although economic cost estimates for Korean unification are typically calculated to be much higher. For example, subsidies to the new states in former East Germany amount to the equivalent of $116.8 billion annually.[6] When one considers the twenty years since German reunification, costs reach a staggering $2.3 trillion and are still rising. And despite the best efforts of the German government, economic conditions in the east remain bleak: droves of younger people and the educated continue to flee to the west; unemployment hovers around 18 percent[7]; and approximately 1.7 million people have left eastern Germany since 1991, constituting 12 percent of its pre-reunification population.[8] The Library of Congress's country profile on Germany describes the economic situation in the following manner:

> Unemployment remains in the high teens in much of the East, where 17 years of massive investment from the West have failed to produce prosperity. This enormous inter-German transfer of wealth, which totaled US$1.6 trillion cumulatively from 1991 to 2004, or about US$130 billion per year, has exceeded the growth rate of the states in the West and thus has eaten away at the substance of the West's economy.[9]

The cost of Korean unification is as difficult to estimate presently as it was for German reunification two decades ago, hence the significant variance in cost estimates, which range as high as $5 trillion.[10] Given the German experience outlined above, however, these figures could well be close to accurate. A 2007 committee report commissioned by the South Korean National Assembly estimates any unification effort undertaken by 2015 "could ultimately be counted in trillions of US dollars."[11] The notion of peninsular unification being achieved in a mere four years is, of course, overly optimistic at this point, thus cost projections will only increase.

Absorption is not a panacea for the ills that plague inter-Korean relations. There simply are no shortcuts to a multifarious process as complex as unification, which at once comprises human emotion, ideology, national security and well-being, and feelings of nationalism. Yet what an examination of the absorption model does offer is a valuable framework for identifying some of the major potential stumbling blocks that must be negotiated if unification is ever to be realized.

AN ALTERNATIVE VIEW

Alternative concepts, theories, and estimates exist with regard to what final unification costs might ultimately total. Charles Wolf Jr. of RAND, takes issue
with past cost estimates for Korean unification because they are based on what
he contends is the false premise of needing to achieve parity in per capita income
between the northern and southern halves of the peninsula. Wiser is the course,
Wolf proffers, that pursues increased economic growth in the North without
trying to fully eliminate per capita income gaps between the northern and southern regions of the peninsula.[12] Wolf writes,

> Achieving a high rate of growth of per capita income in North Korea is
> both more appropriate and more realistic as a reunification goal. This
> target should be sufficient to encourage North Korea's population to
> anticipate that its living standard will be significantly enhanced, as
> well as to motivate economic growth and macro-economic policies
> in the Korean reunification process. This goal is also distinctly more
> realistic than specifying gap-elimination and economic convergence
> between North and South as the reunification goal.[13]

While I agree with Wolf's basic argument, which is premised on a German-
style absorption model, it fails to take into account certain social and diasporic
factors likely to emerge during the early phases of post-unification that will impact cost significantly and are not captured by economic models. For example,
the likelihood that the North Korean population will remain within what is now
North Korea after decades of economic deprivation, starvation, and human rights
abuse is highly improbable, as the millions suffering under the regime are hardly
likely to be mollified by promises of better days to come if only they are patient
a little longer. The increasing numbers of North Koreans presently fleeing into
China and South Korea argue against such an outcome. There are roughly
20,000 North Korean migrants living in South Korea today and an undeter-
mined number living in hiding within China's borders, although some estimates
place the number as high as 300,000.[14] Thus, there exists a high likelihood of
mass diasporic movement into both China and South Korea. Contending with
millions of jobless and homeless northern Koreans in the South will be another
concern as displacement of indigent South Koreans occupying temporary, sea-
sonal or part-time jobs could well present new social issues. Consequently,

secondary, and tertiary effects on the South Korean economy and labor market resulting from unification must also be recognized.

Even for those who might remain in the northern region, a vast infusion of capital will be required to facilitate the economic development Wolf envisions: buildings and roads; factories; education system (including teachers); job training programs; social training programs akin to those being undertaken at Hanawon, only on a much larger scale; and government infrastructure. These are only a representative sample. Absent such fundamental efforts at achieving parity between the halves of the peninsula, there is little rationale for pursuing unification, and instituting these measures will contribute significantly to the cost of a unified Korea.

A final cautionary note: there should be put in place ample metrics and safeguards to achieve and maintain sufficient economic growth in northern Korea relative to southern Korea, lest a lower standard of living becomes the accepted norm for northerners, potentially reinforcing perceptions of the northern half of the peninsula as a backwater of larger contemporary Korean society. Thus, a return to the earlier discussion of issues associated with repatriation will assist in identifying key metrics that must be addressed if unification is to be achieved.

8

Nirvana Undone

A survey conducted in June [2008] indicated that four in five refugees find the "cutthroat and intolerant" South Korean society unbearable. ... A startling 20 percent responded that they preferred their lives in the North.

—Korea Times[1]

Choi Young-hee patronized a hair salon and established a friendly rapport with her hairdresser. Choi described her as "kind and friend-ly." Once the hairdresser became cognizant of her North Korean pedigree, however, Choi observes that she "suddenly turned frigid." She is now hoping to emigrate from South Korea and into the United States.

—Korea Times[2]

Repatriation, for purposes of peninsular unification, is conceptually neb-ulous in its composition: it is amorphous, it encompasses difficult to quantify elements, and in many cases establishing metrics to measure its progress is problematic. Yet it is indispensable to any unification model. In-tegrating political ideology or economic systems without successful repatriation of the citizens impacted by such integration would be tantamount to creating a structure without substance. Consequently, chapters 8–11 address several of the major elements associated with repatriation, namely assimilation (chapter 8), education (chapter 9), employment (chapter 10), and diaspora and social services (chapter 11), which together form the nucleus of any successful future repatriation policy.

Assimilation encompasses those policies that facilitate the cultural and social integration of North Koreans into broader South Korean society. In short, it is the process of making new South Korean citizens. Dr. Randy Green of Gyeongnam National University of Science and Technology defines assimilation as a process through which one set of cultural views is supplanted by another, facilitating the complete absorption of the individual.[3] Thus, issues of cultural competency and literacy, adaptation to new value sets, and South Koreans' willingness to accept North Koreans into the broader society become key areas of concern.

Education is the foundation for assimilation of North Korean youth into the South Korean educational system and ultimately its labor force, and, of course, provides the basis for the generational transformation from Juche citizen to those able to adapt to and thrive in a capitalist society. But this is more than an exercise in providing new textbooks. Issues of differing language and values, gaps in pedagogy, and poor educational infrastructure must all be confronted and resolved. Similarly, for adults, the issue of employability is key to their assimilative success. Yet few North Koreans possess the requisite job skills to ensure entry into the South Korean labor market in any meaningful way. Additionally, domestic regionalism has historically figured largely within the Korean cultural context, something that can and has led to instances of South Korean prejudice against North Korean workers.

Despite the multitude of complexities associated with peninsular unification, the South Korean government enjoys one distinct advantage: the current migration of saeteomin. As they attempt to negotiate and overcome multifamous challenges in their quests to become functioning members of South Korean society, their setbacks and achievements offer a unique primer on what the demands of unification will be, only on a much grander scale. Thus, history may well conclude the present period to have been a prelude to unification taking place within the social and cultural petri dish of South Korean society. The ultimate measure of success will likely be how effectively South Korean government officials developed policies facilitating successful assimilation of former North Korean citizens and how saeteomin were welcomed into South Korean society by its citizens.

With over six decades of a formally divided existence, the respective populations of South and North Korea now have diminished context for a unified

Korea, a situation further compounded with each succeeding generation. Indeed, over 86 percent of today's Koreans were born in a post-divided Korea.[4] Thus, the basis for unification becomes more remote and the argument that necessity for unification rests in the brotherhood of Koreans falls prey to contemporary realities and a distant past.

A major cautionary note proffered throughout this book is the salience of the Choson period experience with regard to the cultural and social division of the peninsula and the diminution of the northern peninsula as a backwater and its inhabitants to second-class citizen status. No doubt there will be some who take issue with this premise. Some of the pieces, however, are already in place. It is more than mere historical irony that most North Korean migrants finding their way into South Korea presently arrive from Hamgyong province (77 percent), an area most notably characterized by the destitution of its inhabitants.[5] This was also one of the northern areas into which the Choson government sought to forcibly migrate its citizens in an attempt to populate its northern border regions. Given the level of deprivation suffered by Hamgyong residents, even within the North Korean cultural context, they are regarded as being politically and culturally devoid. Thus, the challenges saeteomin confront with regard to assimilation and general South Korean attitudes of ambivalence toward them, the specter of re-emergent social and cultural divisions between Koreans from the north and south of the peninsula is not wholly unrealistic. This then becomes a key issue of consideration for unification as well.

Saeteomin flee North Korea's repressive society under circumstances of famine, human rights atrocities, and other social ills, with the expectation of self-enrichment and a better life for themselves and their family members. As they enter South Korean society, however, they confront unexpected challenges at multiple levels: prejudice, employability, cognitive dissonance in terms of past socialization, inability to communicate—all must be confronted and successfully navigated. Far from achieving a panacea for their ills, they become strangers in what they had envisioned as a comparative paradise.

THE STATUS OF NORTH KOREAN MIGRANTS
The United Nations, and the United States, considers North Koreans fleeing the oppressive conditions put in place by their regime to be refugees. According to the 1951 United Nations Convention Relating to the Status of Refugees, as amended by the 1967 Protocol, a "refugee" is defined as someone who flees his

country of origin "owing to well-founded fear of being persecuted for reasons of race, religion, nationality, membership of a particular social group or political opinion, is outside the country of his nationality and is unable or, owing to such fear, is unwilling to avail himself of the protection of that country." The circumstances of political oppression and persecution, imprisonment and torture from which citizens of North Korea flee, clearly align with the definitional parameters of the refugee concept. Parties to the convention commit themselves to the principle of *non-refoulement*, which essentially means authorities in a receiving country will not repatriate refugees for fear they will likely face official reprisal: "No contracting State shall expel or return ['refouler'] a refugee in any manner whatsoever to the frontiers of territories where his life or freedom would be threatened on account of his race, religion, nationality, membership of a particular social group or political opinion."[6]

Both South Korea and China are parties to the convention, yet legally treat North Korean refugees very differently. The approach employed by South Korean officials, treated more fully in subsequent sections, provides citizenship and attempts to assimilate migrants into the larger Korean society. Conversely, China does not recognize North Korean migrants as refugees but rather considers them to be "illegal economic migrants," owing to the conditions of destitution in North Korea that lead many to flee and the economic activities in which they engage within China's border. While the Chinese government cloaks such definitional differences in international law, its reason for not applying the terms of the convention to North Korean migrants is based on geopolitical considerations. Quite simply, the North Korean regime strongly denounces any attempt to render assistance to North Korean migrants, demanding all be repatriated. Thus, in an effort to maintain stable relations with its volatile neighbor, Chinese officials quietly repatriate North Korean migrants. China also confronts its own issues with domestic ethnic instability, particularly in the western autonomous regions of Xinjiang and Tibet. A demonstrated inability to deal with the influx of North Korean migrants across its sovereign borders could potentially ignite unrest among China's own minorities.

There have, however, been a few exceptional cases in which migrants have been passed along to third countries with the expectation they would find passage into South Korea, but these instances were motivated less by any newfound commitment to the terms of the convention and more by Chinese enlightened self-interest. In 2007 Chinese officials permitted forty-three migrants who had reached the relative safety of the South Korean consulate and U.N. refugee offices in Beijing to depart the country, recognizing that allowing the migrants to become an issue in the run-up to the 2008 Beijing Summer Olympics could potentially mar China's international image.[7]

Many North Korean migrants entering China do so on foot and prefer the relative safety of China's Yanbian Korean Autonomous Prefecture, home to some one million ethnic Koreans.[8] While Chinese authorities require Chinese citizens to report North Korean migrants, many indeed are not reported, the motivations for which are varied and many: feelings of kinship, humanitarian concern, financial or other non-monetary gain, or some sense of shared patriotism. Despite any assistance migrants might receive along the way, however, escape remains a journey characterized by peril. Many migrants fall victim to human trafficking, sexual exploitation, or are compelled to enter forced marriages.[9] According to the Congressional Research Service, approximately 80–90 percent of migrants may have fallen prey to some type of human trafficking activity.[10] Such instances have become increasingly prevalent as the number of female migrants has increased over the past few years, now 80 percent of all fleeing migrants.[11]

A WORD ON THE PLIGHT OF NORTH KOREAN MIGRANTS

Beyond the more identifiable challenges to assimilation lies another group of impediments that are hidden, much more difficult to quantify, not often recognized, and yet underly the entirety of the experiences that will likely impact the success of saeteomin assimilation. In toto they comprise a series of traumas most must confront during their trek out of North Korea and into the southern half of the peninsula.

South Korean psychiatrist Woo-taek Jeon notes that North Koreans fleeing the country endure a multi-wave traumatic experience. The first wave occurs while they are still in North Korea prior to their departure. They must confront the hardships that lead to their decision to flee—starvation, deprivation, political harassment, torture—in addition to the stress of maintaining the secrecy of their plans as detection would result in certain imprisonment, torture, or even execution. Considering the nature of the North Korean regime, another likely source of trauma that continues indefinitely for saeteomin is concern over the fate suffered by family members left behind as they could, and often are, punished as a result of other family members' defections.

A second traumatic wave occurs during the period of flight, the first leg of which typically takes North Koreans on a route through China. (Many fleeing

North Korea will remain in China; others will go on to such third countries as Mongolia, Thailand, or Vietnam.) This process can take years and saeteomin live in constant fear that Chinese authorities or North Korean agents will apprehend and repatriate them back to North Korea, again upon fear of death:

> According to a tape-recorded testimony of a former North Korean agent now in hiding in Jilin, China, "a substantial number" of North Korean refugees in China are actually North Korea's undercover agents disguised as refugees assigned to abduct North Korean escapees/defectors.[12]

The fear of abduction, however, is not limited only to those fleeing North Korea. It extends to those offering assistance to migrants as well. For example, in January 2000, South Korean reverend Kim Dong-shik, a legal resident of Lynchburg, Virginia, was abducted in Yanbian, China, for assisting North Koreans fleeing into South Korea. According to reports from coworkers, he went to lunch one day with two North Korean migrants who were in actuality North Korean agents and never returned.[13] Those who are fortunate enough to avoid capture are not necessarily home free; they will likely endure other hardships. Consider the circumstances of a migrant highlighted in a Voice of America news article:

> One 34-year-old woman says she was sold into slavery after crossing the border. "In that house, I was cleaning the stools and urine of a grandfather. I took care of him. I had a chance to run away but I did not," she said. "The family told me, 'It is useless to treat North Korean people well. Even if we treat them well, they still run away.' Then I replied to them, 'Why do you think North Korean people are bad?' I then said, 'I will wait until you let me go.'" Feeling trapped, she was overwhelmed with despair. "Finally, I got some poison. They found I almost killed myself and they took me to the hospital, where they [pumped out] my stomach," she said. To avoid further problems, her captors let her go.[14]

The third wave of trauma occurs once saeteomin reach South Korea and are interrogated by South Korean authorities and kept under surveillance. The purpose of the month-long interrogation process is to ascertain whether any of the migrants are actually North Korean spies. This practice is not without foundation. In August 2008 South Korean authorities indicted saeteomin Won Jeong-hwa on charges of espionage. Authorities contend she developed several romantic relationships with South Korean military officers to gain information and had at least some information that led them to conclude she was also working with co-conspirators inside the country.[15]

The final trauma occurs when saeteomin enter South Korean society and experience what Lankov aptly describes as "a bitter taste of paradise."[16] Such experiences are not transitory in nature but rather onerously cumulative, thus constituting additional baggage with which they must grapple as saeteomin work to assimilate themselves. Recognition of the existence of such trauma, however, has been slow among South Korean officials.

Jeon's research also highlights the manner in which saeteomin trauma tends to manifest itself. One of the more debilitative manifestations is the level of suspicion with which saeteomin regard others—South Koreans and fellow North Koreans alike—which can be attributed to both lifestyle in the North and the result of the added precautions necessary during their flight to South Korea. This, of course, has consequences in their ability to form bonds with others. As Jeon points out they are particularly susceptible to an unwillingness to live together in groups and experience personal loneliness.[17] This sentiment is aptly captured by the proprietress of a beer hall located in a district in Seoul where many saeteomin live, and who is herself a saeteomin. When asked whether many of her former North Korean compatriots patronize her establishment, she responded, "They don't come here and we don't want them. When someone makes it, they are just jealous."[18] Ideological dissonance also poses issues for many saeteomin as they must not only come to grips with an entirely new value set but also reconcile the fact that perhaps much of what the regime proselytizes is without merit, consequently rendering their own value system the same.[19]

There also exists a multi-dimensional cognitive dissonance between North and South Koreans with regard to saeteomin assimilation into South Korean society. Expectations on both sides are high: North Koreans anticipate greater levels of financial assistance from their new government based on "travelers' tales" heard while in China, and South Koreans greet saeteomin with notable apathy while expecting them to seamlessly transition into their new society given the past shared heritage between them. In the case of adults, transition into the labor market is central to the success of assimilation much as schools are key for student success—education and work and the status they accord are cornerstones of South Korean society. These former North Korean citizens, however, must first be taught the basics of how to live and function in a capitalist society, representing their first fledgling steps in a long process.

THE TRANSITION TO CAPITALISM

The influx of North Korean migrants has provided South Korean government officials and non-governmental organizations (NGOs) a real-time litmus test as to the nation's ability to adequately absorb North Koreans. A far cry from the days of the Cold War when "defectors" entering South Korea were educated and prepared to offer something back to their new nation, saeteomin demand much more attention and assistance in order to facilitate their transition. The first step of this process begins with an introduction to the constructs of capitalist society. As government officials have learned over the past decade, various subgroups composing the North Korean migrant population have vastly differing needs requiring independent remedies. The two most obvious subgroups are school-aged children and adults. (One point should be underscored. Because of the rigors and tribulations associated with flight from North Korea, family units are typically fragmented and many adults travel alone, mothers may travel with school-aged children in tow, or children may flee with no parental figure.)

Once saeteomin reach South Korea, they are automatically granted citizenship, the legal basis for which is provided under the nation's constitution. Becoming "legal citizens" is only one part of the challenge, however, as saeteomin must also become "social and cultural citizens," a process that cannot be affected via edict. Thus, in support of its new citizens, government officials have undertaken several initiatives to facilitate their integration into broader South Korean society, among them Hanawon and *Hangyoreh*, which address the needs of adults and special requirements of school-aged children, respectively. While services provided by these institutions have evolved and expanded over the past decade as officials have become more cognizant of and conversant in the special needs of saeteomin and the structural impediments inherent in South Korean society that act as barriers to assimilation, as outlined later, measures undertaken to date have lacked sufficiency.

Hanawon, translated as "house of unity," finds its legal basis in the July 1997 law, Protection of Defecting North Korean Residents and Settlement Support Act. Hanawon, which in December 2008 doubled its capacity to house six hundred migrants, commenced operations in July 1999 and has, over the past ten years, worked to modify and expand its programming to provide greater assistance to North Korean migrants. The facility's current formal education programming, which has ranged in duration from two to three months depending upon its capacity to absorb newly arriving migrants, has focused on: 1) teaching saeteomin how to live in a free society and dispelling misconceptions about South Korea; 2) assisting with psychological adjustment; and 3) familiarizing saeteomin with the basics of daily life in South Korea: shopping, driving, cell phone usage, banking and how to use credit cards and ATMs, public phones and calling cards, subways, computers and Internet access, and the purpose of insurance, along with a host of other activities. In short, Hanawon programming is designed to take "culturally" illiterate persons and transform them into functioning members of South Korean society within a ninety-day period.

Government officials have come to the realization, however, that while their efforts were well intended, they have been inadequate in addressing the new challenges presented by the changing demographics of saeteomin. Consequently, the Ministry of Unification has announced plans to create another center similar to Hanawon in order to expand service capacity to North Korean migrants, construction for which began in July 2011. Additionally, recognizing that saeteomin assimilation will likely be an ongoing process rather than something achieved at a single point in time, Unification Ministry officials have created a network of "Hana centers." Their purpose is threefold: to provide post-Hanawon support services, to do so indefinitely, and to make such services available throughout the country in urbanized areas. In a ministry press release dated April 20, 2010, officials announced the opening of eight such centers throughout the country; there are now thirty operational.[20]

A related issue that must be addressed is the greater rate of domestic violence among saeteomin couples. South Korea's Gender Equality and Family Ministry reported that of 302 saeteomin surveyed in December 2010, over 85 percent had experienced some sort of domestic violence during the preceding twelve months. This is comparatively high when juxtaposed against South Korea's reported incident rate of 54 percent. The source of this relatively higher rate of domestic violence among saeteomin is attributed to North Korea's well-entrenched patriarchal society and its concomitant diminution of women's rights.[21]

An area presently garnering special attention is the needs of the growing population of female saeteomin.[22] Many suffer long-lasting trauma as a result of physical and psychological abuse endured during their trek into South Korea. Youn Mi-ryang, Hanawon's first female director points out, "They were physically and mentally victimized during their stay in China. So, they are more susceptible to gynecological problems than South Korean women."[23] Indeed, Unification Ministry statistics bear this out as some 60 percent of North Korean female migrants who entered Hanawon from 2003 through August 2008 had contracted some type of ovarian or cervical illness.[24]

Other health-related issues abound. As a result of the deleterious effects of famine, many North Koreans are visibly smaller in stature when compared to the typical South Korean. Under a different set of circumstances height differences might not necessarily be an issue. When considered along with problems of language incomprehension, lack of education, and employment difficulties, however, it becomes yet one more "reinforcing discriminator" between South and North Koreans. Dental care is another area of major health concern as many migrants have lost teeth as a result of poor dental hygiene and malnutrition. Consequently, nearly 50 percent of Hanawon's medical budget is used to provide false teeth for its residents.[25] Finally, incidents of depression are rampant among Hanawon's residents with nearly 75 percent suffering from depression or other mental maladies.[26]

Government officials have also come to realize that the nucleus of adult assimilation is the employability factor. Failure to address this issue will leave saeteomin dependent on government subsidies further distinguishing them in socially negative ways from members of broader South Korean society. Yet there are structural impediments present within the South Korean economy that work against saeteomin employment, an issue discussed at greater length in chapter 11. Equally important to recognize at this point, however, is that the employability of migrants is also hampered by their general lack of education and transferrable job skills. This reality is reflected in the sectors of the economy in which they are able to secure employment: manufacturing (30 percent), lodging facilities or restaurants (19 percent), construction (12 percent), and retail (12 percent). Additionally, 43 percent of migrants are employed as day laborers; only 9 percent of South Koreans are so employed.[27]

Hangyoreh serves as a transitional education facility for school-aged saeteomin with the goal of ultimately assimilating students into the formal South Korean education system. Hangyoreh, which operates both a middle school and high school, commenced operation in 2006. Prior to that time saeteomin school children were left to fend for themselves in South Korean schools with very little preparation, which led to abysmal results characterized by high truancy and drop-out rates when compared to their South Korean counterparts. Students remain at Hangyoreh anywhere from six months to two years, after which they transition into South Korean schools or look for a job.

As many of the school's students are in South Korea without their parents, the school also functions as "home" and its teachers as surrogate parents, with both students and teachers living at the facility.[28] During their stay not only do students study academic subjects, which helps to offset the average four years of schooling missed during their trek to South Korea, they also receive cultural lessons similar in nature to the instruction adults receive at Hanawon. Psychological counseling is also provided to assist in healing the emotional trauma of their escape from North Korea.[29]

Despite such efforts, overall prospects for successfully assimilating saeteomin remain uncertain primarily for two reasons. First, the manner in which North Korean migrants are welcomed into larger South Korean society has been widely inhospitable, leading to feelings of estrangement among some percentage of the saeteomin population. For example, Yonhap news service, South Korea's publicly funded and largest news agency, reported that some 450 saeteomin sought asylum in the United Kingdom at the end of 2008.[30] This constitutes a small percentage of their population—slightly more than 2 percent. The figure of 450, however, only addresses those who formally attempted to relocate (not those who have yet to act on any desire to relocate) and only those seeking asylum in the United Kingdom. The larger issue, however, must consider the underlying factors that lead saeteomin, who risked life and limb to escape North Korea and now live in what they had long regarded as paradise, to decide to leave South Korea for a new life in a third country. (It should be noted that other options do, however, present themselves for North Korean migrants, as some have migrated directly to the United States. Under the 2004 U.S. North Korean Human Rights Act [Title III], migrants fleeing the North Korean regime can seek protection as refugees in the United States. Their numbers, however, remain comparatively small. As of June 2009 a total of only eighty-one migrants had settled here.[31])

South Korean government officials regard such actions as illegal and have considered prosecution of those saeteomin who attempt to relocate to third countries. Saeteomin receive government resettlement funds to assist in their transition to life in South Korea, and thus officials take a dim view of those who accept the money only to move on to another country.

The irony of such a situation is unmistakable. Saeteomin, who successfully escaped to South Korea for the purpose of living their lives freely as South Koreans, are accorded less independence and freedom of movement than are South Korean citizens, and threatened with possible legal prosecution. At some level this could be seen by saeteomin as reminiscent of restrictions they fled under the North Korean regime, if not in degree then certainly in form.

The second factor impacting overall assimilation is synergistic in its impact. The diminished financial support saeteomin receive from the South Korean government in conjunction with the difficulty of identifying suitable employment work in tandem against any assimilative benefit derived from institutions like Hanawon or Hangyoreh. Although South Korean officials do provide resettlement funds to North Korean migrants, this financial assistance has been continually reduced over the years as a result of the ever-increasing numbers of migrants entering South Korea. In 2007 such subsidies were again reduced to six million won, which at current exchange rates is about $5,200. Saeteomin are also provided with housing and other forms of assistance, but this is inadequate for building new lives given the inherent challenges to assimilating into South Korean society. Yet their numbers continue to swell. Of the saeteomin currently residing in South Korea, roughly 80 percent have arrived since 2000.[32]

SOUTH KOREAN PERCEPTIONS OF SAETEOMIN

Following is an account of a young saeteomin's short life in South Korea recounted from Byung-ho Chung's journal article, "Between Migrant and Defector." While the result may not be typical (suicide is not unheard of among saeteomin, but it is not the norm), the general tenor of his experience is not at all unusual:

> A boy from Wŏnsan, North Korea, died in Cheju Island, South Korea. His name was Chul and he was nineteen. It was at midnight on a quiet six-lane street. A broken mountain-bike–style motorcycle smashed against an electric pole revealed a terrible accident. He died exactly one and a half years after he arrived in South Korea. "He died because of us. We killed him," a South Korean teacher murmured while weeping at the funeral. The friends with whom he had roamed

around North Korea and China gathered at the funeral and cried, shouting, "You son of bitch, why did you die here? You should have drowned in the River Tuman when we waded across it. You should have died in the North Korean detention center when we couldn't eat for days and we were almost beaten to death." . . . At age fifteen, Chul left his home because of the famine and wandered around with his cousin. When he could, he would cross back over the Sino-Korean border with some food and money for his parents. He was arrested and escaped several times before he finally decided to go to South Korea. . . .

South Korean society gave Chul many things. A subsidized one bedroom apartment, refrigerator, color television, video player, personal computer, bed, and the motorcycle that led him to his death. He owned all of these. While he amassed these material luxuries, he began to experience loneliness, alienation, competition, and discrimination in South Korean society as a newcomer. South Korean society treated him well in its own way. It welcomed him as a defector from oppressive North Korea. It gave him tailored suits and ties and took him to theme parks and fancy department stores. It gave him the initial impression that he could live as a middle-class man in South Korea. But, soon, he realized that he was living on social welfare, and he feared that he would be looked down upon as one of the lowest members of society.

Christian churches called him, asking him to talk about his experiences. But, what they wanted to hear from him was how terrible life had been in North Korea, how hungry he was, how helpless he had been in China, and how the Christian missionaries had saved his body and soul. Each time he spoke, they gave him a couple hundred dollars, which he quickly spent on alcohol to escape his constant sense of humiliation and sadness.

Chul never received an education beyond the sixth grade. However, as a nineteen-year-old young man, he could never fit in an elementary school. He tried to prepare for the qualification examinations for high school, but he gave up within weeks because "the questions on the exam were too twisted to deal with." He worked as a part-timer in gas stations and in delivery jobs at minimum wage.

He would hang around with other South Korean school dropouts at work, sharing feelings of frustration and despair. Sometimes, he was involved in group fights with his friends from the North against the "arrogant" South Korean youths. He found his only solace while riding his motorcycle.

On one of those nights on the motorcycle, Chul died. It was considered a suicide. On the wall of Chul's empty apartment hung a children's measuring stick, shaped like a giraffe, on which he measured his growth every day. At age nineteen, he stood less than five feet tall.[33]

The "through-line" characterizing barriers to full assimilation, whether work, school, or social integration, is the attitude some South Koreans hold with regard to North Koreans, which tends to engender feelings of alienation among saeteomin. This, coupled with the tendency of many migrants to avoid living in groups as observed by Jeon, makes assimilation a difficult end to achieve.

Regionalism lies at the heart of the problem of South Korean attitudes toward migrants. Historically cloistered as it was for centuries during the Choson period, Korean culture came to focus inwardly and emphasis was placed on regional differences; this worked in conjunction with yangban efforts to secure their own social prerogatives by limiting the social mobility of others. Emphasis on regional distinctions remains a part of contemporary Korean culture, in both South and North Korea, although the practice manifests itself differently on either side of the peninsula. In North Korea it is linked more closely with exercising the proper political ideology while in South Korea the practice of *jiyeon*, or regionally based affiliations, tends to cement regional differences among citizens.

For some, North Korean migrants have already achieved the designation of the "Korean other." Comments of a Yonsei University graduate student, Kim Hye Suu, may aptly capture broader social sentiment: "People are scared of North Koreans. . . . People don't want to mix with them."[34] Such perceptions manifest themselves in all facets of life, but most notably and damagingly for those saeteomin in search of employment or attending South Korean schools, leading to a cycle very difficult to break out of. South Korean attitudes help to culturally and socially isolate saeteomin and such isolation keeps them from fully integrating into South Korean society; their inability to assimilate is what then helps to cast them as the Korean other.

Choi Kwang Hyock, a former North Korean soldier who escaped to South Korea while on patrol one night, ultimately graduated from Hanyang University in Seoul. Despite this, he recounts having confronted deep discrimination while in Seoul, consequently leading him to depart for Brazil and other overseas locations. According to Choi, he was rejected by about five hundred South Korean firms after managers discovered he was born in Pyongyang.[35] The general perception among prospective employers is that North Koreans are not as qualified as their South Korean counterparts and thus represent an unnecessary employment risk. Lee In-hee, spokesperson for an on-line recruiting firm, observes that "people's negative perception of defectors is the biggest problem, the lack of credibility they have. . . . It's also very difficult for companies to hire defectors when they obviously lag behind South Koreans in their ability."[36] To be sure, the government is working with a few large firms to develop programs that offer saeteomin employment, but they are few in number, expensive to administer, and thus do not offer a blueprint for a way forward under possible future unification.

South Korean attitudes that relegate saeteomin to a status of the Korean other enhance the need of migrants to feel they "belong" to some larger group. Thus, if they are unable to achieve a sense of belonging within South Korean society, they will likely cloister themselves by retaining the comfort of familiar allegiances with North Korean culture and society. Consider, for example, the results of a recent survey conducted by the Organization for One Korea in which 58.4 percent of North Koreans now living in South Korea surveyed consider themselves to still be North Korean rather than South Korean citizens. Only 6.3 percent considered themselves to be South Korean.

What does all this portend under a scenario of unification? While South Korean government officials have progressed in the type and scope of support services offered to North Korean migrants to facilitate social and cultural assimilation, they remain inadequate, rendering saeteomin integration into the larger society, at best, negligible. Such integrative efforts are miniscule in comparison to the herculean task of full assimilation that awaits under unification. Although both Hanawon and Hangyoreh constitute well-intentioned programmatic efforts, they do not represent viable models under a unified Korea. Their resource intensiveness militate against broader application.

Under a unified Korea, how will government officials develop effective programming that affects cultural and social assimilation and through what means would such programming be delivered to nearly 23 million former North Korean citizens? How will government officials "educate" South Korean citizens to facilitate acceptance of former North Koreans into the larger society? The following two chapters provide extended discussion of the two greatest obstacles to North Korean repatriation under a unification scenario, education and employment.

9

Issues of Repatriation

It is essential to arm the entire body of the working people with communist ideology in order to wipe out the remnants of the outmoded
capitalist ideology and carry the revolutionary upsurge to a higher stage.
—*Kim Il-sung, November 20, 1958*[1]

All I learned in school in North Korea was that Kim Jong Il was the
best leader and that North Korea was the best country.
—*North Korean defector living in South Korea*[2]

Arguably the single most important tool any society has at its disposal for
socializing its citizenry is its educational process, which influences culture,
political ideology, economic constructs, and social behaviors between and
among members of society. In effect, it molds and shapes the population; this
is education's formative function, usually facilitated through the formal educational system, and in most cases, reinforced through the family unit. Education
also has a transformative function: changing the values, mores, and perceptions
of society's members in order to qualitatively alter them. This function is a bit
more complex as it requires a two-step process: it necessitates the "unlearning"
of undesired behaviors before basic socialization processes of the formative function can be pursued. One might reasonably consider the activities undertaken at
Hanawon as being transformative in nature.

In the case of North Korea and peninsular unification, both the formative
and transformative functions of education must be forefront on the agenda of

policymakers as nearly the entirety of the North Korean population, students and adults alike, will first need to be weaned from the ideological constraints of Juche before they can be taught how to successfully function in a society built on a capitalist construct. Of course, the younger the student, the easier the task because less "deprogramming" will be required.

The North Korean educational system, built on a socialist foundation, is designed to create the "perfect and obedient" socialist citizen who is fully compliant, complacent, and dependent—hardly the attributes that mark one for success in an independent and capitalist society. Thus, because of the somewhat dichotomous nature of education practices on the peninsula, it is appropriate to begin discussion of education-related unification challenges with a review of the respective education systems of North and South Korea.

THE MAKING OF A JUCHE CITIZEN

In 1973, the North Korean system of education was modified to an eleven-year compulsory and universal system, divided into three distinct levels: one year of kindergarten, four years of primary education, and a six-year secondary school mandate in senior middle school. Each level functions, in some manner, to develop students into model Juche citizens.

> Our universal eleven-year compulsory education is an advanced education system which, by thoroughly applying the fundamental principles of socialist pedagogy, trains the rising generation to be communist men who are developed in an all-round way. In order to train students in that way, our country puts the main stress on ideological education . . . primary attention is paid to political and ideological education to arm all the students closely with our Party's Juche idea and train them to be communist revolutionaries.[3]

Compulsory classroom education is also reinforced with regular and mandatory activities outside the classroom, the purpose of which is ideological indoctrination to "dye the whole society one color by arming all members of society with the socialist ideology."[4]

NURSERY SCHOOLS

While not a component of the officially articulated educational progression, there are ample options for working parents to place young children into state-run nursery schools. Exact figures as to the number of nursery schools operating in North Korea vary because of the opacity of North Korean society, but some estimates place the number in 2001 as high as 60,000, representing a prolifera- tive growth from rather austere beginnings.[5] Immediately following World War II, there was only one nursery school within the Soviet-administered northern occupation zone.[6]

The source of growth for this "unofficially" sanctioned component of edu- cation results from both legal and cultural bases, stemming from the emphasis the regime places on building model communists for North Korean society, the effort of which manifested itself in the promulgation of various laws, including Concerning the Improvement of Work on Nursery Schools and Kindergartens (1964) and Laws for Upbringing and Indoctrinating Children (1976). Cultur- ally, North Korean working women tend not to entrust the care of infants to mothers or mothers-in-law. One reason for this is that they too are expected to work and undertake group study of Kim Jong-il's writings, thus contributing to the larger society. Consequently, nurseries, operated by medium- and large- sized companies and cooperatives, are their method of choice for childcare. This practice, coupled with the impetus provided through the legal and ideological framework prescribed by the laws promulgated in 1964 and 1976 regarding childcare, may well work in tandem to account for the sustained large number of nurseries. They are also very convenient for working women, offering flex- ible care plans. Children can be left at these facilities daily, weekly, monthly, or seasonally, depending on the work schedule of the mother.

The work of nurseries, undertaken six days a week, has always been to serve as the starting point for inculcating North Korean youth with the Juche doctrine. As such, much of the curriculum is designed to mold children in such a way as to make them receptive to the fundamentals of communism: uniformity, collectivism, and the eschewal of individualism. Kim Mi-young points out that

> the degree of uniformity is one of the important criteria for assess- ing day nurseries. Children are basically required to act on the same timetable and eat the same food. An important goal calls for hav- ing children sing and dance, making identical facial expressions and movements. Hence nurses take great care through repetition to guide kids "to become more alike."[7]

Inculcation of Juche is facilitated in other ways as well. For example, stu- dents are taught to reflexively respond with gratitude toward the country's two patriarchs—the son, Kim Jong-il, and the father, the late Kim Il-sung. [8]

THE KINDERGARTEN YEARS

Kindergarten represents the first year of compulsory education and with it the true work of creating a Juche ideologue commences. Students enter at the age of five and attend school six days a week. These schools are typically aligned with primary schools, called "people's schools." The foundation for and foci of kindergarten education is best captured in the Laws for Upbringing and Indoctrinating Children, which states in part:

> The children of the Democratic People's Republic of Korea are the future of the fatherland, the rear guards for the construction of communism, and the heirs of our revolutionary tasks who will carry out the revolution through succeeding generations . . . to become new revolutionary human beings of the Juche type.[9]

As a practice, the creation of kindergartens has generally been driven by population numbers, one per every 1,000 citizens. Thus, there should roughly be 22,000 to 24,000 in operation presently. How the regime's economic atrophy, famine, and alternating natural disasters of drought and flood have impacted the creation of kindergartens is unclear, but given the millions who have purportedly starved to death and the tens of thousands estimated to have fled the country into China, it would not be unrealistic to conclude that the number of operating kindergartens has been impacted by these events, perhaps significantly.

In a fashion similar to nursery schools, kindergartens come in three varieties: daily, weekly, and monthly. Daily kindergartens function in a fairly standard manner as students are dropped off in the mornings and picked up in the evenings. Weekly kindergartens require students to be dropped off on Mondays and picked up Saturdays; parents are not permitted to visit students during the week. Monthly kindergartens function similarly except students remain at the facility for a month at a time.

Kim and Kim outline the curriculum of North Korean kindergartens in their work chronicling the nation's history of education, "Human Remodeling in North Korea." While on first glance there appears to be a balance of subjects such as arithmetic, song and dance, Korean language, and drawing, much of the content is, in fact, ideologically driven. For example, they point out that song and dance requires students to participate in marching activities as well. Children also listen to daily radio programs extolling the proper behavior of "model children." And arithmetic, not normally considered a tool of propaganda, also affords the regime an opportunity to imbue students with Juche ideology. An example of just such an arithmetic problem follows:

> The respected father, Generalissimo Kim Il Sung, taught us to win always against enemies. The anti-guerilla fighters, upholding the teachings of the respected father, Generalissimo Kim Il Sung, fought many battles against the Japanese imperialists and won them. (Pointing to the figure) How many enemies are down after they were shot (two)? How many horses are down (one)? Which of the two numbers, one or two, is larger? Which of the two numbers, one or two, is less? (Pointing to another figure), Japanese enemies were killed by the rolling rocks. How many Japanese enemies are there (two)? How many rolling rocks are there (three)? Which of the two numbers, two or three, is larger? Which of the two numbers, two or three, is less?[10]

Kindergarten students also receive instruction on the lives of both the "Great Leader" and the "Dear Leader," Kim Il-sung and Kim Jong-il, respectively. The purpose of these teachings is twofold. First, it helps to build a citizenry that remains loyal to and supportive of the North Korean leadership, the only father–son power transition in socialist history. Second, it serves as a means for transmitting to succeeding generations of students the values and mores the regime deems most crucial for exercising continued control over its citizenry.

PEOPLE'S SCHOOLS
People's schools (primary schools), four years in length and administered by the Ministry of Education, represent the next step in the educational progression after kindergarten. They, along with senior middle schools, represent the linchpin of the universal and compulsory educational system. It is difficult to overstate the importance of the formative role these schools play in shaping North Korean children. As is the case in other societies, primary school years are particularly critical in molding impressionable young children, and the regime uses this opportunity to inculcate the lessons and precepts of communism and the Juche ideology. Thus, examples cited earlier of kindergarten teachings are not necessarily altered in content at the primary school level but do differ with regard to degree and intensity. For example, at this level of education, greater martial elements are introduced into the school environment and students' activities. The classroom itself, ranging in size from fifteen to fifty, resembles a military structure. A class

is the equivalent of a squad with four smaller "units," comprising roughly fifteen students each. Units themselves comprise several cells with approximately three to seven students in each.[11] Additionally, Kim and Kim point out that all children are ultimately required to join the Children's League, the North Korean equivalent of the former Soviet Union's Young Pioneers.[12] The purpose of these organizations, overseen by the school's party cell representative, is simple and straightforward: they provide yet another means to teach students the tenants and values of Juche, to convey the importance of collectivism over self, and to further mold children into perfect communists through their various activities.

North Korean author Yong Bok Li, in his work entitled, "Education in the People's Democratic Republic of Korea," identifies three key components of education, all of which have applicability at the primary level: political/ideological, physical education, and scientific-technical.[13] The aim of the political and ideological component is, of course, to create the ideal Juche citizen, one who supports the regime through labor, shared ideology, and propagating its value set. Physical education focuses on building a physically fit citizenry for purposes of national defense, another martial element that, when combined with classroom teachings, has proven quite efficacious in shaping students' perception of the world as the regime would have them view it. Physical education is also seen as a means of ensuring a strong national labor pool in furtherance of economic advancement. The scientific-technical component seeks to have students learn of the advances of modern societies in support of the regime's ideology and welfare of the nation.

The curriculum at people's schools consists of ten courses, three of which are designed to directly indoctrinate students on socialist values: Communist Morals, The Respected Supreme Leader Generalissimo Kim Il Sung's Childhood Days, and The Great Leader Marshal Kim Jong Il's Childhood Days.[14] Their respective content regales young readers with the near–fairy tale achievements and attributes of Kim Il-sung and Kim Jong-il, an example of which follows in part:

> The mother put strawberries in a dish and handed them to Marshal Kim Jong Il. The young Marshal was delirious with happiness...His hand reached the dish, but he immediately withdrew it. . . . He said to his mother that he wanted to make strawberry juice out of them. The mother's heart was filled with warm feelings. . . . After the juice was made, the mother put it into a thermal container. The Marshal

went to the office where the great father Marshal worked. "Father please drink this. It is strawberry juice." "What, strawberry juice!" The great father Marshal was surprised. . . . Indeed, the filial piety the great Marshal had for his father Marshal grew beautifully as a flower.[15]

The message of "filial piety" is fairly clear. What might be slightly less obvious is the implicit message that all Koreans should extend the same filial piety to the country's two leaders: to the memory of Kim Il-sung and to the country's current leader, Kim Jong-il. One of the fundamental teachings the regime communicates to its citizens is that the nation is a patriarchal family that lives, loves, and suffers together, always respecting the father and the son.

While the overt indoctrination purpose of these three courses, offered once a week during each year of primary education, is apparent, equally problematic is the content of the other seven courses, which follow a pattern similar to that established during kindergarten: content that vilifies the Japanese, Americans, or South Koreans and helps to further imbue young children with a Juche-centered martial spirit. Consider the example of a lesson contained in a textbook for national language in which there is the following passage: "A baby tank moves forward, smashing the American rogues," which has an adjacent picture of a young boy holding a flag and a female schoolmate applauding the actions of the tank.[16] Beyond the obvious depiction of the United States as the enemy, such language connotes to young children a martial sense of the world as well as their ability to contribute to the defense of the country, aptly communicated via the "baby tank." On whole, people's schools provide yet one more important layer of the formative groundwork that ultimately shapes the mosaic of future Juche citizens.

SENIOR MIDDLE SCHOOLS

Senior middle schools, six years in length, represent the final stage of compulsory education. Their purpose is to continue the work begun in earlier years of shaping and molding students. Thus, in this discussion citing additional examples at the senior middle school level that only reinforce earlier established patterns serves no real purpose. A discussion on the role and function of added components at this level of schooling, such as the Kim Il-sung Socialist Youth League, however, might be helpful to the reader in understanding the overall progression of building a North Korean communist citizenry.

The Youth League is designed to build upon earlier lessons learned, but at this stage its members are also called upon to "execute" specific tasks and ensure North Korean citizens are fulfilling their respective mandates issued by the country's leadership. Kim and Kim cite an interview with a former North Korean citizen who had been a Youth League member, but escaped to South Korea:

> One of the main activities of the league is to publicize Kim Il Sung's Juche ideology and the party's policies. League members are mobilized to make sure that North Korean citizens are carrying out given tasks . . . also charged with taking care of numerous Kim Il Sung study rooms and museums. They are also responsible for developing new materials designed to improve the cult of personality worship. League members must also be responsible for running the national, regional and local elections held once every four years. They must make sure that people participate 100 percent in the election, casting ballots 100 percent in favor of the official government candidates.[17]

Thus, by this stage in the educational process, Youth League members are called upon to act in direct support of regime policies, a task requiring many participants. Consequently, the Youth League comprises a rather large number of student-citizens including senior middle school students (from fifth grade of senior middle school for those in good standing), students in specialized high schools, and college and university students. It is worth noting that the process of socialist indoctrination is a life-long endeavor: adults also continue to receive instruction in the teachings of Juche.

EDUCATION IN SOUTH KOREA

Thirty-five years of Japanese colonization and the Second World War left the Korean educational system bereft of functionality. The adult population was largely illiterate with only a scant 5 percent having had more than an elementary school education.[18] Thus, upon establishing the peninsula's southern occupation zone as an independent nation, one of the new government's first priorities was educational reform, the cornerstones of which were democratic education and equal access to education by all.[19] The former focused on eliminating any and all vestiges of Japan's colonial educational system while the latter sought education's universality.

Two major initiatives facilitated South Korea's pursuit of these educational priorities. First was its adoption of the American 6-3-3-4 model of education.

Second was formally introducing and recognizing *Hangul*, the native Korean alphabet created during the fifteenth century, as South Korea's official script instead of the Chinese characters formerly used. The Korean system of education has remained largely unaltered, although its emphasis and objectives have undergone several permutations since its inception. One such example was the elimination of middle school entrance examinations during the period 1969–1971, making middle school education universal.

In the South Korean educational model, compulsory through middle school, students matriculate not on academic achievement or by successfully passing tests, but rather by age. Consequently, within any given class there can be significant disparity in the academic abilities of students.

LEVELS OF EDUCATION

While content and emphasis differ widely, the fundamental purpose of education on either side of the DMZ is fairly similar: to put in place foundational elements for the formative development of children in order to facilitate their transition into contributing members of society. In South Korea, however, this is accomplished through two educational systems that exist side by side, both public and private.

South Korean kindergartens, all privately administered, accept students between the ages of three and five. The curriculum at this level focuses on strengthening socialization and physical development, skills that will prove essential as students advance through the educational system. Specifically, the curriculum concentrates on five key areas: physical activity, social skills, expression, language, and inquiry life areas. When students reach the age of six, they are advanced into the first year of elementary school.

This goal of primary education in South Korea, as articulated in Article 93 of the Education Act, is to provide the requisite essentials for a productive life as a contributing citizen of South Korea's capitalist and democratic society. In furtherance of this goal, the primary school curriculum is divided into nine major subjects: moral education, Korean language arts, social studies, mathematics, natural science, music, physical education, practical arts and fine arts.[20] Once they enter the third year of primary school, students also begin learning English. Because parents are committed to the success of their children's academic pursuits, many are prepared to supplement formal English instruction with additional instruction outside the classroom. Many pay to send their children to *hagwon*, or private for-profit instructional institutions, for additional assistance. These institutions will come to play a pivotal role in the lives of students through high school. Other parents employ different means. From my own experience in Korea, I recall neighbors (preponderantly U.S. military spouses, but a few military officers and other Department of Defense employees as well) on the Yongsan military compound in Seoul teaching English to legions of young Koreans, a new group arriving nearly every hour almost every evening of the week.

Secondary schools continue the formative processes begun at the elementary school level. Middle schools, the final stage of compulsory education in South Korea, are the lower secondary tier of education and approximate grades seven to nine in the U.S. educational system, while high schools are the upper secondary tier.

Advancing to middle school requires a monumental shift in the commitment and attitudes of students as they are expected to begin taking their studies seriously. Indeed most middle schools require their students to wear uniforms and adhere to prescribed haircut policies. Students typically attend school five days a week (and a half-day every first, third, and fifth Saturday of the month), receiving six lessons a day derived from a curriculum that includes eleven core and elective subjects. In addition to such core courses as math, English, Korean language, and science, students also study history, technology, art, physical education, Chinese characters, and ethics.

High schools seek to provide an advanced general or specialized education building upon what the student has learned through middle school. Because high schools are not a part of compulsory education, they are accorded a bit more latitude with regard to their foci. For example, while there are, of course, public high schools, they exist alongside specialized high schools that offer more specific curriculums that might better comport with student aspirations. Thus, one can find high schools that specialize in foreign languages, science, or math, although entrance into these schools is highly competitive.

Societal expectations of students in North and South Korea differ significantly although the broad educational function of schools is generally similar. Recall the activities of high school students in North Korea through their participation in the Youth League—conducting rigged elections, overseeing activities of North Korean citizens, and developing regime propaganda. Contrast this with the stated objectives of a high school education as articulated in the South Korean Education Law, article 105 of which proffers the following:

> To educate students to be equipped with fine character and compe-
> tence expected of good citizens by continuing to provide general
> education;
> To improve students' capacity to understand and form sound judg-
> ments on social and political issues;
> To promote students' awareness of national missions, to seek to im-
> prove physical conditions of the students, to help them choose
> future life courses appropriate for themselves as individuals, to
> heighten the level of their culture, and to increase their profes-
> sional skills.

It is stark contrasts like these that will present policymakers of a unified
Korea with significant challenges in bringing a level of equality to education that
affords northern Korean children an opportunity to succeed.[21]

EDUCATIONAL CHALLENGES FOR A UNIFIED KOREA

Given the assumption underlying a final unification scenario that the Korean
peninsula will take the form, democratic governance structure, and capitalist
precepts of South Korea, it is then not unreasonable to assume that the educational system for a unified Korea will also follow the existing South Korean
model. The challenges that will confront policymakers by superimposing this
model in northern Korea, however, will likely be both numerous and sizable.
The preceding comparison of the two existing formative educational systems offers at least a glimpse of some of those challenges, chief among them being issues
of curriculum content and pedagogy. But these only scratch the surface; others
lie just beneath it. For example, consider the problem of residual stigmata regarding North Korean students' past association with a fallen communist regime
and having lived in what is widely regarded as a "backward" society.

Other questions include how these students might be fully assimilated into
the rigorously competitive educational system of South Korea. What will become of the existing cadre of North Korean educators? Can they be retrained? If
so, how long will such an effort take? If they cannot be retrained and assimilated
into the existing educational structure, a circumstance that would immediately
contribute to conditions of widespread unemployment of North Koreans (there
are at least 250,000 educators in North Korea), how can the capacity of the existing educational system in the South be expanded to absorb the anticipated influx

of students in northern Korea? And how then can they be taught the curricular content that more closely accords with the value system of the larger society? The notion of fully and successfully absorbing the school-aged population of children in North Korea, however, remains a daunting one, and the experiences of school-aged saeteomin in South Korea provide a useful primer in this regard.

By the end of 2011, estimates as to the number of saeteomin residing in South Korea will reach approximately 23,000, an increasing number of whom are school-aged children.[22] This is the result of the changing composition of the saeteomin population over the past two decades. During the 1980s and 1990s their numbers consisted primarily of high-profile defectors motivated by political ends; they were well educated and at least of middle-class means. From the early 2000s, however, characteristics of the saeteomin began to change as more destitute North Koreans motivated by economic ends and who were less educated began to dominate their numbers. The influx of this stratum of society has brought with it an increased number of women with children in tow, likely spurred by poor economic conditions, famine, and failure of North Korea's public distribution system, which has led to widespread malnutrition and mass starvation. Andrei Lankov points out that in 2002, for example, the percentage of women comprising saeteomin (54.9 percent) eclipsed men for the first time. In the following year, they comprised 63.5 percent and by 2004 the percentage had reached 66.9.[23] As noted previously, this trend apparently continues as according to the *Korea Times*, in 2008 women constituted 80 percent of North Koreans entering South Korea.[24]

These changing demographics, of course, have implications with regard to education. Challenged not only by the content and pedagogy of their education in the North, most school-aged saeteomin will not have attended school for three or four years by the time they reach South Korea; their dangerous trek out through China and perhaps on to a third country simply does not afford the opportunity for study.[25] Their resultant spotty academic track records do not facilitate assimilation into South Korea's highly competitive academic world. As noted in an earlier chapter, school truancy and drop-out rates among saeteomin are high when compared to South Korean students: only 58.4 percent of saeteomin attend middle school while only 10.4 percent attend high school. Their drop-out rate is ten times higher than the national average, at 13.7 percent.[26] On the other hand, according to the Netherlands Organization for International Cooperation in Higher Education, South Korea now leads the world in the proportion of younger people (25–34) who have completed an upper-secondary education, at 97 percent (2009), a continuing trend that complicates prospects of saeteomin success in South Korean society.[27]

Because of their academic weakness, when saeteomin are finally placed in school, they are typically placed with students younger than themselves, which likely serves as a catalyst for their poor adjustment. Recall that such a practice runs counter to the general South Korean practice of advancing students based on age rather than merit. Saeteomin students placed into classes among students younger than themselves are immediately conspicuous among their peers. This, coupled with their lack of education and diminished language skills, often sets them up for failure. Consider the following experiences of just a few school-aged saeteomin:

> The reason why I didn't learn much in school was that the South Korean kids bullied me a lot, and I got into a lot of fights. . . . I even fought with my teachers, and that's why I got expelled so many times. It was very, very hard. —*Kim Ki-young*

> Mathematics, physics, and history are taught differently in South and North Korea. . . . There are a lot of things I didn't learn in history class in North Korea. —*Kim Soo-kyung*

> After arriving in South Korea, I realized that there was so much I didn't know, that my ignorance made it hard to have even a regular conversation with my South Korean peers. I had a very hard time. . . . So, I changed my mind and decided to attend school. But I'm 20 years old, and attending elementary school is completely out of the question at this age. . . . I chose to join a class for high school entrance examination preparation at the alternative school instead. I am confused and don't know where to go or what to do. I am having a very tough time. —*Lim Keum-Hee*[28]

There is, however, growing recognition that academic maladjustment presents an obstacle to full assimilation, and nongovernmental organizations and the South Korean government alike have responded through the creation of alternative schools such as Hangyoreh, introduced in chapter 8. Schools like Hangyoreh are, however, very few in number and do not have the capacity to handle the growing numbers of students. Roughly 50 percent of the current number of saeteomin have arrived in the last four years.

Language presents yet another fundamental problem. The result of decades of peninsular division and North Korea's self-imposed isolation, language in the respective halves of the peninsula has developed differently, further exacerbating education-related issues. Choi Ok, principal of the One Nation Alternative School in Seoul and himself a saeteomin, points out that "the greatest difficulty the students face is language. . . . Even the specialized vocabulary used in geometry is different in North and South Korea: for example, the names of the various trigonometric functions. And that makes it even more difficult for them to attend school in the South."[29] Add to this the liberal use of English loan words and, of course, slang, and the complexity of learning to cope in an unfamiliar social environment is exponentially increased.

Although education is universal through high school, saeteomin students typically do not have equal access to the advantages many South Korean students enjoy, chief among these being for-profit extramural educational opportunities such as hagwon. These institutions specialize in a full panoply of subjects—English and other foreign languages, math, science, art, or music—and children of all ages, some as young as kindergarten students, attend lessons at hagwon after their regular classes. Indeed, because academic competition is so fierce in South Korea, it is not unusual for students to attend several hagwon late into the night.[30] And these institutions remain as popular as ever. According to the Korea National Statistical Office, parents spend the equivalent of $24 billion annually on hagwon and tutors.[31] The Bank of Korea, however, places the figure nearer $17 billion.[32] Despite the $7 billion difference in reported figures, the larger point should not be lost: both figures represent a year-on-year increase and underscore the premium South Korean parents place on their children's education. Saeteomin, however, do not possess the same financial resources as do many South Koreans, hence their lack of financial means presents one of the more formidable obstacles to saeteomin school children accessing equal educational opportunities, and the inability to do so places them at a distinct disadvantage.

Access to resources like hagwon could be beneficial. According to a Ministry of Education, Science and Technology survey, English is the most difficult subject for North Korean students, followed by Korean language studies, math, science, and social studies, respectively.[33] These "problem areas" are precisely those that hagwon are designed to address.

The existing gulf between South and North Korean educators and students with regard to their respective technological savvy can be measured in multiples of leagues. South Korean Ministry of Education, Science and Technology statistics provide a good case in point. In 2006 a total of 117,933 high school educators taught at general high schools and had available to them 104,998 computers for their own research purposes and 123,859 for in-classroom instruction. The North Korean regime, of course, doesn't publish these kinds of statistics, but given the ideological focus of the country's education system and anecdotal accounts of saeteomin, it is not unreasonable to conclude that the experiences of North Korean educators and students differ from those of their South Korean counterparts. Very few will likely have had any exposure to modern classroom technology as such practices would run counter to regime interests. Computers and associated technology could permit access to information uncontrolled by regime officials.

How best to educate North Korean youth along the lines of the South Korean model will pose another significant challenge to policymakers. The central problem will be one of building greater teaching capacity, which can be resolved in one of two ways: either retraining the existing North Korean cadre of educators to adhere to the content and pedagogy of the South Korean educational system or by building greater teaching capacity among South Korean educators.

Retraining North Korean educators, at first glance, appears to provide a potentially workable solution offering several advantages. It would require little in the way of undertaking additional training of South Korean educators in the problems associated with the North Korean curriculum or pedagogy or addressing issues of past socialization of students. Additionally, this course of action would obviate the need to recruit new South Korean educators and convince them to relocate into northern Korea, which at least in the beginning will be a less hospitable place to live and work due to its lack of amenities and infrastructure.

Conversely, this course of action is not without its disadvantages. North Korean educators will confront challenges of acclimation and socialization similar to those other North Koreans will face, with the added task of re-learning how to be educators in a South Korean educational context. For example, they will first need to be "de-programmed" as Juche citizens, and will themselves need to learn and embrace the value system of a capitalist society in order to effectively educate students. They will also need to learn South Korean pedagogy as well as re-learn course content if saeteomin descriptions of what they learned in North Korean schools are accurate. Additionally, as pointed out earlier, learning the Korean language used in the south is in itself challenging for North Koreans, not only for daily life but for teaching and study as well; and learning the English language presents its own unique set of challenges. Re-educating North Korea's cadre of educators will likely be a lengthy process, potentially leaving at the very least a generation of North Korean students academically disadvantaged.

Expanding teaching capacity of the existing system in South Korea is also laden with challenges, the ability to train an adequate number of educators being chief among them. While the institutional capacity for training secondary educators is comparatively robust in South Korea with thirteen teachers' colleges at national universities and twenty-three private institutions, only eleven national universities and Ehwa Women's University offer primary teacher education.[34] This capacity has proven sufficient in maintaining a cadre of approximately 396,000 public and private school educators (excluding kindergarten teachers) to satisfy South Korea's educational requirements, but will prove insufficient to the task of absorbing North Korea's millions of school-aged children.[35]

Because of the regime's rather sporadic method of reporting educational data, if any is provided at all, making firm assessments as to educational resource requirements in the country becomes difficult. Using what data is available, however, certain assumptions can be made. For example, in 1990 there were 1.4 million children attending kindergarten; in 1996 there were 1.9 million attending people's schools; and in 1998, 2.9 million attended senior middle school. According to the United Nations World Population Prospects report, North Korea's population growth is expected to experience a moderate increase of roughly 1.2 million through the year 2025, reaching a total of 25.1 million.[36] Thus, one might reasonably expect that the numbers of school-aged children will also trend slightly higher and that a population of 6.5–8 million will likely need to be absorbed.

South Korea currently has an estimated population of 48.5 million[37]; by 2025 this is expected to climb by 3.5 million to approximately 52 million.[38] According to the Ministry of Education, Science and Technology, the current number of K–12 students in South Korea is approximately 8.1 million. Thus by 2025 one might reasonably expect a school-aged population of close to 11 million in South Korea.

Under a unified Korea, the student population could well increase by roughly 60–70 percent and place enormous demands on the resources of the

South Korean educational system that can only be met by a significant increase in teaching capacity. Recruiting and training educators will take time; persuading many of them to relocate to northern Korea could prove an even greater challenge. Special care will need to be taken to ensure such disparities in education do not become culturally entrenched.

10

The Conundrum of
Transformative Issues

They [North Koreans] seem to think every South Korean is very rich,
so they must earn money quickly to catch up with them. . . . They
don't know how to compete. They are just dreaming.
                                    —*Manufacturing company recruiter*[1]

The present population of saeteomin residing in South Korea is but an
infinitesimal piece of the challenge that confronts South Korean government officials even absent a unification scenario. The rate at which saeteomin are entering South Korea has never been higher. Prior to 1990 there
were roughly 600 North Koreans in South Korea; by 2001 an additional 1,383
had joined their compatriots. The year 2006 was the first time the annual total
of North Korean immigrants eclipsed 2,000 with 2,018 crossing the border, and
the numbers continue to increase.[2] The annual percentage of growth stands at 10
percent and the number of saeteomin escaping into South Korea surpassed 3,000
for the first time in 2009.

What lies at the heart of this unexpected mass exodus is a mutually supportive set of issues. First, the alternating twin natural disasters of floods in 1995
and 1996 followed by drought in 1997 greatly impacted agriculture in the North,
putting in place all the right factors for a massive outbreak of famine. This was
accompanied in 2002 by regime efforts to adopt new reform measures under
the July 1st Reforms, a major component of which was a scaling back of public
distribution of food rations through the Public Distribution System. Generally,

these events and circumstances accord with the timeframe during which there was a substantially notable increase in the influx of North Koreans into South Korea, which helps to underscore the impact that North Korea's domestic problems continue to have on the growing exodus of its citizens. Another factor that has helped to fuel the increasing numbers, and will continue to do so, is the phenomenon known as "chain migrations"—the efforts of saeteomin to get their family members out of North Korea, China, or a third country and have them come to South Korea as well. In many cases such efforts are financed through the relocation subsidies saeteomin receive from the South Korean government.

In the aggregate, these factors likely portend a continued increase in the number of North Koreans who will be repatriated over the next few years. Developing mechanisms to cope with these rising numbers is not only humane, it will be essential to developing sound policies that minimize the potential adverse impact of saeteomin on South Korean society while maximizing the potential for their successful assimilation.

THE RATIONALE FOR SAETEOMIN IN SOUTH KOREA

The legal basis for accepting saeteomin into South Korea resides within the nation's constitution, although the motivations for doing so have varied over the decades. Article Three of South Korea's constitution stipulates, "The territory of the Republic of Korea shall consist of the Korean peninsula and its adjacent islands." The constitutional preamble also points out that one of the nation's responsibilities is "to elevate the quality of life for all citizens." Thus, these two passages taken together provide the rationale and legal basis for accepting and assisting saeteomin. They are not regarded as North Koreans but rather as Korean citizens over which South Korea exercises sovereignty.

During the Cold War, the motivation for assisting those who fled North Korea was uncomplicated—they were welcomed into South Korea primarily for their propaganda value and treated as *yonsa*, or "national heroes." At the time, both Koreas were locked in a zero-sum geopolitical battle vying for recognition as the sole legitimate sovereign power on the peninsula and inter-Korean relations came to be characterized by a one-upmanship, tit-for-tat manner of engagement.

The policy of recognizing defectors as yonsa was buttressed by a legal framework. For example, in 1962 the government promulgated the Special Law to Protect Those Who Contributed to the Country and North Korean Defectors. This law, which in effect accorded to defectors the same recognition granted to those who fought against Japanese colonialism during World War II, grouped them into three categories based on prior social status in North Korea and provided generous resettlement packages based on those groupings.[3] Other laws followed. In 1978, the government passed the Special Compensation Law for Brave Soldiers, which provided additional benefits for defectors such as free education, free housing, medical assistance, and welfare payments.[4] In addition to the more generous benefits extended to them, those North Koreans with particularly valuable intelligence to share, and this was the majority of defectors at the time, were rather handsomely rewarded. For example, in February 1983 a MiG-19 pilot, Captain Lee Woong-pyung, defected with his fighter, an act for which he ultimately received 1.2 billion won in compensation, the average annual South Korean salary at the time being about 2.5 million won.[5] He also became a researcher and colonel at the Air Force academy.[6] But the law enacted in 1978 would be the last during the Cold War. Post–Cold War laws would come to reflect changes in the prevailing geopolitical circumstances and apply diminished "value" to saeteomin, largely the result of their increasing numbers and changed socioeconomic characteristics, substantially impacting the benefits provided to them.

In 1993, the South Korean government enacted several amendments to the 1978 law, effectively reducing the benefits extended under its protection and mandating more "rational management" of defectors.[7] Criminals and those North Koreans who had resided in third nations for extended periods of time fell outside the relevant legal parameters of the amended law and thus were not extended benefits provided under it. Additionally, free housing was no longer provided. Resettlement packages were continually reduced from an average equivalent of $30,000–$40,000 to about $9,000 in 2005 for single defectors; families received additional compensation depending upon the number of members.[8] Presently, saeteomin receive a stipend of 6 million won (roughly $5,000), again families receiving more based on their size, and a rental apartment worth 13 million won upon completion of assimilation courses offered at Hanawon. They are, however, eligible for various incentives designed to place and keep saeteomin in the South Korean labor market. For example, those saeteomin completing a one-year vocational program are eligible for a 2.4 million won bonus and an additional 2 million won if they obtain a certificate of qualification. If they secure employment and remain with the same firm for one year, saeteomin are awarded 4.5 million won; after completing a total of two years of employment at the same firm, they receive an additional 5 million won and after three years another 5.5 million won. (On August 1, 2011, US$1 was equivalent to 1049.82 won.) Thus, South Korean government officials have shifted their efforts from compensating saeteomin with government handouts for purposes of survival to assisting them in assimilating into the South Korean work force by providing the tools necessary for becoming viable employees and productive citizens.

The government's policy shift comes as a result of two important realizations. First, a model under which the preponderance of support and assistance provided is in the form of handouts is unsustainable even in the near-term, because as saeteomin numbers continue to climb at an increasing rate, associated costs will become unsupportable. Second, such a program promotes a culture of dependency rather than assimilation and, in the process, creates an underclass of North Koreans who are looked down upon by the larger society because working, status, and maintaining one's own livelihood are fundamental values in South Korean society. Inability to meet such expectations has led to perceptions of North Koreans as generally being "dependent, passive, lazy and selfish."[9]

ECONOMIC ASSIMILATION

While the South Korean labor market ranks as one of the strongest among nations of the Organization of Economic Cooperation and Development (OECD), it has certain peculiarities that render it potentially susceptible to strong movements in saeteomin activity, making the issue particularly salient for the study of unification. While South Korea has one of the lowest unemployment rates among OECD nations, one-third of its jobs are made up of non-salaried positions—self-employed or unpaid family workers. As Bidet points out, these types of jobs are generally considered to be of lesser quality as the pay is typically lower and the benefits less generous than those received by salaried workers.[10] Bidet also observes,

> South Korea has the lowest proportion of regular salaried workers among OECD countries and a labor market that is characterized by a growing bipolarization between secured and unsecured jobs.[11]

Bipolarization of the job market has implications not only in the near-term for saeteomin but also for any long-term plans related to unification as well. As discussed earlier, composition of the North Korean migrant population entering South Korea has changed significantly over the decades, primarily the result of newly emergent economic motivations for fleeing North Korea. Current migrants are among the most destitute in North Korea, are poorly educated, and are preponderantly women (with children). Bidet notes that with regard to women in the South Korean job market,

> They can hardly hold a regular and permanent job because of the strong gender discrimination in the Korean market—and among them, especially the women in atypical situations (such as single mothers, divorced women, ex-prostitutes, and migrant workers).[12]

With restricted access to education, few job skills, and an inability to comprehend the South Korean dialect, saeteomin are most likely destined to occupy the lowest rungs of the employment ladder locked in competition with South Korea's population of 400,000–425,000 foreign migrant workers. And the life of a foreign migrant is anything but enviable. Some firsthand accounts describe conditions that require migrants to work from 6 a.m. until midnight six days a week.[13] Conditions like these increase the likelihood that South Korean perceptions of North Koreans as being lazy and ignorant will be realized.

Labor market characteristics raise other troubling questions for unification, particularly under a model of absorption. Structurally, the South Korean labor market is not designed to readily absorb large numbers of adult North Koreans. With over a third of the labor market represented by self-employed or unpaid family members and 45 percent of that market comprising temporary workers with contractual obligations of less than one year in duration,[14] there exists a latent potential instability that could impact domestic labor conditions with devastating results.

Merely finding employment is not necessarily a panacea for curing the employment ills of former North Korean citizens. Substantial discrepancies exist between North Korean migrants and South Korean workers with regard to how they are rewarded for their labors. The average monthly salary of saeteomin is the equivalent of about $680, or about 940,000 won.[15] Bidet notes a slightly higher average monthly income of about 1.1 million won for saeteomin. While the absolute number is slightly higher, when considered as a percentage of the average monthly salary of South Korean workers, saeteomin have, in either case, actually lost ground in the past five years. The current average monthly salary of an urban South Korean worker is 3.3 million won, making saeteomin salaries one-third that of their South Korean counterparts. Using the national monthly average salary of all South Korean workers, which stands at 2.5 million won, renders only slightly better results at 40 percent.[16] By comparison, 2003 statistics indicate saeteomin salaries were 50 percent of the national average.[17] According to some research, the rate of pay for saeteomin is so low that it qualifies nearly 80 percent of them for some form of social welfare assistance.[18]

One reason for this apparent downward trajectory of saeteomin earned income might be attributed to their changing demographic composition: the increasing numbers of unskilled women with children entering South Korea (recall that as a practice North Korean women do not typically ask familial others to render childcare). Given the characteristics of the South Korean labor market with regard to the employment of women (including South Korean women) and the lack of skills and education among migrating North Koreans, this shifting demographic could well be impacting the saeteomin employment situation. This conclusion appears to be substantiated in a study conducted by Kim, Kim, and Lee, whose research of former North Koreans' integration into the South Korean labor market indicates that the employment probability of saeteomin females in the labor market does not increase measurably the longer they reside in South Korea, thus keeping them among the ranks of the unemployed.[19]

Officially reported statistics through the Unification Ministry indicate that the overall saeteomin unemployment rate stood at about 9.5 percent in July 2009.[20] Yet several other surveys calculate their unemployment rate to be much higher. For example, a survey conducted by the Korea Development Institute released in December 2006 found that only 30 percent of saeteomin were employed.[21] Bidet's research also points to higher unemployment figures hovering around 30–40 percent. And according to the presidential National Unification Advisory Council, while approximately 72 percent of all saeteomin in May 2007 were employed, 68 percent were contract workers and only 14 percent had secured full-time employment. Additionally, 69.5 percent received subsidized living expenses, and over 74 percent received assistance for medical services.

Such statistical differences can likely be attributed to how the parameters of any particular survey are defined, what constitutes unemployment, and how transitory employment is accounted for. Thus, in the statistics cited earlier, are the 68 percent of saeteomin working as contract workers considered to be fully employed? Who should be counted as being active in the job market? (Are unemployed women with children generally counted as being voluntarily inactive in the job market because they are caregivers, or unemployed because they are of working age?). The size and composition of the population surveyed as well as their places of residence (urban dwellers versus rural dwellers) could also impact survey results. Given the huge increase in the number of saeteomin and their changing demographics, government figures merit closer scrutiny.

To be sure, the South Korean government has come to recognize the multifarious challenges saeteomin confront and its role in facilitating the economic assimilation process. Thus, government officials have begun working with private industry to develop new programs that help to absorb qualified saeteomin into the market place. Through Hanawon, the Unification Ministry has created a training program with CJ Foodville, a nationwide food-processing firm with seven hundred branches. Saeteomin can work for the firm after completing a five-month training program. Another example is a program offered through GM Daewoo Auto and Technology, under which saeteomin who successfully serve as apprentice mechanics for twelve months can be hired for regular employment.[22]

Although these programs are in a fledgling state, they do show some amount of potential promise. Provided the number of North Korean migrants does not swell to uncontrollable levels, expanding such programs could well assist in efforts to economically assimilate North Koreans in the near term. To employ similar models as a means for absorbing millions of North Koreans under a unification scenario, however, is quite another matter. The capacity of South Korean commercial concerns to absorb large numbers of North Koreans simply does not exist at present, and characteristics of the South Korean labor market would make it particularly susceptible to large diasporic movement from the northern half of the peninsula. Additionally, any such programs will require massive infusions of funding, the most likely source of which will be the South Korean government, contributing significantly to the overall cost of unification.

Another issue left unaddressed in these work programs is the potential for social displacement among South Koreans. Through massive and expensive aid programs to facilitate economic assimilation of North Koreans under unification, what will become of the jobless and impoverished among South Korean citizens? They, and perhaps the society at large, might well question why former North Koreans merit assistance that South Koreans do not, putting in place a wedge between the larger society and its new citizens. Yoon and Lim help to confirm this point:

> The existence of other social minorities including unemployed, homeless, and disabled persons is raising the issue of equality regard-

ing North Korean migrant's special treatments. They also receive other benefits such as job training education, employment arrangements, employment aid funds, loans for business capital, etc.[23]

Finally, at least at the unskilled labor level, the law of supply and demand will likely help to drive the price of labor down with potentially significant displacement among South Koreans, the result of massive influxes of cheap labor from the North. The notion of such a happenstance is not without precedence, as this is the concept upon which the Kaesong Industrial Complex is predicated and upon which the success of South Korean firms operating in the complex depends—South Korean technology and management fueled with cheap North Korean labor. The North Koreans who work at the complex (June 2009 Ministry of Unification figures) on average earn about $70–80 per month, of which the workers receive $25–30. The residual finds its way into the coffers of the North Korean regime leadership.[24]

OF PRIDE AND PREJUDICE:
SAETEOMIN IN THE WORKPLACE

Structural issues like those outlined in the preceding sections offer significant impediments against entry into the South Korean labor market, but non-structural issues can be equally difficult to negotiate. In particular the attitudes of both saeteomin and South Koreans toward each other can, and has, led to workplace dissonance between the two populations of workers. Adding to the problem's complexity is the tendency of North Korean migrants to define their prospects for success in South Korea in unrealistic terms.

From the perspective of some saeteomin, lack of integration into the workplace may stem from the type of work to which they've been relegated, which may not accord with their levels of education, training, or expectations. In a 2005 survey of 128 "professional" saeteomin, only two were working in the professions for which they had been trained in North Korea.[25] Because professional jobs are more highly valued than those requiring physical labor, saeteomin tend to shun lesser jobs considered menial, particularly those characterized as "3D"—dirty, dangerous, or difficult.[26] This of course fuels their higher unemployment rates, as they either do not enter the job market or their employment is characterized by frequent job changes.

Other unfulfilled expectations arise from saeteomin beliefs that the affluence of South Koreans, by which they are beset on a daily basis, is easily attainable, and they consequently become impatient for the "luxuries" of capitalism, leading some to rashly quit their jobs in pursuit of self-employment, an undertaking for which they are both unprepared and unskilled. Such perceptions are reinforced by the belief that they should receive compensation for the hardships endured during their flight to South Korea. With reductions in government subsidies and the inability to find good paying jobs, saeteomin expectations go largely unsatisfied. Consider the comments of one saeteomin during a recent interview with the *Korea Times*:

> Only 350,000 won ($350 U.S.) is given to each defector per month. Worse still, the subsidy continues only for the first six months. After paying housing fees, insurance premiums and pension fees, we have almost nothing to spend.[27]

In 2005 the Information Center for North Korean Human Rights conducted a survey to identify the types of employment saeteomin held prior to their migration into South Korea. The survey found that slightly over 63 percent had been: physical laborers (34.6 percent), unemployed (15.4 percent), farmers (7.3 percent), and housewives (6 percent). Thus, expectations of high payoffs as a result of migrating south are generally inconsistent with individual saeteomin experiences or the realities they confront.[28] These findings generally comport with how former North Korean citizens self-identified their socio-economic status in North Korea: 11.1 percent considered themselves to be middle class; 52.5 percent as lower-middle class; 26 percent as lower class; and 7.8 percent as poverty stricken.[29]

The value system saeteomin bring to the workplace, while appropriate for a society based on a collectivist construct, is generally incongruent with the South Korean context. One glaring example of this is the tendency of former North Koreans to openly and publicly criticize their work colleagues, a practice normally conducted through formal daily sessions of open criticism in North Korea. Such behavior not only fails to conform with South Korean norms and values, it hampers saeteomin from building relationships, adding to their isolation. Working in concert with such practices to confound saeteomin integration is the socialization process that North Koreans have undergone, which leads to rigidly structured thinking. Woo-taek Jeon's interviews of saeteomin offer some idea as to the depth of the problem:

> When I found that other defectors possess different political opinions about North Korea, I usually refused to accept these differences and simply discontinued the relationship with those defectors. I believe that is right.[30]

Such thinking points to two problems. First, it underscores Jeon's contention that there exists a lack of social and cognitive flexibility among some saeteomin. It also highlights that while migrating North Koreans have received South Korean citizenship and completed "cultural" training through Hanawon, there are those among the saeteomin population who remain more comfortable with the precepts of Juche society. This may indicate that greater efforts to acculturate migrants at the time of entry are required.

Perceived prejudice in the workplace presents yet another obstacle for saeteomin. For example, Kim and Jang point out that in a 2001 survey 22.4 percent of saeteomin indicated they felt South Korean prejudice against them represented the greatest obstacle to successful integration into the workplace.[31] A National Committee for Human Rights of South Korea report (2005) offered additional insights into saeteomin perceptions, revealing that 50.5 percent felt policies regarding salaries were unfairly administered against them: saeteomin perceived they received less pay for the same work. Regarding equality in promotion, 52.7 percent felt they were unfairly treated because of their background, and 38.6 percent felt their South Korean colleagues purposely shunned and ostracized them in the workplace.[32] And such perceptions remain unchanged. In a May 2008 interview with the *Korea Times*, one saeteomin observed, "Most South Korean businesses are still reluctant to hire us. . . . Some of them look down on us, saying they cannot trust North Koreans."[33]

On whole, South Korean attitudes and perceptions of saeteomin generally do not facilitate their integration into the workplace and might lend some measure of credence to saeteomin perceptions of their circumstances in South Korea. In a survey undertaken by Sogang University researchers in June 2008, respondents were asked pointed but hypothetical questions, such as "How would you feel about employing a North Korean refugee?" or "How would you feel about your children befriending a refugee youth?" to which those surveyed responded negatively. Conversely, general and open-ended questions like "How do you feel towards the refugees?" tended to elicit more affirmative and supportive responses.[34] Thus, in a general social context some South Koreans might feel compelled to demonstrate empathy to the plight of migrants, but such feelings might not lead them to personally extend themselves.

As is the case in the larger society, there appears to be a general ignorance of and negative indifference to the plight of North Koreans in the workplace. These feelings manifest themselves in various ways, but most often take the form of creating and maintaining social distance by ostracizing them. Several factors conflate to create such circumstances. First is the realization that all Koreans are not brothers and that the myth of homogeneity is simply that—a myth. Stark differences exist in speech, culture, recent history, socialization, and value systems between North and South Koreans that fundamentally make them two different peoples; indeed most Koreans have never experienced a unified Korea. South Korea may comprise a homogeneous population, as does North Korea, but together they do not. In the abstract, the notion of a Korean brotherhood is appealing; the reality, however, is quite a different matter.

Second, because the demographics of North Korean migrants have shifted so dramatically, from the elite of North Korean society several decades ago to its impoverished masses today, saeteomin come with few job skills or an ability to adapt to South Korean society. Consequently they are viewed as a burden to society, the labor market, and workplace.

Economic assimilation is the cornerstone of any successful unification scenario based on absorption under which the South Korean model of government is predominant. Clearly some progress has been made in assisting small numbers of saeteomin to assimilate into South Korean society, but these efforts pale in comparison to what will be required under a unified peninsula. Structural issues in the labor market must be addressed and are interwoven with social attitudes, misconceptions, and prejudices of both North and South Koreans, making successful resolution a complex undertaking.

11

Beyond the Formative
and Transformative

There are only two kinds of people in North Korea—those who
trade [goods] and those who are dead.

—North Korean defector [1]

Formative and transformative issues will compose the nucleus of any successful repatriation policy, which in turn will be fundamental to any
meaningful effort to advance peninsular unification. Yet there are other
issues, largely social service programs, indirectly related to repatriation that officials of a unified Korean government must successfully negotiate in order to
ensure some amount of parity is achieved and maintained between the northern
and southern halves of the peninsula. One such challenge is health care, specifically the need to address deteriorating health conditions among North Korean
citizens, the result of long-term malnutrition and dysfunctional, if not non-
existent, preventive care policies. Associated considerations include the potential
for diasporic movement out of northern Korea during post-unification and the
need for a unified government to develop social welfare policies equitable to all
Koreans, former North Koreans and South Koreans alike.

HEALTH ISSUES
A review of several key metrics helps to illustrate current conditions in North
Korea's health-care system. To begin with, it appears that the estimated total
population of North Korea has been negatively impacted over the past several

years, which could be attributed to several factors. According to the *CIA World Factbook*, North Korea's estimated total population in July 2007 was about 23.5 million; for July 2009 the estimate stood at approximately 22.7 million. One reason for the decrease in population might be traced to a higher incidence of mortality among North Koreans as a result of malnutrition. The continuing exodus of North Koreans migrating into China, third countries, and South Korea might also account for a percentage of the decrease. Finally, any decline might also be attributed, in part, to methods used in calculating the estimated population.

A comparison of fertility and mortality rates of the two Koreas, however, offers compelling data to consider. While North Korea's fertility rate of 1.96 is actually higher than South Korea's 1.21, North Korea's infant mortality rate of 51.34 per 1,000 live births is about twelve times higher than that of South Korea, which registers an infant mortality rate of only 4.26 per 1,000 live births.[2] Another useful metric to consider is the life expectancy in North Korea, which for 2009 stood at an average of 63.81 years for all North Korean citizens (61.23 years for males; 66.53 years for females). In a peninsular context these figures become quite revealing, as the average life expectancy of a South Korean citizen for the same period was 78.72 years (75.45 years for males; 82.22 years for females).[3] Thus, North Korea's greater infant mortality rate and lower life expectancy could well be contributing to a decrease in population, the result of greater health risks associated with the effects of long-term starvation, malnutrition, and a dysfunctional health-care system.

North Korean citizens have lived with the pernicious effects of malnutrition for at least a generation. Exact statistics are, of course, difficult to come by but some assumptions can be reached based on what facts are known. First, the problem of chronic food shortages continues for North Koreans as the specter of broad starvation has again become all too real. The WFP is estimating that by the end of 2011 North Korea's food shortfall will reach 542,000 tons. Compounding this anticipated food deficit is the funding shortfall the WFP confronts. The organization's program to provide food to 1.7 million North Korean women and children remains woefully underfunded, having received a mere 20 percent of the funds required for its implementation.[4] Several other factors have also conflated to exacerbate these circumstances. The country experienced an outbreak of foot-and-mouth disease during late winter and early spring 2011, and given its extensive dependence on draught animals for plowing fields, particularly oxen, this could represent a consequential disruption to agricultural activities; most recent reports estimate that some 10,000 have been afflicted with the disease. Indeed, oxen are so important to North Korea's agriculture that the central government owns them all.[5] Additionally, sanctions the South Korean government put in place against the regime in 2010 in response to its two unprovoked attacks that left a total of fifty South Korean citizens dead (the March 26, 2010, sinking of the *Cheonan* that left forty-six sailors dead and the November 23, 2010, attack on Yeonpyeong Island that killed four) have also begun to have an impact. The Lee administration has suspended food aid to the regime until it apologizes for these attacks on South Korean sovereignty.

In response to the nation's worsening food shortage, the regime has ordered that citizens achieve food self-sufficiency through the widespread introduction of *toibee*, a homemade fertilizer produced by mixing night soil (human excrement) with ash for use as a soil additive. The goal is to create tons of the makeshift fertlizer.[6] That any government in the twenty-first century would require its citizens to resort to such outdated methods of farming, particularly a country possessing the necessary technology to build nuclear devices, reinforces the depth of North Korea's problems.

These efforts will not, in all likelihood, achieve the desired results, despite the regime's efforts to mobilize the entirety of its citizenry in this nationwide initiative, because it is based on past faulty agricultural policies. Because of its mountainous topography, North Korea has a dearth of arable land; inputting greater variables, in this case toibee, on a constant—the amount of arable land—will only replicate past failures. As noted in chapter 5, not only have the regime's past agricultural policies been misguided, they have actually worsened the nation's agricultural problems. Add to this the fact that food distribution is typically carried out within a political context: those with the right ideological pedigree and who live in closer proximity to the center (Pyongyang), are usually taken care of first. Conversely, those North Korean citizens living in rural areas generally bear the brunt of food shortages, hence, the continued conditions of starvation in the nation's rural areas like Hamgyong Province (chapter 8).

Second, the chronic food shortage is insidious in its impact. North Korean teen-aged boys fleeing into South Korea over the past decade are on average twenty-five pounds lighter and five inches shorter than their South Korean counterparts.[7] Another effect of malnutrition to which young children are acutely susceptible is arrested mental development. A report released by the U.S. National Intelligence Council in December 2008 points to the fact that roughly

25 percent of North Korean military conscripts will likely be disqualified from service as a result of malnutrition-induced mental retardation.[8] Other problems associated with the "eating problem," as starvation is often referred to in North Korea, are osteoporosis, tooth decay, organ failure, and other illnesses, contingent upon the severity of the malnutrition. Thus, cognitive impairment, physical abnormalities, dental problems, and other health issues that plague North Koreans will immediately become the problem of a unified Korean government to address.

Basic preventive medical care is also lacking in North Korea. In 2006–2007 the country suffered an outbreak of measles, which the World Health Organization (WHO) described as having been "significant": 3,500 cases and four deaths.[9] In what WHO termed as a rapid response to the outbreak, more than 6 million children were vaccinated within a three-day time period in March 2007. In its entirety, the program vaccinated over 16 million North Koreans. It is the general lack of preventive medical care, however, that contributes to fifty-five children out of every 1,000 dying before the age of five.[10]

South Korea moved to a universal health-care model in 1977 when South Korean government officials required firms with five hundred or more workers to provide health insurance to employees and their family members. Twelve years later in 1989, the government mandated that medical insurance be extended nationwide, through National Health Insurance (NHI), which replaced the voluntary health-care system that had existed to that point. The real question regarding health care, however, is how its bottom line will be impacted under a scenario of unification. South Korea's universal health-care system bears some interesting characteristics. For example, among OECD nations, the country shows the third highest increase in per-capita annual growth of total expenditures on health care, 10.3 percent, outpaced only by the Slovak Republic and Poland, which had annual growth percentages of 16.5 percent and 12.1 percent, respectively.[11] South Korea's actual per-capita health-care expenditure, however, is comparatively low. While it spends $1,688 per person on health care, the United States spends about $7,290 per person.[12] If this is the case, a simple "guesstimation" is that a unified Korean government might expect, at the very least, to add an additional $38.4 billion in healthcare costs annually. This calculation does not account for any additional costs a unified government will need to absorb as it seeks to treat chronic health problems former North Korean citizens bring with them, which could increase the cost of health care significantly.

ISSUES OF DIASPORA

The majority of the North Korean population is, as described throughout part II, destitute and without means for earning a living wage, their ranks preponderantly comprising unskilled laborers. In fact given the various associated challenges of assimilation within a framework of unification, even well-educated North Koreans will likely find it difficult to secure employment in a post-unification period. Thus, North Koreans will see peninsular unification immediately representing two groundswells of change: a reprieve from harsh governance and an opportunity to relocate to a more hospitable land offering greater opportunity. The first of these perceptions will most likely be accurate, given the democratic foundations of South Korean governance, but efforts of a unified government to control the potential diasporic movement of former North Korean citizens may ultimately impact their perceptions of the new leadership.

Human migration has occurred throughout the history of mankind. People have migrated across borders from one place to another for centuries, motivated by political oppression, economic gain, or survival. In the case of East Asia, however, such migration is a relatively new post–Cold War phenomenon. Prior to the end of the Cold War, human migratory activity was largely limited by the restrictive policies most governments had in place against freedom of movement across their respective borders. As a result, while the East Asia region (Japan, China, Russia, Mongolia, Taiwan, South Korea, and North Korea) comprises about 28 percent of the world's population, it contains only 11 percent of the world's "migrant stock."[13] Presently, however, most East Asian nations face various challenges associated with either inward, outward, or internal migrations of people, North Korea among them.

Mass movement of people out of the northern half of the Korean peninsula must be assumed and anticipated. There simply is little inducement for North Koreans to remain in place after unification is achieved; domestic conditions have been, and likely will remain, very inhospitable. The accompanying diaspora to which unification will give rise will likely move in two directions: China and South Korea. The fundamental challenge government officials will confront is this: through what means do they ensure that the population of former North Korean citizens remains largely in place in order to avoid antagonizing China or destabilizing the South Korean economy while avoiding implementation of policies that are reminiscent of North Korea's current Stalinist regime?

Potential migration into China holds several attractions for North Koreans. First is the comparative ease with which border crossings can be affected.

Although the trek into China is clearly not without peril, tens of thousands (by some estimates hundreds of thousands) of North Koreans have made the crossing successfully. Contrast this with the heavily armed demilitarized zone that now separates North and South Korea, which is virtually impossible to navigate successfully. Second is the existence of an informal infrastructure within China of which North Koreans can avail themselves. One area that offers a potential haven for North Koreans migrating into China, as described earlier, is the Yanbian Korean Autonomous Prefecture, which is home to about one million ethnic Koreans. Third, China also presents opportunities for grassroots-level trade and commerce. Despite the North Korean regime's repressive policies, enterprising North Koreans undertake market activities, much of which takes place inside Chinese borders. North Korean "entrepreneurs" sell what few items they can on the Chinese market, primarily seafood and a few herbs, to earn money; Chinese merchants in turn provide inexpensive consumer products to a needy North Korean market. Such cross-border commerce can account for nearly 75–80 percent of a North Korean family's income, if they are in a position to take advantage of their proximity to the Chinese border.[14] Thus, North Koreans will likely seek to expand these types of commercial activities under a unification scenario if they are permitted any degree of economic self-determination because it is a familiar activity, requiring few, if any, advanced job skills, and can be accomplished within a cultural context with which they are comfortable.

From the perspective of average North Korean citizens, a new life in South Korea also offers potential reprieve from starvation and destitution. While the current context of inter-Korean relations greatly reduces the likelihood of mass diasporic movement onto the southern half of the peninsula, it is not unreasonable to conclude that, within a unification framework, current mechanisms designed to keep North Koreans from crossing directly into South Korea, most notably the DMZ, will no longer be in place.

Government leaders of a newly unified Korea will likely be pressed, both domestically and through the international community of nations, to rid the country, physically and symbolically, of the DMZ, its most visible Cold War legacy. Recall the celebratory response among German citizens in November 1989 as the Berlin Wall was, for all intents and purposes, politically dismantled when Gunter Schabowski, East German minister of propaganda, announced the opening of the border for "private trips abroad." This was actually acquiescence on the part of the East German leadership to permit greater freedom of movement outside East Germany for such destinations as Hungary and Czechoslovakia, a response to growing demands for these freedoms among its citizenry. Physical dismantlement of the Wall occurred over the following weeks and months and, while not insignificant, was largely symbolic. A newly unified Korean government will likely face similar demands.

Eliminating the decades-old border dividing the Korean peninsula will not be a cure-all remedy for the ills that plague those living in the northern half, and will likely transpose many of the problems onto southern Korea, some of which were discussed earlier. A huge influx of migrants could have a debilitating effect on the labor market, which, because of its unique characteristics, would be particularly susceptible to large increases in the size of the employably aged population. Government employment partnerships like the program operated by CJ Foodville demonstrate potential on a small scale but are hardly workable models for addressing the needs of a mass influx of migrants. There already exists a demonstrated deficiency in North Korean pedagogy and curricular content that institutions like Hangyoreh work to correct, but it takes a sizeable investment of time and resources to assist students educated in North Korea, all of which will be in finite supply in the immediate aftermath of unification. Additionally, under such a scenario how will the government provide the necessary assimilative tools to new migrants as it currently does through programs offered at Hanawon? Hanawon can accommodate approximately 3,600 residents annually and thus is hardly a model that can be replicated for millions of migrants on short order, yet the services it provides are essential in assisting North Korean migrants in their transition into a democratic and capitalist society.[15]

Despite the anticipated challenges any new government will confront upon the DMZ's dismantlement, failure to open the border between the former halves of the Koreas could be equally devastating because of the troubling message it would communicate. How would a new government formed on the principles of democracy reconcile maintaining an internal border designed to keep northerners politically sequestered? Even more challenging would be the necessity to maintain guard over a border. How would such action be substantively differentiated from the actions of the current regime? If such a scenario were to occur, how would former North Korean citizens respond? Would it, in the end, actually lead to greater cross-border migration into China, the result of uncertainty and lack of confidence in the governance infrastructure of a unified Korea? The end result of any effort to control migration, while essential for economic and social stability, would likely be construed negatively. Similarly, any such actions could also negatively color perceptions that South Korean citizens hold of their North Korean neighbors.

SOCIAL WELFARE PROGRAMS

South Korea has a fairly comprehensive social welfare program comprising both social insurance and public assistance programs. Social insurance programs include National Health Insurance, National Pension Plan, Employment Insurance, and the Long-Term Care Insurance program. As noted earlier, the National Health Insurance program is universal in its application and is financed through government subsidies and employee contributions; workers pay 4.31 percent of their income into the system. The National Pension Plan covers all employees ages eighteen to sixty, with the exception of those covered under separate plans: military, government workers, and private school educators.[16] Full benefits are extended to those workers who have reached the age of sixty and have contributed into the program for twenty years. The 9 percent contribution rate into the National Pension Plan is shared between employer and employee with each paying half. The Employment Insurance program provides benefits to workers who become unemployed; the exception being government workers and educators. The program requires a 0.9 percent monthly contribution, again split evenly between employee and employer.[17] Finally, the Long-Term Care Insurance program provides care to the infirmed elderly. Payments for this program are made through the National Health Insurance program and are over and above the basic charges for universal health insurance.[18]

All these programs are designed to provide a social safety net for South Korean citizens at various points in their lives when assistance will likely be needed, the common denominator of such assistance being, however, that both employees and employers contribute to the various plans. This raises larger questions with regard to unification and whether such benefits would be extended to former North Korean citizens. Arguably they will be needy, but under what justification would the Korean government extend these benefits for no charge to its new citizens when South Koreans have been and will continue to be required to pay for them? Yet absent a policy that recognizes the need of former North Koreans, a newly formed government will create an indigent class of Koreans, numbering nearly 23 million, with no jobs, medical coverage, or source of income.

South Korean government officials may have at their disposal one public assistance tool to offer some measure of help to indigent North Koreans—the

NBLS program, created in 2000. Fully funded by the South Korean government, the program is designed to provide benefits to those citizens whose income is below the established poverty line. South Korean citizens are entitled to such assistance irrespective of age or ability to work. Roughly about one million people were on the rolls of the program in 2007.[19] Within a unification framework, however, this model raises issues of sustainability. Can the system adequately absorb millions of new people and for how long? The objective of NBLS is to get benefit recipients off its rolls as quickly as possible and back into the labor market where they can earn a living wage. This is problematic when applied to the situation that will confront former North Koreans who have neither meaningful job skills nor prospects for securing long-term employment.

One means of potentially defraying some of the cost associated with the program would be to make enrollment into NBLS contingent upon former North Koreans working public service jobs on the northern half of the peninsula, which might also assist in mitigating the potential impact of diaspora as it would provide a means for earning a living wage. Such an approach, however, will require investment of both time and capital to train the existing unskilled workforce, but might be undertaken in partnership with South Korean private enterprise. South Korean management teams working with North Korean labor has proven to be an efficacious model in the past.

The preceding issues are only representative of the varied ancillary problems connected with repatriation and assimilation of Koreans living on the northern half of the peninsula. But they will add a massive amount to the bottom line of unification. When considered in conjunction with issues of broader assimilation, schooling and employment, the cost could reach staggering proportions, measurable in the trillions of dollars. Thus, while the process and form of unification is a matter to be decided by the two Koreas, the cost of implementation will likely be borne by the international community of nations because of the sheer size of capital infusion anticipated to help ensure unification's success. It might be useful at this point then to consider peninsular unification from the perspective of countries in the East Asia region beginning, most appropriately, with the Koreas.

12

A Regional Perspective

There is an American proverb that says, "if it ain't broke, don't fix it." This status quo policy toward the Korean peninsula has dominated the post–Korean War strategic thinking of the four great powers surrounding the peninsula, the United States, Russia (the former Soviet Union), China, and Japan. . . . The essence of North Korea's policy can be summarized as the idea that "if it ain't broke, break it."

—*Youngho Kim*[1]

Presently, unification is considered the province of the two Koreas—the conditions under which peninsular amalgamation will occur, its ultimate form, and associated timeline. This, however, has not always been the case. Until the late 1990s, unification was still seen through a Cold War prism and thus considered to be subject to the influence, and perhaps even the approval, of the large regional powers: China, the United States, Russia, and perhaps to a slightly lesser degree, Japan. Fei-Ling Wang wrote in *Pacific Affairs* in summer 1999,

The economic empowerment of South Korea, somewhat tarnished by the financial and debt crisis of 1997-98, and the political transition in Pyongyang may have created some favourable conditions for the Koreans to strive for reunification. Yet, the major external powers, especially the United States and China, still have a crucial role to play, if not a straightforward veto power.[2]

Wang's was not the only voice that placed secondary importance on the desires of the Korean people with respect to self-determination. Another Chinese analyst, Guo Xue-Tang, wrote,

> The future new international political order in Northeast Asia depended on the relations among the four major powers: The U.S., Japan, China, and Russia. The interests of the four major powers will affect the issue of Korean reunification. Korean reunification will be decided by inter-Korean factors under the influence of the political attitudes of the four major powers.[3]

Such peninsula-focused geopolitical perspectives may have played themselves out during the Cold War but were in fact a continuation of policies originating during the late-nineteenth and early-twentieth centuries. Emblematic of this externally imposed determination was the Taft-Katsura agreement (1905) reached between the United States and Japan, discussed in chapter 3. Another example, at least from the Korean perspective, was the Cairo Declaration, the outcome of the Cairo Conference held on November 27, 1943, between President Franklin D. Roosevelt, Prime Minister Winston Churchill, and Generalissimo Chiang Kai-shek. The declaration asserted that, among other things, "Korea shall become free and independent." The course that events followed in the end, however, was quite different as the cessation of hostilities associated with the Second World War saw both the division of the peninsula and its occupation by the United States and former Soviet Union, yet another example of Korean self-determination subordinated to broader geopolitical issues.

To the extent that the anticipated staggering cost of unification will likely be a burden shared among South Korea and other nations, negotiations with regional powers regarding the type, level, and timing of support can be expected. What is unlikely to occur, however, is a return to the earlier mind-set that subordinates Korean self-determination to the interests of external powers.

While none will likely exercise the veto power predicted a decade earlier, their respective national interests will be important to the final calculus of unification, the common denominators among these nations being: 1) maintenance of regional stability, 2) mitigating the adverse impact of any peninsular unification scenario on their respective national interests, and 3) maximizing any advantage associated with anticipated changes in the regional balance of power resulting from a unified Korea. Further complicating these factors are the evolving dynamics that surround the geopolitical relationships between the countries in the region. Thus, understanding the perspectives of each is germane to the present discussion.

THE LOOK OF A UNIFIED KOREA

A post-unification Korea will, of course, possess slightly different characteristics than each half of the peninsula presently does. By all accounts the country will become a robust mid-sized world power. Its population will increase by roughly 50 percent to an estimated 71.1 million, making a unified Korea the eighteenth most populated country in the world. Its land mass will more than double, reaching 220,128 square kilometers, approximating the size of the United Kingdom. Its population of work-aged adults (fifteen to sixty-four years of age) will reach 50.1 million people, an increase of just under 50 percent, while adding an additional 5–6 million citizens up to age fourteen, or those representing the next generation of workers, who will total an estimated 13 million people. Finally, the South Korean economy, which has ranged between the tenth largest and fifteenth largest in the world over the past several years, could potentially grow in strength as a result of the inexpensive labor and natural resources located in the north of the peninsula, if a unified government is able to negotiate the many economic and social challenges that lie in unification's wake. Additionally, a report issued by Goldman Sachs estimates that North Korea's wealth in natural resources is 140 times its 2008 GDP and that it possesses abundant stores of South Korea's most important strategic minerals: bituminous, coal, uranium, iron, copper, steel, and nickel.[4] Thus, considering the potential combination of South Korea's economic strength and technology with North Korea's abundant natural resources, the report also speculates that a united Korea has the potential to overtake G7 countries such as Japan, Germany, and France in economic production.[5]

The additional manpower that could potentially enter the workforce, however, is a double-edged sword. If a post-unification government is able to devise ways to effectively absorb and gainfully employ their numbers, they could represent a significant economic advantage. As discussed earlier, however, the South Korean labor market possesses certain characteristics that will likely present challenges to absorbing large numbers of new potential workers. The ongoing and successful South-North joint project at the Kaesong Industrial Complex might represent a workable model in post-unification but would require substantial capital outlay, coordination, and cooperation between government and private enterprise. Despite the success of the Kaesong Industrial Complex, making the complex model immediately workable for 15 million additional Korean citizens may be an insurmountable task.

It is, however, the unquantifiable factors that a unified Korea will present that loom largely in the regional geopolitics of East Asia. How will its relationship with Japan, given the history between the two countries, evolve? Will it be characterized by revanchism or follow a course that develops a formalized tripartite alliance that includes the United States? Or, given expanding Sino–South Korean links will a unified government align itself more closely with Beijing than Washington? How the balance of power shifts in the wake of unification will impact the national interests of each of the major regional stakeholders.

THE KOREAS

The decades-long official emphasis the two Koreas have placed on unification has led to the obvious and logical conclusion that achieving integration of the peninsula continues to be a top inter-Korean priority. The signals that have been telegraphed over the past decade, however, may point to a slightly different emerging tale of the two Koreas. A North Korean economy long ravaged by mismanagement and natural disasters and a society and culture bereft of anything pre–Kim Il-sung has compelled the regime to move from a policy of belligerent unification to one of belligerent survival. Conversely, the South Korean government, now painfully cognizant of the likely costs of unification based on the reunion of Germany and learning from the saeteomin experience, may be undergoing an ebbing zeal for peninsular integration. Neither side, of course, has openly articulated a commitment to moving away from unification, but there appears to be growing recognition that immediate pursuit of unification has become a goal in the abstract.

South Korean officials may well have come to the realization that the trillions of dollars unification will require, in addition to the potential domestic, social, and regional geopolitical instability that may ensue, is a cost the government is unwilling to bear anytime in the near future. One example that may point to such an official mind-set is the ever-decreasing benefits being extended to North Korean migrants who successfully find their way into South Korea. The practice of providing fewer cash benefits has two immediate impacts. First, without the sizeable cash payouts of the past, saeteomin are less able to finance the trek from China into South Korea of other family members, thus helping to break the cycle of chain migrations described earlier. This policy could also be a means of transmitting to other migrants located in China that the proverbial welcome mat of the eighties and nineties has been pulled in.

If South Korean officials were in fact committed to hastening the demise of the North Korean regime, making South Korea appear more attractive to potential migrants would not be difficult to do. Even late former president Kim Dae-jung, however, recognized that any popular support for unification needed to be reined in so it might better comport with the realities of inter-Korean relations. He anticipated that unification might occur at least twenty to thirty years in the future.[6] Finally, another consideration is the Lee administration's move away from the Sunshine Policy and its successor policies to a more pragmatic approach in its relations with the regime, characterized by a demand for greater reciprocity on the part of North Korean leaders. There is enough history between the two Koreas to fully understand that such an approach would antagonize the northern regime and likely hold in abeyance any discussions of peninsular amalgamation. This is not to argue that the Lee administration should not have followed its more pragmatic approach; it is only an observation that having done so will likely set back any possibility of dialogue related to unification. A review of the trend in inter-Korean relations since Lee's inauguration, provided in chapter 6, underscores the chilling impact that his administration's northern policy has had on the tenor of engagement between Pyongyang and Seoul.

On the other hand, the North Korean regime may have come to realize that as a result of its policy transition to belligerent survival it no longer exercises the same threat or potential influence in inter-Korean relations that characterized the two governments' Cold War–period interaction and that unification will very likely include some sort of absorption of the North Korean state. Consequently, the regime has reportedly assumed a more pragmatic posture by quietly abandoning its original position that U.S. military forces be removed from the peninsula, a surprising turn of events given the decades of histrionics it has displayed. Bruce Cumings observes,

> U.S. troops thus continue being a general stabilizer for Northeast Asia, but both Korean leaders want them to stay because they are the guarantor of peaceful coexistence—that the South will not be attacked and the North will not be swallowed or "absorbed" by the South, a kind of "Hong Kong" solution to the border (or DMZ) problem in Korea. Several years ago North Koreans began telling Americans privately that U.S. troops should stay in the South to help

Koreans deal with a strong Japan and a rising China, but also to protect the DPRK against absorption by the South. In 1997 Selig Harrison interviewed a North Korean general who told him that whereas the North may call publicly for the withdrawal of American troops, in reality American troops should stay in Korea. During the June 2000 summit, Kim Jong Il said essentially the same thing directly to Kim Dae Jung.[7]

North Korean pragmatism may have additional implications for both future unification prospects and its own policy of belligerent survival. Despite the vituperative and recalcitrant posture the North Korean regime demonstrates toward the rest of the world, it oversees a society typifying the great failed socialist experiment and in the process has successfully cloistered itself from the global community of nations, with the one exception of China. It is unwilling or unable to introduce market reforms that would facilitate economic growth because such measures would place in peril its control over North Korean society. Rather, international food assistance sustains the Korean people. And, while unable to minister the needs of millions over whom it exercises dominion, it actively pursues policies most likely to ensure protection of the elite's prerogatives.

Consequently, maintenance of the status quo may be the only viable option available under North Korea's policy of survival, as unification could well portend the regime's demise. Preserving current circumstances affords the regime several advantages. It permits government officials to safeguard their independence of action, one of the major principles of Juche philosophy. It also permits the regime to retain access to international food aid, which historically has not been jeopardized for appreciable lengths of time even during displays of its now legendary brinksmanship behaviors.

Consider the example of the *Cheonan* cited in the previous chapter. One would not usually associate such behavior with an attempt to engage the global community, but for the regime it accomplishes several key objectives. First, it refocuses world attention on North Korea rather than such other geopolitical "distractions" as Afghanistan and Iraq. Second, it lays the foundations for opening dialogue with other nations, which in the end could help to facilitate greater inflows of food assistance. Securing external food assistance has again become a major objective in light of increasing food shortages. This is not dissimilar to how the regime approached reinvigorating discussions on its nuclear and ballistic missile programs in 2006 and 2009. Finally, and very importantly, while the *Cheonan* incident may provide the framework for a new round of discussions, it does so by resetting the clock. In effect, all discussions begin at "point zero"—that is, from the most recent act of intransigence, not from where they might have ended earlier, focused on the regime's nuclear program. This gives the regime the advantage of not giving up any ground or providing a negotiating advantage to its interlocutors.

Thus, there may be a growing realization between South and North Korea that the ties binding them are fewer than the issues that keep them divided and that some accommodative middle ground of the status quo may be a wiser course for the foreseeable future. As one considers the perspectives of other nations in the region, their respective national interests, and how they might be impacted by Korean unification, the operative term becomes "maintaining the status quo" for the Koreas and other nations of East Asia. The known devil may be better than the unknown one.

CHINA

China remains North Korea's most important ally, although the relationship is perhaps less robust, and the regime considered more troublesome, than it was during the Cold War. Then, under the terms of the 1961 Sino-North Korean Treaty on Friendship, Cooperation and Mutual Assistance, the relationship was often described as being as close as "lips and teeth." China, however, serves as one of North Korea's chief suppliers of food and energy (the other being South Korea), perhaps more for reasons of pragmatism than the shared ideological connections of the past.

From the Chinese perspective, a weak and unstable regime sows seeds for potential regional instability, and instability is seen as a threat to China's continued economic growth. Indeed, regime collapse in the Chinese calculus would be the worst of all outcomes. Consequently, providing assistance to North Korea in order to avoid its catastrophic implosion is a pragmatic consideration. Chinese officials are, however, frustrated by North Korea's unwillingness to undertake serious efforts at market reforms to integrate itself into the global economy in the fashion of China's own reforms, which began in the late 1970s. From the Chinese standpoint this failure lies at the heart of North Korean instability.

China's position regarding Korean unification is characterized by a similar ambivalence. Diplomatically, the Chinese government officially supports a peaceful and independent union of the Korean peninsula, but this too may be pragmatic and driven by the fact that to do otherwise could be geopolitically and economically costly. The immediate repercussions of openly opposing unification would be to alienate both South and North Korea, potentially damaging Beijing's national interests in maintaining stability for uninterrupted economic growth. Sino–South Korean relations have improved steadily since rapprochement was achieved between Seoul and Beijing in 1992. Bilateral trade statistics offer compelling proof of strengthening economic linkages between the two countries. According to figures released in 2009, China is presently South Korea's largest export and import partner.[8] By the end of 2008, South Korea had invested a total of nearly $42 billion in China, $29 billion of which targeted that country's manufacturing sector. Bilateral trade reached $186.1 billion, which represents an annual growth rate of 25 percent between the two countries since 1992.[9] Figures for 2009 are less impressive, the result of a worldwide economic slowdown and a larger global trend of reduced foreign direct investment (FDI). For example, South Korean direct investment into China was nearly halved (48.7 percent), but FDI into Asia dropped by 59.5 percent while North America experienced a 45.2 percent reduction during the same period.[10]

North Korea, on the other hand, represents the negative parallel to the Sino–South Korean relationship. An alienated and disenchanted regime could, through activities for which it has demonstrated a penchant over the past few years, such as undertaking ballistic missile and nuclear detonation tests or launching unprovoked attacks on South Korea, destabilize conditions in the region to the point that China's economic growth could be undermined. Consequently, in an effort to avoid the happenstance of regime collapse, China has remained economically engaged with its problematic ally. Bilateral trade between the two countries has continued to grow, achieving a record level of $2.79 billion in 2008, an increase of 41 percent year-on-year from 2007.[11] Figures for 2009 remained fairly steady at approximately $2.7 billion according to statistics provided by the Korea Trade-Investment Promotion Agency.[12] What has continued to increase, however, is the Sino–North Korean trade ratio, which was 42.8 percent in 2003; in 2009 it reached 78.5 percent.[13]

In the final analysis, however, despite claims of support for peninsular unification, Chinese officials prefer the status quo on the peninsula because, while not ideal, it has afforded the stability necessary to allow for China's unprecedented economic growth. An equally important consideration is that unification brings with it an uncertainty for what regional events and changes will emerge in the wake of peninsular amalgamation. Additionally, unlike the circumstances that existed on the peninsula during the Cold War, South Korea is no longer the ideological enemy—it now represents an important trading partner with which there are also expanding cultural ties. Finally, a union of the two Koreas presents major security concerns for Chinese officials, both domestic and external.

Unification will, of course, erase the present inter-Korean border and as a result eliminate the buffer zone that North Korea currently represents between China and South Korea. This, in itself, is not necessarily a point of concern given the growing ties between the two countries. In addition to increased economic activity, there has been a commensurate growth in cultural links as well. Researcher Michael Yoo writes,

> This boom [the "China Boom" in South Korea] parallels the "Korea boom" that has hit China, as Korean music, dance, fashion and movies have become increasingly popular recently. It is important to pay attention to the increase in human exchange between the two countries, as well as the number of people studying Chinese.[14]

Additionally, in a Gallup poll conducted in 2006 in which South Korean citizens were asked how inclined they were to the leadership of the countries surrounding them, China received the highest percentage of positive public opinion with 36 percent of South Koreans viewing the country favorably; Russia was second with 26 percent, while the United States garnered 23 percent of the vote. Thus, it appears that cultural affinity accompanies the growing number and size of economic linkages between the two countries.

The potential problem that unification presents, however, is a unified Korea that maintains its current security relationship with the United States. Under this scenario, North Korea would no longer function as a buffer and U.S. military forces would be in much closer proximity to China's border, the specter of which is not a comforting one to Chinese officials. Recall the April 1, 2001, incident in which a mid-air collision occurred between a U.S. Navy surveillance aircraft and a People's Liberation Army Navy interceptor fighter jet, forcing the U.S. aircraft to make an emergency landing on Hainan Island, China. Crewmembers were detained for ten days until the United States issued a formal letter of apology. The basic cause of the incident was that a U.S. surveillance aircraft flew close to what Chinese officials regard as part of China's exclusive economic zone in the South China Sea; the Chinese military responded to what it regarded as an intrusion on its sovereign territory. Thus, from the perspective of Chinese officials, a permanent U.S. military presence on a unified Korean peninsula that could potentially locate troops as close to its border as the Yalu River would likely be considered problematic, both from a security perspective and symbolically.

As discussed earlier, unification also brings with it the potential of diasporic movement of large numbers of North Koreans into northeast China. There are, however, potentially broader issues with which Chinese officials grapple that could well be exacerbated by a large-scale influx of North Koreans. Chinese officials have in the past confronted significant ethnic unrest and violence among citizens in the country's western region of Xinjiang, involving Han Chinese and ethnic minority Muslim Uighurs. The unrest stemmed from the killing of Uighur migrant workers in Guangdong, located in southern China, the genesis of which was itself ethnic conflict.[15] Thus, despite China's vast size, ethnic unrest occurring in one part of the country has the potential of igniting unrest in other parts. The threat of millions of North Koreans streaming across the Chinese border, particularly if it has economic repercussions for average Chinese citizens, might provide the spark for more widespread ethnic unrest within China.

Fei-Ling Wang points to another potential impact of Korean unification: the rise of Korean nationalism. He describes it in the following manner:

A rise of new Korean nationalism after a Korean reunification is fully anticipated. A united and much more powerful Korea, under the influence of a new Korean nationalism, may produce very undesirable consequences to the Chinese, since there are already standing disputes between the two nations. The unfavorable consequences would be of even greater concern should a unified Korea continue its military alliance with the United States.[16]

While Wang raises some salient points in the above passage, I disagree with the basic premise of the argument. Wang presumes that a rise in Korean nationalism carries with it a negative connotation, which is not necessarily the case. First, I would argue that a rise in Korean nationalism notwithstanding, economic pragmatism for both China and a unified Korea will remain of paramount importance. China is not prepared to abandon its national commitment to continued economic growth, and Korea, given the anticipated staggering costs of unification, will not be in a position to alienate one of its major trading partners. Second, if a rise in nationalism is also accompanied by an increased cognizance of the need to achieve some measure of economic, political, and cultural parity between the former halves of the peninsula, then nationalism could have a positive post-unification effect. Additionally, if nationalism helps to eradicate the social stigma associated with former North Koreans' connection to a failed and empty ideology and the regime that propounded its tenants, then again this would represent a positive outcome. I suggest, however, that any nationalism arising in the immediate aftermath of unification will be short-lived, much as it was with German unification. After the immediate euphoria subsides, the Korean people will confront the harsh reality that they are two very different peoples and what presently divides them will far outweigh distant memories of what once may have united them.

The subtext of Wang's observations also ignores the strength of the long-standing cultural ties between China and Korea. This, coupled with the ever-strengthening linkages resulting from more robust economic connections, cultural exchanges, and other activities, has made Sino-Korean cooperation more vibrant, which will continue for the foreseeable future.

There is one area in which Wang's argument on nationalism, however, could hold some truth: the desire of a unified Korea to reclaim territory it considers rightfully to belong to the Korean people. One such example is Mount Baekdu (Changbai Mountain in Chinese) located on the border between North Korea and China. Historically, both the Koreans and Chinese have claimed ownership, but, through a border agreement reached between North Korea and China in 1962, ownership of the mountain is now shared with 60 percent of the area under North Korean control. It is possible that a unified Korea might not feel bound by the 1962 treaty, potentially reigniting sovereignty issues over the area.

Other potential issues also argue for the known quantity of the status quo in lieu of the unknown associated with unification. For example, Korean unification might lead to calls within the international community of nations for a final settlement of the Taiwan independence question. Despite the decades-long effort of Chinese officials to control the narrative on the issue of Taiwanese independence by casting Taiwan as a renegade province, there is no way of predicting what the future mood will be if and when Korean unification occurs and how it might potentially impact the Taiwan issue. It is this uncertainty that makes maintaining the Korean status quo a more favored course for the Chinese government.

JAPAN

Japan's perspective on Korean unification might also be described as recognizing the desirability of maintaining the status quo on the peninsula, but for reasons different from those that motivate Chinese officials. Unification of the peninsula, particularly if sudden and unexpected, could bring about a major shift in the regional balance of power. If not managed carefully, this shift has the potential of working against Japan's national interests. Armacost and Pyle note that

> given the difficulty of peacefully achieving the kind of united Korea that they favor, most Japanese policymakers have quietly concluded that their wisest course is not to hasten unification, but rather to pursue a course that maintains the status quo of a divided Korea for as long as possible, all the while supporting American policies of deterrence, hoping to contain tensions and foster cordial ties with South Korea, and favoring policies that promote a gradual reconciliation rather than a rapid and potentially violent reunification, which might produce new problems for Japan.[17]

Victor Cha coined the term "defensive realism" to explain Japan's motives and underlying philosophy on unification:

> Defensive realists also care dearly about the pursuit of power for survival and see the world in competitive, self-help terms. But for defensive realism, survival is best attained by pursuing just enough power to maintain a "balance" where no one other power or coalition of powers can threaten the system and one's national security. That is, states pursue power for defensive reasons, and therefore seek to maintain a balance of power rather than seek to maximize power as the optimum strategy.[18]

Thus, at the heart of Japan's posture of defensive realism are several key points. First, in a manner similar to Chinese officials, Japanese government officials publicly support unification of the peninsula. To do otherwise would likely not only reflect poorly on Japan within the global community of nations, but would undercut its second key goal: to develop stronger ties with a pre-unified Korea. Fostering stronger links with South Korea helps to create a countervailing balance to China's growing regional strength and minimizes the chance of alienating South Korea, which could prompt a unified Korea to ally itself more closely with China. A Sino-Korean alliance could potentially overshadow Japan or bifurcate the region by creating a sphere of influence that competes regionally with the U.S.-Japan alliance. Finally, it also helps to mitigate the latent feelings of ill will Koreans still harbor as a result of the two countries' past history, specifically the colonial period and festering territorial disputes over Takeshima/ Dokdo, islets located in the Sea of Japan, or what Koreans refer to as the East Sea.

Japanese officials perceive two imperatives with regard to unification that must be addressed, preferably to be resolved long prior to unification, but certainly not long after it is achieved. The first is the issue of the abduction of Japanese citizens by North Korean agents between the years 1977 and 1983. This has been a long-festering issue for the government of Japan, and it has pressed to have the topic officially addressed during the Six Party Talks as well as other venues. The second imperative is North Korea's denuclearization. The August 31, 1998, missile launch undertaken by the North Korean regime ignited genuine concern that in the event of hostilities on the peninsula, Japan's cities were now in harm's way and that given the palpable enmity the North Korean regime has for Japan, there exists an even greater risk of Japan's sovereign territory coming under attack.

In assessing policies and potential outcomes with Korea in a post-unification scenario, Japanese government officials consider the United States to be the common denominator between itself and a unified Korea. A continued presence of U.S. military on the Korean peninsula after unification is achieved, given its continued presence on the Japanese islands, provides a measure of assurance that Korea will remain "in the fold" of the U.S. security umbrella, thus increasing the likelihood of achieving and maintaining concordant security relations with Korea.

These types of regional dynamics are further buffeted by the vagaries of day-to-day positioning and jockeying among the three regional powers, which will likely complicate any effort at reaching a coordinated regional security paradigm in the wake of unification. Consider one assessment of a trilateral meeting convened in October 2009 in Beijing among the leaders of Japan, China, and Korea:

> Chinese, South Korean and Japanese leaders held a trilateral meeting in Beijing Oct. 10 to discuss potential areas for cooperation between the three East Asian giants. While the three did achieve something

concrete on one issue — economics — the refusal to cede any ground on what each perceives as a core national interest and a general distrust of the other parties prevented any other tangible accomplishments.[19]

Thus, from the Japanese perspective, the status quo remains the best option, a position advanced by the Office of the Prime Minister. Former Prime Minister Koizumi Junichiro noted during a meeting of the House of Councilors in March 2006 that early unification of the Korean peninsula would not be in Japan's best interests. As Japan surveys the post-unification landscape of East Asia, a stable Korean peninsula coupled with a continued regional U.S. military presence works most effectively in support of its national interests.

RUSSIA

The trajectory of Russia's relationships with the Koreas is not necessarily represented by a smooth line. For example, prior to 1990, the year in which Seoul and Moscow achieved rapprochement, the Russian and South Korean relationship was characterized by the usual paradigmatic dynamics of Cold War opponents on opposite sides of an ideological divide. Seoul's extension of economic carrots from about 1989, however, helped to thaw the freeze between the two countries and the relationship has strengthened over the ensuing years.

Conversely, after Soviet–South Korean rapprochement was achieved, the relationship between Moscow and Pyongyang withered primarily because ideological kinship had given way to economic pragmatism. Moscow was no longer interested in providing handouts to the North Korean regime; former Soviet leaders wanted payment for services rendered and goods supplied. Failure of the command economy structure demanded a change in how business was done. A decade later, with Vladimir Putin's elevation to the Russian Federation's presidency, the relationship took a decided turn for the better with the signing of the Russia–North Korea Treaty of Friendship and Cooperation (February 2000), which was followed by Putin's official visit to North Korea a year later.

Since then the official Russian position with regard to the peninsula has been to maintain a policy that recognizes and engages both Koreas, while supporting the unification process and any attendant dialogue. Closer inspection, however, reveals that Russia does not interact with the two Koreas in similar fashion. Relations with North Korea, for example, are maintained at a level consistent with parameters outlined within the now-moribund Six Party Talks, the genesis of what might be considered a more regionally driven geopolitical approach and paralleling imposition of sanctions against North Korea by the international community of nations. Thus, in 2008, Russia delivered approximately 200,000 tons of fuel oil and 2,860 tons of flour to North Korea.[20] In contrast, in 2006 Russia represented the regime's third largest trading partner, bettered only by China and South Korea. Import trade with Russia amounted to 9 percent of a total expenditure of $3.18 billion spent by the regime on imports.[21] On the other hand, trade and other bilateral cooperation between South Korea and Russia flourishes in a comparative sense. For the year 2008, bilateral trade increased by an impressive 22.4 percent, reaching $18.4 billion. South Korean direct investment in Russia has also achieved substantive levels. Through the first quarter of 2009, South Korean investment in the Russian economy totaled nearly $1.3 trillion, $731 billion of which was in direct investments.[22] While Russia may accord a similar level of diplomatic recognition to the Koreas, officials are pragmatic in their recognition of the difference in regional status between the halves of the Korean peninsula.

Russia's peninsular policies are motivated by two precepts: maneuvering to gain economic advantage in the region and developing security alliances that check the growth of any single regional player, specifically the United States. Consider the expanding joint military exercises between Russia and China through the "Peace Mission" framework. (Russia is also interested in having India participate in Peace Mission activities.) Exercises are conducted bi-annually (2005, 2007, 2009, and 2011) and involve thousands of troops in combined arms operations. Given the large numbers of ground troops, air force and army aircraft, and seaborne operations they incorporate, there may be an unspoken intent to send a quiet message of deterrence to the United States and its regional allies. Chinese and Russian security analysts, however, proffer a very different assessment, applying a broad definition of "anti-terrorism." For example, Professor Ouyang Wei of the People's Liberation Army's National Defense University points out that

> terrorism activities vary in different countries and regions. It may be a large incident, such as that in Chechnya, or it could be individual operations such as roadside and suicide bombings.[23]

Military operations in Chechnya, however, have usually been described in terms of "war" by Western observers, rather than anti-terrorism, if for no other reason than the large number of casualties that resulted. In the first Chechnya war, at least 41,500 civilians and military lost their lives.[24]

The economic advantage that Russia pursues focuses on the huge natural gas reserves and electrical power it can provide to the region. Over the past decade Russian officials have proposed ideas for developing a pipeline into the Northeast Asia region. One such plan called for running a pipeline from Irkutsk through China into the port of Dalian and under the Yellow Sea (West Sea) to South Korea. Under this plan, North Korea would have been bypassed out of an abundance of caution. While Russian officials support inter-Korean dialogue, they also remain quite cognizant of the regime's truculent and troublesome nature.[25] Russia has also proposed providing electrical power to the Korean peninsula. The Russian government–controlled RAO Unified Energy System is considering a number of conceptual approaches to address peninsular electricity demands. One proposal would supply electricity from the Bureyskaya Hydropower Plant through North Korea and into South Korea. The high-voltage electrical power lines required to transmit the electricity would be fixed high enough above ground level to minimize the possibility of any tampering by the North Korean regime.[26]

In principle, Russian officials hold both South and North Korea in similar regard. Cultivating and maintaining bilateral relations with both is considered essential for regional stability and, in turn, maintaining the regional status quo, into which North Korean miscreant behavior figures largely. Realistically, South Korea's dominance diplomatically, economically, and in other areas underscores its vital role in the ultimate peninsular unification solution. In the end, Russia, much like other nations in the region, officially supports inter-Korean unification dialogue while hedging its bets on the status quo.

UNITED STATES

The United States staked its claim as a regional power in East Asia as far back as July 1844 when its representative, Caleb Cushing, concluded the Treaty of Wangxia with China as a means of parrying Great Britain's growing presence in that country. Through its various security alliances with Japan and South Korea, its special security relationship with Taiwan as defined by the Taiwan Relations Act (1979), and strong economic ties to the region, the United States has retained its status as a regional power. Indeed its presence in East Asia helps to stabilize the region's balance of power.

The U.S. priority on the Korean peninsula is not unification of the two Koreas, but rather remains the denuclearization of the North Korean regime primarily for three reasons. First is the regional threat a nuclear-armed regime presents to Asia given the regime's history of unpredictability, truculence, and predilection for geopolitical extortion. Second is its propensity for proliferating the sale and exchange of weapons of mass destruction (WMDs) technology on a global scale. North Korea's WMD trade relationship with Pakistan, illustrated by the regime's sale of its No Dong missile technology during the mid-1990s and on which the Pakistani Ghauri missile is modeled, underscores the danger of the regime's proliferative activities. Finally, there exists a concern within the Obama administration that failure to check the growth of a nuclear North Korean regime could serve as a precursor to a nuclear arms race in East Asia as Japan might conclude that its own national security interests would be best served by developing a retaliatory nuclear capability against the regime.

While not imminent, such a turn of events could lead to catastrophic second- and third-order effects in the region as nations begin to reassess their own national security interests.[27] The issue of denuclearizing the regime remains central to the entirety of East Asia, including China. Because Chinese officials link their country's continued economic growth to maintaining regional stability, the Chinese government walks a tightrope of not supporting a nuclearized North Korea while also trying to ensure the North Korean regime doesn't collapse under the weight of its outdated and inefficient economic model.

U.S. efforts to denuclearize the North Korean regime have been long-term, dating back to the Clinton administration and the conclusion of the 1994 Agreed Framework, but have been characterized by some amount of inconsistency. For example, while the Agreed Framework was concluded in October 1994, control of the U.S. Congress was regained by the Republican Party, some members of which were staunchly opposed to the framework. Consequently, funding was not always provided for the initiative in a timely fashion. The circumstances surrounding the agreement were such that Korean Peninsula Energy Development Organization (KEDO) first director Stephen Bosworth observed, "The Agreed Framework was a political orphan within two weeks after its signature."[28] The Six Party Talks (United States, China, Japan, Russia, South Korea, and North Korea), a Bush administration initiative that first commenced in August 2003, is a regional multilateral venue through which the nations of the region negotiate with the North Korean regime to abandon its nuclear weapons program, often offering some combination of economic carrots and threat of sanctions to facilitate negotiations. Although presently inactive, the talks offer what many might consider to be one of the best hopes of continued engagement with the regime within the present paradigm of negotiations.

U.S. policy regarding unification of the peninsula places that issue as a secondary or even tertiary priority. While official U.S. policy recognizes peninsular unification as the prerogative of the Koreas, regime denuclearization and maintaining a regional balance of power favoring U.S. interests are key to the U.S. regional strategy. Within the framework of unification, however, a unitary Korea that maintains the current U.S.–South Korean security alliance, or at least remains under the U.S. security umbrella as opposed to aligning itself with China, is recognized as essential for long-term U.S. policy interests in East Asia.

13

Conclusion:
Paradise Postponed?

[There is] much hope on a desired gradual and reconciliatory unification of Korea. It disregards, however, that the base of unification lies in unity at the interconnected levels of the nation and of the state system, which would therefore require a systemic conversion in North Korea. This, however, cannot be achieved through evolutionary changes. . . . Because the contrasting state systems of the Koreas are not reconcilable, they should decide for rapprochement through normalised interstate relations until a chance for a democratic get-together dawns.

—*Hans Maretzki* [1]

What then do the preceding findings portend for unification of the two Koreas? Despite the periodic high-level official proclamations articulated by leaders on both sides of the DMZ in support of peninsular amalgamation, present inter-Korean circumstances seem to point to the fact that the unification process will likely be undertaken later rather than sooner. For example, North Korean officials appear to be undertaking a program of economic policy retrenchment designed to put a full-nelson hold on any nascent market activity within the country. This does not bode well for a South Korean government committed to free market principles. Pursuit of broader economic cooperation that might lead to greater levels of integration in the future across a spectrum of activities, however, has been the cornerstone of South Korean unification policy pursuits for years.

In late 2008, the regime issued Cabinet Decision No. 61 that limited the operation of markets nationwide to only three days a week, similar to circumstances found during the Choson period.[2] Petrov observes that

> busy markets are a nightmare for Pyongyang retrogrades. The North Korean government is now confiscating Japanese-made cars and minibuses from small businesses, prohibits the sale of many consumer goods (including mobile phones, radios and DVDs) and is reintroducing the public distribution system that dominated the country's economic life for four decades.[3]

And for all the promise of expanded inter-Korean cooperation the Kaesong Industrial Complex has come to symbolize, there are indications that this project too might be falling prey to broader economic retrenchment. The number of daily border crossings has been reduced and South Korean staff working in the complex has been cut by approximately 80 percent. Inter-Korean trade also reflects a new trajectory, as 2008 figures indicate a 23.2 percent decrease to $160 million, the first-ever double-digit drop.[4]

South Korean public opinion appears to have evolved in a similar direction since the early 1990s. A *Choson Ilbo* survey of university students undertaken in 2005 found that while the majority felt favorably disposed to unification with North Korea, their support came with a caveat: they were not prepared to make sacrifices to achieve integration of the peninsula. Another 2005 survey, conducted by the *Joong Ang Daily* and the East Asia Institute on the sixtieth anniversary of Korean liberation from Japanese colonial rule, found that 78 percent of South Korean respondents no longer regarded Korea as one nation divided by an arbitrarily imposed border, but rather as two separate countries.[5] In a 2006 Gallup World Poll survey, the majority of respondents (56 percent) felt that South Korea stands to lose more than it gains through unification.[6] A 2007 survey rendered similar results. Nearly 80 percent of respondents held that unification should either be pursued gradually in order to avoid domestic economic destabilization or, absent the guarantee of a stable transition, should not be pursued at all; conversely, a mere 20 percent considered unification to be an "urgent" issue.[7] Finally, a 2008 *Korea Times-Hankook Ilbo* poll of 1,000 South Korean citizens found that 73.8 percent felt (re)unification should be a goal pursued gradually; only 13.7 percent felt the government should pursue the process with more haste.[8]

These findings belie the often strident exhortations of the past calling for immediate unification, captured by Syngman Rhee's call for South Koreans to march north and unify the peninsula. The single factor that has spanned the decades and helped to infuse more pragmatism into unification dialogue and replace the enthusiasm and commitment that characterized past support for peninsular integration, on both sides of the DMZ, is time itself. With the passing of three generations since division of the peninsula in the aftermath of World War II, the immediacy of the task appears more distant to younger Koreans. Links to the past have become more obscure and any familial ties that once bridged the halves of the peninsula are quickly fading into a distant memory with each passing decade. Consequently, rather than seeing unification through a prism of peninsular nationalism characteristic of the mid-twentieth century, there appears to be a growing sense that the value of unification must be weighed objectively. Thus, increasing numbers of South and North Koreans look for measurable value-added: North Koreans are in search of better lives for themselves and family members while South Koreans may be looking for benefits that will accrue to the larger society as a whole. The more tempered outlook on peninsular integration may be a manifestation of the old adage that "having" may not be so pleasing a thing as "wanting."

Various models exist for how best to integrate the peninsula, none of which is perfect. The two models proffered by South and North Korea, the confederal and federal models, respectively, do not immediately present themselves as viable for bringing the halves of the peninsula together. They are at their foundations self-serving and designed to mitigate the perceived advantages of the other, consequently offering little likelihood that either will be universally accepted as a path to achieve a single Korean polity. Given present-day inter-Korean dynamics and the relative strength of each nation, most assessments envisage North Korea's absorption by South Korea. The major shortcoming with the absorption model, irrespective of its appeal, is that it describes a likely end state; it is not a roadmap for achieving unification, thus limiting its viability as well. In the end, there presently exists no constructive means for advancing the amalgamation of the Koreas.

Factors challenging unification at the governmental level are both numerous and varied, although fewer perhaps for the North Korean regime than for South Korean government officials. Regime officials will continue to be driven by what has been their single and prime motivation since the 1990s—regime survival, which within the unification context means avoiding its own absorption through liberal application of vituperative tactics, unpredictability, and geo-political extortion, the primary tool for which is its WMD capability. For South Korean officials, the problems are more complex and multi-dimensional. They need to simultaneously consider issues of repatriation and integration to ensure a successful transition to a unified Korea.

In addition to the changing attitudes of South Korean citizens regarding the concept of unification, they must also consider: 1) the historical context of the re-lationship between Koreans living in the northern and southern halves of the peninsula in order to avoid creation of a two-class society; 2) the anticipated cost of unification, which will easily be measureable in the trillions of dollars; 3) the experience of saeteomin in South Korean society and the difficulties this has illustrated in acculturating and assimilating North Koreans into South Korean society; 4) how to ameliorate the incongruence of the cultural, social, educa-tional, and employment contexts of North Koreans within South Korean society; and 5) a host of social welfare issues.

These repatriation efforts must, however, be treated as a distinct set of chal-lenges alongside issues of integrating political and economic systems, disman-tling the North Korean military infrastructure, mothballing the regime's WMD capability and consideration of other tasks that will facilitate unification. Ad-ditionally, the regional geopolitical dynamics in East Asia will have an impact, perhaps not directly on the issue of unification itself but on the regional balance of power that emerges in the wake of unification. When all these factors are considered in the aggregate, the salient question with regard to Korean unifica-tion is whether it has become "too hard" to achieve? Will, in fact, the heretofore perceived paradise of a unified Korea be postponed indefinitely?

Issues of repatriation focus on the transition of people and the various im-pediments attendant to the process. Consequently, the underlying challenge of repatriation is to recognize that the citizens of North and South Korea have undergone quite drastically different socialization processes over the past three generations and consequently have developed into two very different peoples. The Juche citizen simply does not fit into the capitalist construct of South Ko-rea. Thus, officials of a unified Korea will need to re-educate and reshape nearly 23 million North Koreans into "Korean" citizens who accept capitalism and democratic governance as the new basis of their lives. The current experiences of saeteomin underscore the breadth of the gulf between South Koreans and North Koreans that must be bridged. Because Juche socialization has failed to provide North Koreans with adequate education, usable job skills, or a meaningful cultural context for functioning in modern society, there is yet one more insidious challenge officials of a unified Korea will need to address: an emerging sense of differentiation and superiority over North Koreans among some South Koreans. Any unified government will need to address these basic deficiencies to help assure and ensure successful assimilation and integration—repatriation—of former North Koreans citizens.

This discussion leaves unaddressed the question of unification's timing. "When" unification will occur remains an imponderable. Developing timelines that predict when unification will occur amounts to an exercise in speculation, little more than a modern-day geopolitical parlor game. There are too many variables and unknowns to make an accurate assessment as to the precise course any unification effort will ultimately follow or how long it will take. Yet for some, the efforts to time peninsular integration continue. For example, the investment firm Goldman Sachs released a report in 2009 that proffers one such prediction, speculating that unification will advance in three stages: transition (2012–2027), integration (2028–2037), and maturity (2038–2050).[9] This prediction is sufficiently broad to provide a "safe cushion" of plausible deniability, yet carries with it an air of precision, given the timeframes for its three-stage progression, to pass for substantive analysis. What the report is really forecasting, however, is unification sometime within the next forty years—hardly virgin ground.

In the end, the question of whether to pursue peninsular unification remains the singular province of the two Koreas, although emergent geopolitical issues that could result from unification will involve other regional players. But South Korea will, by most accounts, shoulder the preponderant burden of a unified nation. The issue then, given the multitude of challenges, tempered public support and astronomical costs attendant to unification, is whether a unified Korea is a goal to be pursued in the near term, or if it is wiser to kick the proverbial can down the road, in essence postponing paradise.

Appendix A
Treaty of Chemulpo

Treaty of Peace, Amity, Commerce and Navigation Between Korea (Chosen) and the United States of America

Concluded May 22, 1882; Ratification advised by the Senate January 9, 1883; ratified by the President February 13, 1883; ratifications exchanged May 19, 1883; proclaimed June 4, 1883.

The United States of America and the Kingdom of Chosen, being sincerely, desirous of establishing permanent relations of amity and friendship between their respective peoples, have to this end appointed—that is to say, the President of the United States—R.W. Shufeldt, Commodore, U.S. Navy and his Commissioner Plenipotentiary, and His Majesty, the King of Chosen, Shin-Chen, President of the Royal Cabinet, Chin-Hong-Chi, Member of the Royal Cabinet, as his Commissioners Plenipotentiary, who, having reciprocally examined their respective full Powers, which have been found to be in due form, have agreed upon the several following articles:

ARTICLE I.

There shall be perpetual peace and friendship between the President of the United States and the King of Chosen and the citizens and subjects of their respective Governments. If other Powers deal unjustly or oppressively with either Government, the other will exert their good offices, on being informed of the case, to bring about an amicable arrangement, thus showing their friendly feelings.

ARTICLE II.

After the conclusion of this Treaty of amity and commerce, the High Contracting Powers may each appoint Diplomatic Representatives to reside at the Court of the other, and may each appoint Consular Representatives at the ports of the other, which are open to foreign commerce, at their own convenience.

These officials shall have relations with the corresponding local authorities of equal rank upon a basis of mutual equality.

The Diplomatic and Consular Representatives of the two Governments shall receive mutually all the privileges, rights and immunities without discrimination, which are accorded to the same class of Representatives from the most favored nation.

Consuls shall exercise their functions only on receipt of an exequatur from the Government, to which they are accredited. Consular authorities shall be bona fide officials. No merchants shall be permitted to exercise the duties of the office, nor shall Consular officers be allowed to engage in trade. At ports, to which no Consular Representatives have been appointed, the Consuls of other Powers may be invited to act, provided, that no merchant shall be allowed to assume Consular functions, or the provisions of this Treaty may, in such case, be enforced by the local authorities.

If Consular Representatives of the United States in Chosen conduct their business in an improper manner, their exequaturs may be revoked, subject to the approval previously obtained, of the Diplomatic Representative of the United States.

ARTICLE III.

Whenever United States vessels, either because of stress of weather, or by want of fuel or provisions cannot reach the nearest open port of Chosen, they may enter any port or harbor, either to take refuge therein, or to get supplies of wood, coal and other necessaries, or to make repairs, the expenses incurred thereby being defrayed by the ship's master. In such event the officers and people of the locality shall display their sympathy by rendering full assistance, and their liberality by furnishing the necessities required.

If a United States vessel carries on a clandestine trade at a port not open to foreign commerce, such vessel with her cargo shall be seized and confiscated.

If a United States vessel be wrecked on the coast of Chosen, the local authorities, on being informed of the occurrence, shall immediately render assistance to the crew, provided for their present necessities, and take the measures necessary for the salvage of the ship and the preservation of her cargo. They shall also bring the matter to the knowledge of the nearest Consular Representative of the United States, in order that steps may be taken to send the crew home and to save the ship and cargo. The necessary expenses shall be defrayed either by the ship's master or by the United States.

ARTICLE IV.
All citizens of the United States of America in Chosen, peaceably attending to their own affairs, shall receive and enjoy for themselves and everything appertaining to them the protection of the local authorities of the Government of Chosen, who shall defend them from all insult and injury of any sort. If their dwellings or property be threatened or attacked by mobs, incendiaries, or other violent or lawless persons, the local officers on requisition of the Consul, shall immediately dispatch a military force to disperse the rioters, apprehend the guilty individuals, and punish them with the utmost rigor of the law.

Subjects of Chosen, guilty of any criminal act towards citizens of the United States, shall be punished by the authorities of Chosen according to the laws of Chosen; and citizens of the United States, either on shore or in any merchant-vessel, who may insult, trouble or wound the persons or injure the property of the people of Chosen, shall be arrested and punished only by the Consul or other public functionary of the United States thereto authorized, according to the laws of the United States.

When controversies arise in the Kingdom of Chosen between citizens of the United States and the subjects of His Majesty, which need to be examined and decided by the public officers of the two nations, it is agreed between the two Governments of the United States and Chosen, that such cases shall be tried by the proper official of the nationality of the defendant, according to the laws of that nation. The properly authorized official of the plaintiff's nationality shall be freely permitted to attend the trial, and shall be treated with courtesy due to his position. He shall be granted all proper facilities for watching the proceedings in the interest of justice. If he so desires, he shall have the right to present, to examine and cross examine witnesses. If he is dissatisfied with the proceedings, he shall be permitted to protest against them in detail.

It is however mutually agreed and understood between the High Contracting Powers, that whenever the King of Chosen shall have so far modified and reformed the statutes and judicial procedures of his Kingdom that, in the judgment of the United States, they conform to the laws and course of justice in the United States, the right of exterritorial jurisdiction over United States citizens in Chosen shall be abandoned, and thereafter United States citizens, when within the limits of the Kingdom of Chosen, shall be subject to the jurisdiction of the native authorities.

ARTICLE V.

Merchants and merchant-vessels of Chosen visiting the United States for purposes of traffic, shall pay duties and tonnage-dues and all fees according to the Customs-Regulations of the United States, but no higher or other rates of duties and tonnage-dues shall be exacted of them, than are levied upon citizens of the United States or upon citizens or subjects of the most favored nation.

Merchants and merchant-vessels of the United States visiting Chosen for purposes of traffic, shall pay duties upon all merchandise imported and exported. The authority to levy duties is of right vested in the Government of Chosen. The tariff of duties upon exports and imports, together with the Customs-Regulations for the prevention of smuggling and other irregularities, will be fixed by the authorities of Chosen and communicated to the proper officials of the United States, to be by the latter notified to their citizens and duly observed.

It is however agreed in the first instance as a general measure, that the tariff upon such imports as are articles of daily use shall not exceed an ad valorem duty of ten per centum; that the tariff upon such imports as are luxuries, as for instance foreign wines, foreign tobacco, clocks and watches, shall not exceed an ad valorem-duty of thirty per centum, and that native produce exported shall pay a duty not to exceed five percentum ad valorem. And it is further agreed that the duty upon foreign imports shall be paid once for all at the port of entry, and that no other dues, duties, fees, taxes or charges of any sort shall be levied upon such imports either in the interior of Chosen or at the ports.

United States merchant-vessels entering the ports of Chosen shall pay tonnage-dues at the rate of five mace per ton, payable once in three months on each vessel, according to the Chinese calendar.

ARTICLE VI.

Subjects of Chosen who may visit the United States shall be permitted to reside and to rent premises, purchase land, or to construct residences or warehouses in all parts of the country.

They shall be freely permitted to pursue their various callings and avocations, and to traffic in all merchandise, raw and manufactured, that is not declared contraband by law. Citizens of the United States who may resort to the ports of Chosen which are open to foreign commerce, shall be permitted to reside at such open ports within the limits of the concessions and to lease buildings or land, or to construct residences or warehouses therein. They shall be freely permitted to pursue their various callings and avocations within the limits of the port, and to traffic in all merchandise, raw and manufactured, that is not declared contraband by law.

No coercion or intimidation in the acquisition of land or buildings shall be permitted, and the land-rent as fixed by the authorities of Chosen shall be paid. And it is expressly agreed that land so acquired in the open ports of Chosen still remains an integral part of the Kingdom, and that all rights of jurisdiction over persons and property within such areas remain vested in the authorities of Chosen, except in so far as such rights have been expressly relinquished by this Treaty.

American citizens are not permitted either to transport foreign imports to the interior for sale, or to proceed thither to purchase native produce. Nor are they permitted to transport native produce from one open port to another open port.

Violations of this rule will subject such merchandise to confiscation, and the merchant offending will be handed over to the Consular Authorities to be dealt with.

ARTICLE VII.
The Governments of the United States and of Chosen mutually agree and undertake that subjects of Chosen shall not be permitted to import opium into any of the ports of the United States, and citizens of the United States shall not be permitted to import opium into any of the open ports of Chosen, to transport it from one open port to another open port, or to traffic in it in Chosen. This absolute prohibition which extends to vessels owned by the citizens or subjects of either Power, to foreign vessels employed by them, and to vessels owned by the citizens or subjects of either Power and employed by other persons for the transportation of opium, shall be enforced by appropriate legislation on the part of the United States and of Chosen, and offenders against it shall be severely punished.

ARTICLE VIII.
Whenever the Government of Chosen shall have reason to apprehend a scarcity of food within the limits of the Kingdom, His Majesty may by Decree temporarily prohibit the export of all breadstuffs, and such Decree shall be binding on

all citizens of the United States in Chosen upon due notice having been given them by the Authorities of Chosen through the proper officers of the United States; but it is to be understood that the exportation of rice and breadstuffs of every description is prohibited from the open port of Yin-Chuen.

Chosen having of old prohibited the exportation of red gingseng, if citizens of the United States clandestinely purchase it for export, it shall be confiscated and the offenders punished.

ARTICLE IX.

The purchase of cannon, small arms, swords, gunpowder, shot and all munitions of war is permitted only to officials of the Government of Chosen, and they may be imported by citizens of the United States only under a written permit from the authorities of Chosen. If these articles are clandestinely imported, they shall be confiscated and the offending party shall be punished.

ARTICLE X.

The officers and people of either nation residing in the other, shall have the right to employ natives for all kinds of lawful work. Should, however, subjects of Chosen, guilty of violation of the laws of the Kingdom, or against whom any action has been brought, conceal themselves in the residences or warehouses of United States citizens, or on board United States merchant-vessels, the Consular Authorities of the United States, on being notified of the fact by the local authorities, will either permit the latter to dispatch constables to make the arrests, or the persons will be arrested by the Consular Authorities and handed over to the local constables. Officials or citizens of the United States shall not harbor such persons.

ARTICLE XI.

Students of either nationality, who may proceed to the country of the other, in order to study the language, literature, laws or arts shall be given all possible protection and assistance in evidence of cordial good will.

ARTICLE XII.

This being the First treaty negotiated by Chosen, and hence being general and and incomplete in its provisions, shall in the first instance be put into operation in all things stipulated herein. As to stipulations not contained herein, after an interval of five years, when the officers and the people of the two Powers shall have become more familiar with each others language, a further negotiation of commercial provisions and regulations in detail, in conformity with international law and without unequal discriminations on either part shall be had.

ARTICLE XIII.
This Treaty, and future official correspondence between the two contracting Governments shall be made, on the part of Chosen, in the Chinese language.

The United States shall either use the Chinese language, or, if English is to be used, it shall be accompanied with a Chinese version, in order to avoid misunderstanding.

ARTICLE XIV.
The High Contracting Powers hereby agree that, should at any time the King of Chosen grant to any nation or to the merchants or citizens of any nation, any right, privilege or favor, connected either with navigation, commerce, political or other intercourse, which is not conferred by this Treaty, such right, privilege and favor shall freely inure to the benefit of the United States, its public officers, merchants and citizens, providing always, that whenever such right, privilege or favor is accompanied by any condition, or equivalent concession granted by the other nation interested, the United States, its officers and people shall only be entitled to the benefit of such right, privilege or favor upon complying with the conditions or concessions connected therewith.

In faith whereof the respective Commissioners Plenipotentiary have signed and sealed the foregoing at Yin-Chuen in English and Chinese, being three originals of each text of enen tenor and date, the ramifications of which shall be exchanged at Yin-Chuen within one year from the date of its execution, and immediately thereafter this Treaty shall be in all its provisions publicly proclaimed and made known by both Governments in their respective countries, in order that it may be obeyed by their citizens and subjects respectively.

Chosen, May the 22nd, A. D. 1882.
[seal.] R. W. Shufeldt, Commodore, U.S.N., Envoy of the U.S. to Chosen
[seal.] Shin Chen, Chin Hong Chi } [In Chinese.]

Source: Korea Society; lesson plan developed by David Morse (http://www.koreasociety.org/index2.php?option=com_docman&task =doc_view&gid=548)

Appendix B
Treaty of Shimonoseki

His Majesty the Emperor of Japan and His Majesty the Emperor of China, desiring to restore the blessings of peace to their countries and subjects and to remove all cause for future complications, have named as their Plenipotentiaries for the purpose of concluding a Treaty of Peace, that is to say:

His Majesty the Emperor of Japan, Count ITO Hirobumi, Junii, Grand Cross of the Imperial Order of Paullownia, Minister President of State; and Viscount MUTSU Munemitsu, Junii, First Class of the Imperial Order of the Sacred Treasure, Minister of State for Foreign Affairs.

And His Majesty the Emperor of China, LI Hung-chang [Li Hongzhang], Senior Tutor to the Heir Apparent, Senior Grand Secretary of State, Minister Superintendent of Trade for the Northern Ports of China, Viceroy of the province of Chili [Zhili], and Earl of the First Rank; and LI Ching-fong [Li Jingfeng], Ex-Minister of the Diplomatic Service, of the Second Official Rank:

Who, after having exchanged their full powers, which were found to be in good and proper form, have agreed to the following Articles:

ARTICLE 1
China recognises definitively the full and complete independence and autonomy of Korea, and, in consequence, the payment of tribute and the performance of ceremonies and formalities by Korea to China, in derogation of such independence and autonomy, shall wholly cease for the future.

ARTICLE 2

China cedes to Japan in perpetuity and full sovereignty the following territories, together with all fortifications, arsenals, and public property thereon:

(a) The southern portion of the province of Fêngtien [Fengtian] within the following boundaries [Liaodong agreement in November 1895 deleted this and replaced it with an indemnity of 30 million taels of silver to be paid Japan]:

The line of demarcation begins at the mouth of the River Yalu and ascends that stream to the mouth of the River An-ping [Anping], from thence the line runs to Fêng-huang [Fenghuang], from thence to Hai-cheng [Haizheng?], from thence to Ying-kow [Yinzhou?], forming a line which describes the southern portion of the territory. The places above named are included in the ceded territory. When the line reaches the River Liao at Ying-kow, it follows the course of the stream to its mouth, where it terminates. The mid-channel of the River Liao shall be taken as the line of demarcation.

This cession also includes all islands appertaining or belonging to the province of Fêngtien situated in the eastern portion of the Bay of Liao-tung and the northern portion of the Yellow Sea.

(b) The island of Formosa, together with all islands appertaining or belonging to the said island of Formosa.

(c) The Pescadores Group, that is to say, all islands lying between the 119th and 120th degrees of longitude east of Greenwich and the 23rd and 24th degrees of north latitude.

ARTICLE 3
[deleted by the Liaodong agreement, November 1895]
The alignment of the frontiers described in the preceding Article, and shown on the annexed map, shall be subject to verification and demarcation on the spot by a Joint Commission of Delimitation, consisting of two or more Japanese and two or more Chinese delegates, to be appointed immediately after the exchange of the ratifications of this Act. In case the boundaries laid down in this Act are found to be defective at any point, either on account of topography or in consideration of good administration, it shall also be the duty of the Delimitation Commission to rectify the same.

The Delimitation Commission will enter upon its duties as soon as possible, and will bring its labours to a conclusion within the period of one year after appointment.

The alignments laid down in this Act shall, however, be maintained until the rectifications of the Delimitation Commission, if any are made, shall have received the approval of the Governments of Japan and China.

ARTICLE 4

China agrees to pay to Japan as a war indemnity the sum of 200,000,000 Kuping [Gubing] taels; the said sum to be paid in eight instalments. The first instalment of 50,000,000 taels to be paid within six months, and the second instalment of 50,000,000 to be paid within twelve months, after the exchange of the ratifications of this Act. The remaining sum to be paid in six equal instalments as follows: the first of such equal annual instalments to be paid within two years, the second within three years, the third within four years, the fourth within five years, the fifth within six years, and the the sixth within seven years, after the exchange of the ratifications of this Act. Interest at the rate of 5 per centum per annum shall begin to run on all unpaid portions of the said indemnity from the date the first instalment falls due.

China shall, however, have the right to pay by anticipation at any time any or all of the said instalments. In case the whole amount of the said indemnity is paid within three years after the exchange of the ratifications of the present Act all interest shall be waived, and the interest for two years and a half or for any less period, if any already paid, shall be included as part of the principal amount of the indemnity.

ARTICLE 5

The inhabitants of the territories ceded to Japan who wish to take up their residence outside the ceded districts shall be at liberty to sell their real property and retire. For this purpose a period of two years from the date of the exchange of ratifications of the present Act shall be granted. At the expiration of that period those of the inhabitants who shall not have left such territories shall, at the option of Japan, be deemed to be Japanese subjects.

Each of the two Governments shall, immediately upon the exchange of the ratifications of the present Act, send one or more Commissioners to Formosa to effect a final transfer of that province, and within the space of two months after the exchange of the ratifications of this Act such transfer shall be completed.

ARTICLE 6

All Treaties between Japan and China having come to an end as a consequence of war, China engages, immediately upon the exchange of the ratifications of this Act, to appoint Plenipotentiaries to conclude with the Japanese Plenipotentiaries, a Treaty of Commerce and Navigation and a Convention to regulate Frontier Intercourse and Trade. The Treaties, Conventions, and Regulations now subsisting between China and the European Powers shall serve as a basis for the said Treaty and Convention between Japan and China. From the date of the exchange of ratifications of this Act until the said Treaty and Convention are brought into actual operation, the Japanese Governments, its officials, commerce, navigation, frontier intercourse and trade, industries, ships, and subjects, shall in every respect be accorded by China most favoured nation treatment.

China makes, in addition, the following concessions, to take effect six months after the date of the present Act:

First. —The following cities, towns, and ports, in addition to those already opened, shall be opened to the trade, residence, industries, and manufactures of Japanese subjects, under the same conditions and with the same privileges and facilities as exist at the present open cities, towns, and ports of China: Shashih [Shashi], in the province of Hupeh [Hubei].
Chungking [Chongqing], in the province of Szechwan [Sichuan].
Suchow [Suzhou], in the province of Kiangsu [Jiangsu].
Hangchow [Hangzhou], in the province of Chekiang [Zhejiang].
The Japanese Government shall have the right to station consuls at any all of the above named places.

Second. —Steam navigation for vessels under the Japanese flag, for the conveyance of passengers and cargo, shall be extended to the following places:
On the Upper Yangtze [Yangzi] River, from Ichang [Yichang] to Chungking [Chongqing].
On the Woosung [Wusong] River and the Canal, from Shanghai to Suchow [Suzhou] and Hangchow [Hangzhou].
The rules and regulations that now govern the navigation of the inland waters of China by Foreign vessels shall, so far as applicable, be enforced, in respect to the above named routes, until new rules and regulations are conjointly agreed to.

Third. —Japanese subjects purchasing goods or produce in the interior of China, or transporting imported merchandise into the interior of China, shall have the right temporarily to rent or hire warehouses for the storage of the articles so purchased or transported without the payment of any taxes or extractions whatever.

Fourth. —Japanese subjects shall be free to engage in all kinds of manufacturing industries in all the open cities, towns, and ports of China, and shall be at liberty to import into China all kinds of machinery, paying only the stipulated import duties thereon.

All articles manufactured by Japanese subjects in China shall, in respect of inland transit and internal taxes, duties, charges, and exactions of all kinds, and also in respect of warehousing and storage facilities in the interior of China, stand upon the same footing and enjoy the same privileges and exemptions as merchandise imported by Japanese subjects into China.

In the event additional rules and regulations are necessary in connection with these concessions, they shall be embodied in the Treaty of Commerce and Navigation provided for by this Article.

ARTICLE 7

Subject to the provisions of the next succeeding Article, the evacuation of China by the armies of Japan shall be completely effected within three months after the exchange of the ratifications of the present Act.

ARTICLE 8

As a guarantee of the faithful performance of the stipulations of this Act, China consents to the temporary occupation by the military forces of Japan of Weihai-wei, in the province of Shantung [Shandong]. [later in the same day, Japan and China agreed to the terms of the occupation]

Upon payment of the first two installments of the war indemnity herein stipulated for and the exchange of the ratifications of the Treaty of Commerce and navigation, the said place shall be evacuated by the Japanese forces, provided the Chinese Government consents to pledge, under suitable and sufficient arrangements, the Customs revenue of China as security for the payment of the principal and interest of the remaining installments of the said indemnity. In the event that no such arrangements are concluded, such evacuation shall only take place upon the payment of the final installment of said indemnity.

It is, however, expressly understood that no such evacuation shall take place until after the exchange of the ratifications of the Treaty of Commerce and Navigation.

ARTICLE 9

Immediately upon the exchange of the ratifications of this Act, all prisoners of war then held shall be restored, and China undertakes not to ill-treat or punish prisoners of war so restored to her by Japan. China also engages to at once release all Japanese subjects accused of being military spies or charged with any other military offences. China further engages not to punish in any manner, nor to allow to be punished, those Chinese subjects who have in any manner been compromised in their relations with the Japanese army during the war.

ARTICLE 10

All offensive military operations shall cease upon the exchange of the ratifications of this Act.

ARTICLE 11

The present Act shall be ratified by their Majesties the Emperor of Japan and the Emperor of China, and the ratifications shall be exchanged at Chefoo on the 8th day of the 5th month of the 28th year of MEIJI, corresponding to the 14th day of the 4th month of the 21st year of KUANG HSÜ [Guangxu].

In witness whereof the respective Plenipotentiaries have signed the same and affixed thereto the seal of their arms.

Done in Shimonoseki, in duplicate, this 17th day of the fourth month of the 28th year of MEIJI, corresponding to the 23rd day of the 3rd month of the 21st year of KUANG HSÜ [Guangxu].

Count ITO HIROBUMI, [L.S.]
Junii, Grand Cross of the Imperial Order of Paullownia
Minister President of State
Plenipotentiary of His Majesty the Emperor of Japan

Viscount MUTSU MUNEMITSU, [L.S.]
Junii, First Class of the Imperial Order of the Sacred Treasure

Minister of State for Foreign Affairs
Plenipotentiary of His Majesty the Emperor of Japan

LI HUNG-CHANG [Li Hongzhang], [L.S.]
Plenipotentiary of His Majesty the Emperor of China
Senior Tutor to the Heir Apparent
Senior Grand Secretary of State
Minister Superintendent of Trade for the Northern Ports of China
Viceroy of the province of Chili [Zhili]
Earl of the First Rank

LI CHING-FONG [Li Jingfeng]
Plenipotentiary of His Majesty the Emperor of China
Ex-Minister of the Diplomatic Service, of the Second Official Rank

Source: UCLA Center for East Asian Studies (http://www.international
.ucla.edu/eas/documents/1895shimonoseki-treaty.htm)

Appendix C
Japan-Korea Annexation Treaty
August 22, 1910

THE PROCLAMATION

Notwithstanding the earnest and laborious work of reforms in the administration of Korea in which the Governments of Japan and Korea have been engaged for more than four years since the conclusion of the Agreement of 1905, the existing system of government in that country has not proved entirely equal to the duty of preserving public order and tranquility; and in addition, the spirit of suspicion and misgiving dominates the whole peninsula.

In order to maintain peace and stability in Korea, to promote the prosperity and welfare of Koreans, and at the same time to ensure the safety and repose of foreign residents, it has been made abundantly clear that fundamental changes in the actual regime of government are absolutely essential. The Governments of Japan and Korea, being convinced of the urgent necessity of introducing reforms responsive to the requirements of the situation and of furnishing sufficient guarantee for the future, have, with the approval of His Majesty the Emperor of Japan and His Majesty the Emperor of Korea, concluded, through their plenipotentiaries, a treaty providing for complete annexation of Korea to the Empire of Japan. By virtue of that important act, which shall take effect on its promulgation on August 29, 1910, the Imperial Government of Japan shall undertake the entire government and administration of Korea, and they hereby declare that the matters relating to foreigners and foreign trade in Korea shall be conducted in accordance with the following rules:

THE TREATY

His Majesty the Emperor of Japan and His Majesty the Emperor of Korea, having in view the special and close relations between their respective countries, desiring to promote the common wealth of the two nations and to assure the permanent peace in the Far East, and being convinced that these objectives can be best attained by the annexation of Korea to the Empire of Japan, have resolved to conclude a treaty of such annexation and have, for that purpose, appointed as their plenipotentiaries, that is to say, His Majesty the Emperor of Japan Viscount Terauchi Masatake, Resident-General, and His Majesty the Emperor of Korea Yi Wan-Yong, Prime Minister, who upon mutual conference and deliberation have agreed to the following articles:

Article 1. His Majesty the Emperor of Korea makes the complete and permanent cession to His Majesty the Emperor of Japan of all rights of sovereignty over the whole of Korea.

Article 2. His Majesty the Emperor of Japan accepts the cession mentioned in the preceding article and consents to the complete annexation of Korea to the Empire of Japan.

Article 3. His Majesty the Emperor of Japan will accord to their Majesties the Emperor and ex-Emperor and His Imperial Highness the Crown Prince of Korea and their consorts and heirs such titles, dignity, and honor as are appropriate to their respective ranks, and sufficient annual grants will be made for the maintenance of such titles, dignity and honor.

Article 4. His Majesty the Emperor of Japan will also accord appropriate honor and treatment to the members of the Imperial House of Korea and their heirs other than those mentioned in the preceding article, and the funds necessary for the maintenance of such honor and treatment will be granted.

Article 5. His Majesty the Emperor of Japan will confer peerage and monetary grants upon those Koreans who, on account of meritorious services, are regarded as deserving such special recognition.

Article 6. In consequence of the aforesaid annexation the Government of Japan assume the entire government and administration of Korea, and undertake to afford full protection for the persons and property of Koreans obeying the laws there in force to promote the welfare of all such Koreans.

Article 7. The Government of Japan will, so far as circumstances permit, employ in the public service of Japan in Korea those Koreans who accept the new regime loyally and in good faith and who are duly qualified for such service.

Article 8. This treaty, having been approved by His Majesty the Emperor of Japan and His Majesty the Emperor of Korea, shall take effect from the state of its promulgation.

In faith thereof:

Resident General Viscount Terauchi Masatake

Prime Minister Yi, Wan-yong

Source: UCLA Center for East Asian Studies
(http://www.international.ucla.edu/eas/documents/kore1910.htm)

Notes

INTRODUCTION

1. As explained in *Nuclear Endgame: The Need for Engagement with North Korea,* Juche has a much broader and complex meaning than its usual definition of "self-reliance." The concept embodies an autonomous self-identity that offers "an enabling independence of action that in its ideal state renders North Korea insusceptible to, or at the very least mitigates, the undesirable external influences of larger powers," which would include China, Russia, the United States, and Japan. This philosophy does not preclude the regime from accepting assistance from other nations. In practice, North Korean officials remain dependent upon massive external economic assistance to feed the North Korean citizenry. On whole, the Juche ideology, which is based on a strong Stalinist approach to governance, relies on broad indoctrination of the public, permits little freedom of thought or expression, and exercises draconian measures to ensure citizen compliance with policy directives.

2. Cheol-oh Ho, "Korean Unification," in *Resolving International Disputes through Super-Optimum Solutions*, ed. Stuart S. Nagel (Hauppauge, NY: Nova Science Publishers, June 2001), 153.

3. The period of the Choson Dynasty can be identified in one of two ways. Typically, as is done in this book, the period July 1392–August 1910 is recognized because Choson rule did not officially end until the onset of Japanese colonization in 1910. Technically, however, the Choson Dynasty came to a close in 1897 because it was then that the Korean emperor declared the nation to be the "Korean Empire" in an effort to stave off ever-increasing encroachment on the peninsula by foreign nations and to re-establish Korean sovereignty over its own affairs.

CHAPTER 1. DECONSTRUCTING THE UNIFICATION ISSUE

1. Andrei Lankov, "What Will Become of N. Koreans after Unification?," *Korea Times*, October 31, 2008.

2. Andrei Lankov, "Working through Korean Unification Blues," *Asia Times Online*, November 15, 2007, http://www.atimes.com/atimes/Korea/IK15Dg01.html, accessed April 23, 2009.

3. While the second attempt on Park's life failed again, the North Korean assassins did manage to kill his wife. Park was finally assassinated, not by North Korean agents,

but, ironically, rather by his own director of the Korean Central Intelligence Agency, Kim Jae Kyu, on October 26, 1979. North Korean motivation for both assassination attempts on Park's life rested in the growing economic prosperity Park brought to South Korea and his consolidation of domestic political power, all of which was construed as a threat to Kim Il-sung's vision of a peninsula under North Korean rule.

4. Ambassador Charles L. (Jack) Pritchard, "Korean Reunification: Implications for the United States and Northeast Asia," Uri Party Foundation International Symposium on Peace and Prosperity in Northeast Asia (Seoul, Korea), January 13–14, 2005.

5. The Moscow Agreement was concluded during the Foreign Ministers' Conference held in December 1945 in Moscow. The Conference was attended by representatives of the United States, Soviet Union, and Great Britain, all of whom agreed that the line bisecting the Korean peninsula should be removed at the first practicable opportunity. To that end they created the Joint Commission, comprising representatives from the U.S. and Soviet Union, which was to oversee the political and economic integration of the northern and southern zones of occupation.

6. Kim Jae-kyoung, "BRICs, Australia Outgrow Korea," *Korea Times*, July 6, 2009.

7. Ministry of Unification (Republic of Korea), *North Korea: Tables and Charts*, http://www.unikorea.go.kr/eng/default.jsp?pgname=NORtables, accessed July 12, 2009.

8. Ibid.

9. The Rome Statute of the International Criminal Court defines crimes against humanity in the following manner: "For the purpose of this Statute, 'crimes against humanity' means any of the following acts when committed as part of a widespread or systematic attack directed against any civilian population, with knowledge of the attack: murder; extermination; enslavement; deportation or forcible transfer of population; imprisonment or other severe deprivation of physical liberty in violation of fundamental rules of international law; torture; rape, sexual slavery, enforced prostitution, forced pregnancy, enforced sterilization, or any form of sexual violence…; persecution against any identifiable group or collectivity on political, racial, national, ethnic, cultural, religious, gender…or other grounds…; enforced disappearance of persons; the crime of apartheid; other inhumane acts of similar character."

10. International Food Aid Information System (INTERFAIS), *Quantity Reporting Overview*, http://www.wfp.org/fais/, accessed August 22, 2009.

11. World Food Programme, "WFP Launches Emergency Operation to Support 3.5 Million Vulnerable People in DPRK (April 2011)," http://www.wfp.org/news/news-release/wfp-launches-emergency-operation-support-35-mln-vulnerable-people-dprk, accessed May 12, 2011.

12. Kim Kwang-tae, "Secret Couriers Work as New Warriors against North Korea," Yonhap News, July 25, 2011.

13. Andrei Lankov, "North Korea Adopts New Propaganda Tool," *Korea Times*, November 23, 2008.

14. Lankov, "What Will Become of N. Koreans after Unification?"

15. Jih-Un Kim and Dong-Jin Jang, "Aliens among Brothers? The Status and Perception of North Korean Refugees in South Korea," *Asian Perspective* 31, no. 2 (2007): 12.

16. Ibid.

17. Central Intelligence Agency, *CIA World Factbook* (2009), https://www.cia.gov/library/publications/the-world-factbook/index.html, accessed August 23, 2009.

18. Ibid.

19. Sung Ho Ko, Kiseon Chung, and Yoo-seok Oh, "North Korean Defectors: Their Life and Well-Being after Defection," *Asian Perspective* 28, no. 2 (2004): 69.

20. Kim and Jang, "Aliens among Brothers?," 12.

21. Ibid., 12–13.
22. Ibid., 15.
23. Sundance's Freedom of Expression Award is given each year to a documentary that educates the public on issues of social or political importance.

CHAPTER 2. IN THE BEGINNING
1. *Korea Times*, December 22, 2008.
2. Shin-who Kang, "Is Korea Homogeneous Country?," *Korea Times*, December 22, 2008.
3. Ibid.
4. "What Koreans Really Think about Ethnic Homogeneity," *Chosun Ilbo Digital Edition*, September 6, 2007, http://english.chosun.com/cgi-bin printNews?id=2007 09060019, accessed March 15, 2009.
5. Several manuscripts were used in compiling the information in the section, all of which proved valuable in providing information salient in developing an accurate historical portrayal of early Korea:
   Andrew C. Nahm, *Korea: Tradition and Transformation* (Elizabeth, NJ, and Seoul: Hollym International Corporation, 1991); Carter J. Eckert, Ki-baik Lee, Young-ick Lew, Michael Robinson, and Edward Wagner, *Korea: Old and New* (Seoul: Korea Institute, Harvard University, 1990, published by Ilchokak Publishers); Ki-baik Lee, *A New History of Korea* (Cambridge, MA: Harvard University Press, 1984); Sung Chul Yang, *The North and South Korean Political Systems: A Comparative Analysis* (Elizabeth, NJ, and Seoul: Hollym International Corporation, 1999); Peter H. Lee and Wm. Theodore de Bary, eds., *Sources of Korean Tradition*, vol. 1 (New York: Columbia University Press, 1997).
6. Nahm, *Korea*, 100.
7. Ibid., 101.
8. Ibid., 101.
9. Yong-ho Ch'oe, Peter H. Lee, and Wm. Theodore de Bary, eds., *Sources of Korean Tradition, vol. 2* (New York: Columbia University Press, 2001), 157.
10. The Hong Kyongnae Rebellion of 1812 was, at its core, an anti-dynastic response to what its rebels perceived as consistent and long-term unfair treatment and regional discrimination against Koreans living in the northern provinces of the country by Choson dynasty officials, in this case P'yongan. The Donghak (Tonghak) Rebellion of 1894–95 focused peasant discontent against three elements present in Choson society: 1) foreign incursion; 2) government corruption; and 3) and conspicuous consumption by the yangban. Unlike the Hong Kyongnae Rebellion of 1812, which was ultimately quelled, the Donghak Rebellion helped to lay the foundations of the first Sino-Japanese War (1894–95), the result of which was the total defeat of China by Japanese forces and the rise of Japanese supremacy on the Korean peninsula. Thus, the Rebellion would help to put in place some of the precursors necessary for Japanese takeover of the peninsula at the start of the twentieth century.
11. Kyung Moon Hwang, "From the Dirt to Heaven: Northern Koreans in the Choson and Early Modern Eras," *Harvard Journal of Asiatic Studies* 62, no. 1 (July 2002): 139.
12. Ibid., 139–40.
13. Sun Joo Kim, *Marginality and Subversion in Korea: The Hong Kyongnae Rebellion of 1812* (Seattle: University of Washington Press, 2007), 15.
14. Hwang, "From the Dirt to Heaven," 149.
15. Ibid., 149.
16. Ibid., 147.

17. Ibid., 148.
18. Ibid., 144.
19. Ibid., 148.
20. Kim, *Marginality and Subversion*, 9.
21. Ibid., 35–40.
22. Ibid., 40–41.
23. Ibid., 72–75.

CHAPTER 3. A SHRIMP AMONG WHALES

1. Tae-hung Ha, *Maxims and Proverbs of Old Korea, Korean Cultural Series*, vol. 7 (Seoul: Yonsei University Press, 1970) 128.
2. *Japan: An Illustrated Encyclopedia*, 1st ed., s.v. "Tempo Famine."
3. *Sankin kotai* was the policy of mandatory "alternate attendance" required of domainal lords (*daimyo*), instituted by the Tokugawa Shogunate, and regularized under the third shogun, Tokugawa Iemitsu. Under this practice, daimyo were required to spend every other year in service to the shogun in Tokyo, called Edo at the time, and also to maintain a residence there where his family members were forced to reside permanently, essentially as hostages. During the years in which a daimyo was not in attendance in Edo, he was required to serve in his home domain. Additionally, when a daimyo traveled back and forth to Edo, he was required to do so with a retinue, which could number anywhere from 100–300 men depending on the size of his domain—the larger the domain, the larger the retinue was required to be. All this was designed to minimize the possibility of revolt by the daimyo, by compelling them to use much of their wealth—the costs associated with sankin kotai typically used 70–80 percent of a daimyo's income.
4. *Meiji ishin* (Restoration): the events of the Meiji Restoration itself occurred on January 3, 1868, when the Satsuma (Kagoshima) and Choushuu (Yamaguchi) domains took control of the Imperial Palace in Kyoto and "restored" power to the emperor, wresting political control from the Tokugawa shogunate. The restoration was, however, a much more complex series of events precipitated by the breakdown of the social order, economic problems, incursions by Western powers into sovereign Japanese territory, and growing political unrest.
5. Japan also succeeded in convincing the British to recognize its "peculiar interests" on the peninsula via the Anglo-Japanese Alliance of January 1902.

CHAPTER 4. KOREA UNDER THE JAPANESE COLONIAL MODEL

1. Gi-wook Shin, *Ethnic Nationalism in Korea: Genealogy, Politics, and Legacy* (Stanford, CA: Stanford University Press, 2006), 45.
2. Nahm, *Korea*, 223–24.
3. *Japan: An Illustrated Encyclopedia*, 1st ed., s.v. "Korea and Japan."
4. Ibid.
5. Mukden is present-day Shenyang. On September 18, 1931, a section of Japan's South Manchurian Railway was blown up. The incident remains controversial because Japanese Imperial Army officials blamed Chinese dissidents for having perpetrated the act. It is widely speculated, however, that the incident was contrived by Japanese Army officials as a means for gaining formal control over the area, which they did a year later with the establishment of the puppet state, Manchukuo.
6. Nahm, *Korea*, 234.
7. The Tientsin Convention (April 1885) was signed by representatives of Japan's Meiji

government and the Qing Dynasty in China. The terms of the convention provided for de facto dual stewardship of the Korean peninsula by both China and Japan.

8. Henry Em as quoted in Gi-wook Shin, *Ethnic Nationalism in Korea*, 45.

9. Ibid., 45.

10. There is another historical point to consider. The Koreans also remembered that it was the Japanese, under the leadership of Toyotomi Hideyoshi, who attempted to subjugate the peninsula during the years 1592–98.

11. Shin, *Ethnic Nationalism in Korea*, 41–45.

12. The Cairo Declaration was the result of the Cairo Conference, which was attended by U.S. president Franklin Roosevelt; British prime minister Winston Churchill (Great Britain); and Chinese Gen. Chiang Kai-shek. It dealt specifically with issues relating to the surrender of Japan and disposition of territory over which it had taken control. Specifically with regard to Korea, the declaration offered that "mindful of the enslavement of the people of Korea, are determined that in due course Korea shall become free and independent."

13. Jacques L. Fuqua Jr., *Nuclear Endgame: The Need for Engagement with North Korea* (Westport, CT: Praeger Security International, 2007), 47.

CHAPTER 5. A POST–WORLD WAR II OVERVIEW

1. "S. Koreans See Long Road to Reunification," *Gallup News*, November 28, 2007, http://www.gallup.com/video/102916/minority-south-koreans-envision-reunification.aspx, accessed September 1, 2008.

2. Namkoong Young, "Similarities and Dissimilarities: The Inter-Korean Summit and Unification Formulae," *East Asian Review* 13, no. 3 (Autumn 2001): 61–62.

3. While Roh's efforts can be seen as pivotal in the nation's transition toward a broadly engaging unification policy, two of his predecessors did take fledgling, yet important, steps in that direction. Park Chung-hee, for example, articulated for the first time in an August 15, 1970, speech that Seoul was willing to pursue peaceful co-existence with the North. This new policy manifested itself in the July 4, 1972, Joint Communiqué agreed to by both governments, which underscored the need to pursue unification peacefully and independently. Chun Doo-hwan, who succeeded Park, urged normal relations between the two countries and put forth a new unification policy. That such efforts didn't gain much traction is the function of the geopolitical climate at the time, e.g., the intensity of the Cold War, and other antagonistic polices pursued by these administrations against the North Koreans.

4. The Mount Kumgang (Diamond Mountain) resort was a popular tourist program run jointly by the South Korean firm, Hyundai Asan, and the North Korean government. Hyundai Asan invested roughly $1.5 billion to build the tourist destination, which included a shopping mall, hotel, and hot springs. In June 2008, however, a North Korean guard fatally shot a South Korean female tourist whom the regime claims wandered into a restricted area. As a result of the shooting and North Korea's refusal to respond to the South Korean government's demands for a joint investigation of the shooting, all tours to the area have been suspended. In May 2011, the North Korean government announced it was assuming ownership of all Hyundai Asan facilities at the Mount Kumgang resort.

5. Donald MacIntyre, "A Very Expensive Affair," *Time*, March 26, 2003, http://www.time.com/time/magazine/article/0,9171,433328,00.html, accessed August 1, 2008.

6. Ministry of Unification (Republic of Korea), *Policy for Peace and Prosperity* (Seoul, 2003), 5.

7. Ibid.

8. Andrei Lankov, "Koreas Not Eye to Eye on Vision 3000," *Nautilus Institute Policy Forum Online* 08-45A, June 6, 2008, http://www.nautilus.org/fora/security/08045Lankov. html, accessed November 12, 2008.

9. Fuqua, *Nuclear Endgame*, 120–24.

10. "China Has Socialist Market Economy in Place," *People's Daily Online*, July 13, 2005, http://english.peopledaily.com.cn/200507/13/eng20050713_195876.html, accessed February 3, 2009.

11. Fuqua, *Nuclear Endgame*, 84–85.

12. Sang-woo Rhee, "North Korea in 1991: The Struggle to Save Chuch'e Amid Signs of Change," *Asian Survey* 32, no. 1 (January 1992): 59.

13. Dae-sook Suh, "North Korea in 1986: Strengthening the Soviet Connection," *Asian Survey* 27, no. 1 (January 1987): 58.

14. There are no official figures citing how many North Koreans may have died during the worst of the famine in the 1990s. However, most estimates range between 2–3 million.

15. The Great Leap Forward was the Second Five Year Plan to which Mao had committed China during the years 1958–63. The plan's objective was to modernize and industrialize China's agricultural society, the focus of which was increased grain and steel production. With no indigenous capacity to pursue such aims, however, the plan was pursued with reckless abandon and doomed to failure from the start. Peasants developed backyard furnaces using wood from their homes—doors, tables, chairs—to fuel the furnaces. The steel they were to produce came from farming tools, pots, pans, etc., producing useless pig iron. Without tools to farm, there was resultant famine. The Plan was abandoned in 1959.

16. Joungwon Alexander Kim, "The 'Peak of Socialism' in North Korea: The Five and Seven Year Plans," *Asian Survey* 5, no. 5 (May 1965): 258.

17. B. C. Koh, "North Korea in 1977: Year of 'Readjustment'," *Asian Survey* 18, no. 1 (January 1978): 36–37.

18. Ibid.

19. B. C. Koh, "North Korea 1976: Under Stress," *Asian Survey* 17, no. 1 (January 1977): 67.

20. Ibid.

21. Sung-ki Jung, "N. Korea Lambasts S. Korean Leader," *Korea Times*, April 1, 2008.

22. Tae-gyu Kim, "North Korea Closes Border Again," *Korea Times*, March 13, 2009.

23. Andrei Lankov, "Gaesong Industrial Complex Faces Serious Threat," *Korea Times*, May 15, 2009.

24. "Closing Kaesong Industrial Complex Would Hit NK Hard," *Chosun Ilbo*, May 18, 2009.

25. Ministry of Unification, *Humanitarian Assistance*, http://www.unikorea.go.kr/eng/ default.jsp?pgname=AFFhumanitarian_assistance, accessed August 4, 2009.

26. INTERFAIS, Quantity Reporting Overview.

27. Se-jeong Kim, "NK Famine Becoming Widespread Following Currency Reform," *Korea Times*, March 12, 2010.

CHAPTER 6. THE ROADS TOWARD UNIFICATION

1. "Quotations of Kim Jong Il on Unification," Columbia University Law School website, http://www2.law.columbia.edu/course_00S_L9436_001/North%20Korea%20materials/quotations_of_kim_jong_il_on_uni.htm, accessed May 24, 2011.

2. Sung-ki Jung, "Denuclearization Before NK Aid," *Korea Times*, February 25, 2008.

3. Text of the "North-South Joint Communiqué, July 4, 1972," *Nautilus*, http://www.nautilus.org/DPRKBriefingBook/agreements/CanKor_VTK_1972_07_04_north_south_joint_communique.pdf, accessed January 3, 2009.

4. United States Institute of Peace, *Peace Agreements: North-South Korea*, Peace Agreements Digital Collection, http://www.usip.org/resources/peace-agreements-north-korea-south-korea, accessed on January 3, 2009.

5. "Full Text of Inter-Korean Agreement," *Korea Times*, October 4, 2007.

6. Dick K. Nanto and Mark E. Manyin, *CRS Report for Congress: The Kaesong North-South Korean Industrial Complex*, July 19, 2007, Congressional Research Service: Washington, DC, https://www.policyarchive.org/bitstream/handle/10207/1888/RL32161_20031126.pdf, accessed February 14, 2008.

7. Chi-dong Lee, "S. Korea Holds Key to Resumption of Mount Kumgang Tourism," Yonhap News Service, August 17, 2009, http://english.yonhapnews.co.kr/northkorea/2009/08/17/68/0401000000AEN20090817003600315F.HTML, accessed December 1, 2009.

8. K. Connie Kang, "Roh Cautions U.S. on North Korea," *Los Angeles Times*, November 13, 2004.

9. U.S. Census Bureau, *2010: U.S. trade in goods with Korea, South*, Foreign Trade Statistics, May 27, 2011, http://www.census.gov/foreign-trade/balance/c5800.html, accessed September 27, 2009.

10. Fuqua, *Nuclear Endgame*, 149–58.

11. Namkoong Young, "Similarities and Dissimilarities: The Inter-Korean Summit and Unification Formulae," *East Asian Review* 13, no. 3 (Autumn 2001): 65–68.

12. Ibid.

13. Jung, "N. Korea Lambasts S. Korean Leader."

14. Stephan Haggard and Marcus Noland, "North Korea in 2008: Twilight of the God?," *Asia Survey* 49, no. 1 (January 2009): 1.

15. The U.S. State Department describes the Proliferation Security Initiative as "a global effort that aims to stop trafficking of weapons of mass destruction (WMD), their delivery systems, and related materials to and from states and non-state actors of proliferation concern. Launched by President Bush on May 31, 2003, U.S. involvement in the PSI stems from the U.S. National Strategy to Combat Weapons of Mass Destruction issued in December 2002. That strategy recognizes the need for more robust tools to stop proliferation of WMD around the world, and specifically identifies interdiction as an area where greater focus will be placed. Today, more than 90 countries around the world support the PSI." U.S. State Department website, http://www.state.gov/t/isn/c10390.htm.

16. Yon-se Kim, "President Lee Vows to Respond to Expulsion Sternly," *Korea Times*, March 27, 2008.

17. Tae-gyu Kim, "North Korea Closes Border Again," *Korea Times*, March 13, 2009.

18. Sue-young Kim, "NK Frees Detained Hyundai Worker," *Korea Times*, August 13, 2009.

19. Sung-ki Jung, "Ban Urges NK to Improve Human Rights," *Korea Times*, July 4, 2008.

20. Sung-ki Jung, "N. Korean Urged to Improve Human Rights," *Korea Times*, August 6, 2008.

21. Sung-ki Jung, "N. Korea Rebuffs Calls for Rights Improvements," *Korea Times*, March 5, 2008.

CHAPTER 7. THE ABSORPTION SCENARIO

1. Samuel Kim, "Korean Unification: Retrospect and Prospect," Fathom (Columbia University, http://www.fathom.com/feature/35684/index.html, accessed May 10, 2009.
2. Hyun-kyung Kang, "Doves Say S. Korea, US Corner NK," *Korea Times*, June 19, 2009.
3. Chico Harlan, "South Korean Leader has Unification Plan," *Washington Post*, August 16, 2010.
4. "UN Investigator Condemns North Korea Human Rights Violations," *Jurist*, October 23, 2009.
5. Kim, "Korean Unification: Retrospect and Prospect."
6. Stefan Berg, Steffen Winter and Andreas Wassermann, "Germany's Eastern Burden: The Price of a Failed Reunification," *Spiegel Online International*, September 5, 2005, http://www.spiegel.de/international/spiegel/0,1518,373639,00.html, accessed September 12, 2009.
7. Tim Weber, "Waiting for the East to Flourish," *BBC Online*, September 9, 2005, http://news.bbc.co.uk/2/hi/business/4225346.stm, accessed September 12, 2009.
8. Nicholas Kulish, "In East Germany, a Decline as Stark as a Wall," *New York Times*, June 18, 2009, http://www.nytimes.com/2009/06/19/world/europe/19germany.html, accessed September 12, 2009.
9. Library of Congress, *Country Profile: Germany* (April 2008).
10. Peter M. Beck, "Contemplating Korean Reunification," *Wall Street Journal*, January 4, 2010.
11. Lankov, "Working through Korean Unification Blues."
12. Charles Wolf Jr., "Korean Unification: How It Might Come About and at What Cost," *Defence and Peace Economics* 17, no. 6 (December 2006): 685–86.
13. Ibid, 686.
14. Rhoda Margesson, Emma Chanlett-Avery, and Andorra Bruno, *CRS Report for Congress: North Korean Refugees in China and Human Rights Issues: International Response and U.S. Options*, September 26, 2007, Congressional Research Service: Washington, D.C., http://www.fas.org/sgp/crs/row/RL34189.pdf, accessed on September 5, 2009.

CHAPTER 8. NIRVANA UNDONE

1. Soo-hyun Rhee, "North Korean Defectors in South Korea," *Korea Times*, July 23, 2008.
2. Ibid.
3. Randy Green, "Border Pedagogy and the Acculturation of Korean Students in U.S. Institutions of Higher Education" (PhD diss., Indiana State University, 2010), 20.
4. Joungwon Alexander Kim and Myungshin Hong, "The Koreas, Unification and the Great Powers," *Current History* 105, no. 690 (April 2006): 186.
5. In-jin Yoon and Chang-kyu Lim, "Social Adjustments of North Korean Migrants in South Korea" (paper presented at the annual meeting of the American Sociological Association, New York City, August 11, 2007).
6. United Nations, "Convention and Protocol Relating to the Status of Refugees," 1967.
7. Luis Ramirez, "China Faces Predicament over North Korean Refugees," VOA.com, April 16, 2008, http://www.voanews.com/english/archive/2008-04/2008-04-16-voa38.cfm?renderforprint=1&pageid=448551, accessed November 6, 2009.
8. Margesson, Chanlett-Avery, and Bruno, *CRS Report for Congress*, 5.
9. Ibid.

10. Ibid.
11. Sue-young Kim, "Plight of NK Women Defectors Deepening," *Korea Times*, July 3, 2009.
12. Sang-ho Yoon as reported in Dick Nanto, *CRS Report for Congress: North Korea: Chronology of Provocations, 1950–2003*, March 18, 2003, 20 in *The Realities of Abduction Revealed by a North Korean Agent*," Tong-A Ilbo (Korean).
13. Nanto, *CRS Report for Congress*, 20.
14. Ramirez, "China Faces Predicament."
15. "N. Korean Defectors under Spotlight after Arrest of Woman Spy Suspect," *Yonsei News Service*, September 4, 2008.
16. Woo-taek Jeon, "Issues and Problems of Adaptation of North Korean Defectors to South Korean Society: An In-depth Interview Study with 32 Defectors," *Yonsei Medical Journal* 41, no. 3 (2000): 368.
17. Ibid., 365.
18. Eric Bidet, "Social Capital and Work Integration of Migrants: The Case of North Korean Defectors in South Korea," *Asian Perspective* 33, no. 2 (2009): 167–68.
19. Jeon, "Issues and Problems of Adaptation," 367–68.
20. Special Reporting Team, "DPR Korea: Defectors Still Confront Uphill Battle," *Joong Ang Daily*, October 19, 2010.
21. Kim Rahn, "Female NK Defectors Fall Victim to Domestic Violence," *Korea Times*, December 28, 2010.
22. Kim, "Plight of NK Women Defectors Deepening."
23. Ibid.
24. Ibid.
25. "North Koreans Struggle in New Lives in South Korea," *The China Post*, August 1, 2009.
26. John M. Glionna, "A Rare Look Inside the Hanawon Center for North Korean Defectors," LATimes.com, July 9, 2009, http://articles.latimes.com/2009/jul/09/world/fg-korea-defectors9, accessed September 12, 2009.
27. Kim Hyun, "Hanawon Center: A Litmus Test for How Koreas Can Unite," Yonhap News Service, July 1, 2009.
28. Jon Herskovitz, "North Korean Teen Defectors Get Capitalist Education," Reuters.com, December 2, 2008, http://www.reuters.com/articlePrint?articleId=USTRE4B20W120081203, accessed September 29, 2009.
29. Kurt Achin, "S. Korean School Isolates N. Korean Defectors to Better Integrate Them," VOA.com, December 4, 2008, http://www.voanews.com/english/archive/2008-12/2008-12-04-voa9.cfm, accessed September 29, 2009.
30. Bomi Lim, "South Korea May Punish North's Refugees Who Seek Asylum Abroad," Bloomberg.com, October 5, 2008, http://www.bloomberg.com/apps/news?pid=20670001&sid=aRiU__Y8.lMg, accessed October 17, 2009.
31. Jane Kim, "North Korean Human Rights and Resettlement in the United States: A Slow and Quiet Progress," *SAIA US-Korea Yearbook 2008* (Baltimore: Johns Hopkins University Press, 2008), 151.
32. Ibid.
33. Byung-ho Chung, "Between Migrant and Defector," *Korean Studies* 32 (2009): 1–3.
34. Don Kirk, "N. Korean Defectors Face New Challenges on Journey South," *Christian Science Monitor*, December 29, 2004.
35. Lim, "South Korea May Punish North's Refugees."
36. Ibid.

CHAPTER 9. ISSUES OF REPATRIATION

1. Kim Il-sung, *Kim Il-sung Selected Works*, vol. II *On Communist Education* (Pyongyang: Foreign Languages Publishing House, 1971), 256.
2. Blaine Harden, "N. Korean Defectors Bewildered by the South," *Washington Post*, April 12, 2009.
3. Yong Bok Li, *Education in the Democratic People's Republic of Korea* (Pyongyang: Foreign Languages Publishing House, 1986), 31–32.
4. Gay Garland Reed and Yoon-young Kim, "Schooling in North Korea," in *Going to School in East Asia*, ed. Gerard A. Postiglione and Jason Tan (Westport, CT: Greenwood Press, 2007), 259.
5. Mi Young Kim, "Nurseries in North Korea," NKChosun.com, October 7, 2001, http://www.nkmissions.com/10part_report/Articles/NKChosun%20-%20Nurseries.htm, accessed January 11, 2009.
6. Hyung-chan Kim with Dong-kyu Kim, *Human Remodeling in North Korea* (Lanham, MD: University Press of America, 2005), 192.
7. Kim, "Nurseries in North Korea."
8. Ibid.
9. Kim with Kim, *Human Remodeling in North Korea*, 192–93.
10. Ibid., 200.
11. Ibid., 204.
12. Ibid., 203.
13. Li, *Education in the Democratic People's Republic of Korea*, 32.
14. Kim with Kim, *Human Remodeling in North Korea*, 204.
15. Ibid., 211.
16. Ibid., 215.
17. Ibid., 228.
18. Reed and Kim, "Schooling in North Korea," 325.
19. Ibid., 324–25.
20. "Education/Literacy in Korea," Asian Info.org, http://www.asianinfo.org/asianinfo/korea/education.htm, accessed September 5, 2009.
21. "South Korea-Secondary Education," Stateuniversity.com, http://education.stateuniversity.com/pages/1402/South-Korea-SECONDARY-EDUCATION.html, accessed March 15, 2009.
22. Estimates as to the number of saeteomin living in South Korea are based on an annual average of 3,000 North Korean migrants arriving in South Korea.
23. Andrei Lankov, "A Bitter Taste of Paradise: North Korean Refugees in South Korea," *Journal of East Asian Studies* 6 (2006): 111.
24. Kim, "Plight of NK Women Defectors Deepening."
25. Sung-ki Jung, "More N. Koreans Defecting to South via 3rd Nations," *Korea Times*, March 19, 2008.
26. Kim and Jang, "Aliens Among Brothers?," 15.
27. The Netherlands Organization for International Cooperation in Higher Education, "Country Education Profile: South Korea," September 2009.
28. "North Koreans' Struggle for Schooling," Radio Free Asia.com, February 2, 2009. Original reporting in Korean by Sookyung Lee, Si Chun, and Jung Young; written for the web in English by Luisetta Mudie, http://www.rfa.org/english/news/korea/nkstruggleforschooling-02022009124839.html, accessed September 6, 2009.
29. Jon Herskovitz, "North Korean Teen Defectors Get Capitalist Education," Reuters, December 2, 2008.
30. President Lee's administration had plans to limit the number of hours hagwon could

legally operate to no later than 10 pm, but opposition from the Grand National Party, a conservative political party, forced the administration to abandon these plans.

31. "No Curfew on Korean Cram Schools," *Reuters*, May 25, 2009, http://www.asia one.com/News/Education/Story/A1Story20090525-143642.html, accessed June 17, 2009.

32. Dong-seok Sah, "Private Education and Teachers," *Korea Times*, June 3, 2009.

33. Shin-who Kang, "English Most Troublesome for NK Refugee Students," *Korea Times*, July 17, 2009.

34. In Whoe Kim and Terri Kim, "Globalization and *dirigisme*: Teacher Education in South Korea," in *Teacher Education: Dilemmas and Prospects*, ed. Thomas E. Kogan (London: Page Limited, 2002), 36.

35. Ministry of Education, Science and Technology, "Statistical Overview" http://english.mest.go.kr/main.jsp?idx=0401010101, accessed August 25, 2009.

36. United Nations, Population Division, Department of Economic and Social Affairs, "World Population Prospects, the 2008 Revision."

37. *CIA World Factbook*, "South Korea," https://www.cia.gov/library/publications/the -world-factbook/geos/ks.html.

38. World Resources Institute, 2007. *EarthTrends: Environmental Information,* Washington: World Resources Institute, http://earthtrends.wri.org, accessed August 14, 2009.

CHAPTER 10. THE CONUNDRUM OF TRANSFORMATIVE ISSUES

1. Ashley Rowland and Hae-rym Hwang, "North Korean Defectors Struggle to Make it Work," *Stars and Stripes*, Pacific Edition, July 26, 2009.

2. Bidet, "Social Capital and Work Integration of Migrants," 157.

3. Kelly Koh and Glenn Baek, "North Korean Defectors: A Window into a Reunified Korea," in *Korea Briefing 2000-2001: First Steps toward Reconciliation and Reunification*, ed. Kongdan Oh and Ralph C. Hassig (Armonk, NY: M.E. Sharpe, 2002), 214–15.

4. Ibid.

5. Lankov, "A Bitter Taste on Paradise," 117.

6. Yoon and Lim, "Social Adjustments," 3.

7. Koh and Baek, "North Korean Defectors," 214.

8. Ibid., 118.

9. Jae-jean Suh, "The Settlement of North Korean Defectors," *East Asian Review* 14:3 (Autumn 2002): 81.

10. Bidet, "Social Capital and Work Integration of Migrants," 152.

11. Ibid.

12. Ibid., 153.

13. Aung Tin Htun and Robert Prey, "Life as a Foreign Migrant Worker," *Korea Times*, May 29, 2007.

14. Bidet, "Social Capital and Work Integration of Migrants," 152.

15. Sue-young Kim, "N. Korean Defectors Earn Less Than W1 Mil. Per Month," *Korea Times*, March 24, 2009.

16. Bidet, "Social Capital and Work Integration of Migrants," 162.

17. Ibid., 162.

18. Ibid., 163.

19. Ji-hong Kim, Taejong Kim, and Insook Lee, "Economic Assimilation of North Korean Refugees in South Korea: Survey Evidence," *KDI Working Paper Series*, 06-19 (December 2006): 9.

20. Kim, "Job Fair Planned for N. Koreans Tomorrow."

21. Kim, Kim, and Lee, "Economic Assimilation," 7.

22. Sue-young Kim, "Communication Problem Haunts N. Korean Defectors," *Korea Times*, June 25, 2008.
23. Yoon and Lim, "Social Adjustments," 5.
24. Andrei Lankov, "Gaesong Industrial Complex Faces Serious Threat," *Korea Times*, May 15, 2009.
25. Yoon and Lim, "Social Adjustments," 12.
26. Jae-jean Suh, "North Korean Defectors: Their Adaptation and Resettlement," *East Asian Review* 14, no. 3 (Autumn 2002): 76.
27. Si-soo Park, "Defectors Struggle in Capitalist South," *Korea Times*, May 25, 2008.
28. Yoon and Lim, "Social Adjustments," 8.
29. Ibid.
30. Jeon, "Issues and Problems of Adaptation," 366.
31. Kim and Jang, "Aliens Among Brothers?," 13.
32. Ibid., 14.
33. Park, "Defectors Struggle in Capitalistic South."
34. Soo-hyun Rhee, "North Korean Defectors in South Korea," *Korea Times*, July 23, 2008.

CHAPTER 11. BEYOND THE FORMATIVE AND TRANSFORMATIVE

1. Andrei Lankov, "The Changing Realities of Life for Average North Koreans," Yonhap News Service, July 9, 2009, http://english.yonhapnews.co.kr/northkorea/2009/07/06/4/0401000000AEN20090706000800325F.HTML, accessed November 15, 2009.
2. *CIA World Factbook*, "North Korea," https://www.cia.gov/library/publications/the-world-factbook/geos/kn.html.
3. *CIA World Factbook*, "South Korea."
4. United Nations World Food Program, "WFP Launches Emergency Operation to Support 3.5 mln Vulnerable People in DPRK," April 29, 2011, http://www.wfp.org/news/news-release/wfp-launches-emergency-operation-support-35-mln-vulnerable-people-dprk, accessed May 27, 2011.
5. Bomi Lim and Sungwoo Park, "Sick Oxen May Rattle Kim Jong Il Regime as Food Shortages Worsen," Bloomberg.com, February 11, 2011, http://www.bloomberg.com/news/2011-02-11/north-korea-reports-foot-and-mouth-outbreak-amid-food-shortages.html, accessed May 29, 2011,.
6. Blaine Harden, "At the Heart of North Korea's Troubles, an Intractable Hunger Crisis," Washington Post.com, March 6, 2009, http://www.washingtonpost.com/wp-dyn/content/article/2009/03/05/AR2009030503613.html?sid=ST2009030600104, accessed November 15, 2009.
7. Ibid.
8. Ibid.
9. World Health Organization, "WHO Assists North Korea in Controlling Measles Outbreak," http://www.who.int/immunization/newsroom/north_korea_measles/en/, accessed November 15, 2009.
10. Hyun-kyung Kang, "Save N. Korean Children with Vaccines," *Korea Times*, February 25, 2009.
11. Organization for Economic Cooperation and Development, "OECD Health Data 2009," November 9, 2009, http://www.oecd.org/document/16/0,3343,en_2649_34631_2085200_1_1_1_1,00.html, accessed November 20, 2009.
12. Ibid.

13. Tsuneo Akaha, "Cross-Border Human Flows in Northeast Asia," *Migration Information Source*, Monterey Institute of International Studies (October 2004), http://www.migrationinformation.org/feature/display.cfm?ID=257, accessed November 16, 2009.
14. Lankov, "The Changing Realities."
15. Hyun-kyung Kang, "Female NK Refugees Undergo Anxiety Disorder," *Korea Times*, November 17, 2009.
16. Kim Jong-il, "The Welfare State in South Korea: Where It Stands and Where It Is Headed," *Gastvortrag am* (June 26, 2007): 4–5.
17. Ibid.
18. Ibid.
19. Ibid.

CHAPTER 12. A REGIONAL PERSPECTIVE

1. Youngho Kim, "The Great Powers in Peaceful Korean Unification," *International Journal on World Peace* 20, no. 3 (2003): 1.
2. Fei-Ling Wang, "Joining the Major Powers for the Status Quo: China's Views and Policy on Korean Reunification," *Pacific Affairs* 72, no. 2 (Summer 1999): 167.
3. Ibid.
4. Goohoon Kwon, "A United Korea?: Reassessing North Korea Risks (Part I)," *Goldman Sachs Global Economics, Commodities and Strategy Research*, Global Economics Paper no. 188 (September 21, 2009): 10, http://www.scribd.com/doc/20520995/North-Korea-Goldman-Sachs, accessed December 6, 2009.
5. Ibid.
6. Bruce Cumings, "The United States and Korean Unification," *The Center for International Policy's Asia Program*, http://www.ciponline.org/asia/reports/task_force/Cumings.htm, accessed December 1, 2009.
7. Ibid.
8. Chung-un Cho, "Korea Relies on 10 Major Partners for 60% of Trade," *Korea Herald*, November 27, 2009.
9. Qingfen Ding, "China-ROK Free Trade Deal Urged," *China Daily*, November 24, 2009.
10. "S. Korea's Foreign Direct Investment Nearly Halves in 2009," *Xinhua News Agency*, November 4, 2009.
11. "China, NK Trade Boom Despite Rocket Tensions," AFP, April 5, 2009.
12. Tae-gyu Kim, "N. Korea Suffers Trade Deficit for Two Decades," *Korea Times*, May 24, 2010.
13. Ibid.
14. Michael Yoo, "Why Korea Perceives China as an Opportunity Rather than a Threat," *Research Institute of Economy, Trade and Industry*, May 8, 2003, http://www.rieti.go.jp/users/michael-yoo/cfk-en/04.html, accessed on November 20, 2009.
15. Tania Branigan and Jonathan Watts, "Muslim Uighurs Riot as Ethnic Tensions Rise in Western China," *The Guardian*, July 5, 2009, http://www.guardian.co.uk/world/2009/jul/05/china-uighur-riots-xianjing, accessed November 20, 2009.
16. Wang, "Joining the Major Powers," 179.
17. Michael H. Armacost and Kenneth B. Pyle, "Japan and the Unification of Korea: Challenges for U.S. Policy Coordination," *NBR Analysis* 10, no. 1 (March 1999): 9.
18. Victor Cha, "Defensive Realism and Japan's Approach toward Korean Unification," *NBR Analysis* 14, no. 1 (June 2003): 10.

19. "China, Japan, South Korea: Cooperation and the East Asian Giants," *STRATFOR Global Intelligence*, October 13, 2009.
20. Leonid Petrov, "Russia's 'Power Politics' and North Korea," *Policy Forum Online* (Nautilus Institute) 08-061A (August 8, 2008), http://www.nautilus.org/fora/security/08061Petrov.html, accessed November 30, 2009.
21. Ibid.
22. Russian Embassy in the Republic of Korea, "Relations between Russia and the Republic of Korea," http://www.russian-embassy.org/english/political.html, accessed December 1, 2009.
23. "Researchers: Sino-Russian Joint Military Exercise a Warning to Terrorists," *Xinhua*, July 22, 2009, http://english.sina.com/china/2009/0721/257482.html, accessed November 30, 2009.
24. Tony Wood, "The Case for Chechnya," *The New Left Review* 30 (November-December 2004), http://newleftreview.org/A2533, accessed December 1, 2009.
25. Petrov, "Russia's 'Power Politics' and North Korea."
26. Ibid.
27. David E. Sanger, "U.S. Weighs Intercepting North Korean Shipments," *New York Times*, June 7, 2009.
28. Richard Behar and Brenda Cherry, "Rummy's North Korea Connection: What Did Donald Rumsfeld Know about ABB's Deal to Build Nuclear Reactors There? And Why Won't He Talk about It?," CNNMoney.com, May 12, 2003, http://money.cnn.com/magazines/fortune/fortune_archive/2003/05/12/342316/, accessed on December 1, 2003.

CHAPTER 13. CONCLUSION: PARADISE POSTPONED?

1. Hans Maretzki, "Korean Unification in Light of the German Experience," *Asia Europe Journal* 3, no. 1 (March 2005): 63–77.
2. Leonid A. Petrov, "Neo-cons in Pyongyang," *Korea Times*, December 9, 2008.
3. Ibid.
4. Ibid.
5. "Koreans Sober about Unification," *Korea JoongAng Daily*, October 12, 2005.
6. Cheoleon Lee, "Implications of Reunification of Two Koreas," Gallup News Service, October 12, 2006, http://www.gallup.com/poll/24949/gallup-world-poll-implications-reunification-two-koreas.aspx?version=print, accessed November 26, 2009.
7. Sun-young Park, "Shinsedae: Conservative Attitudes of a 'New Generation' in South Korea and the Impact on the Korean Presidential Election," *EWC Insights* (East-West Center) 2, no. 1 (September 2007), http://scholarspace.manoa.hawaii.edu/bitstream/10125/3772/1/Insights00201.pdf, accessed October 1, 2009.
8. Hyun-kyung Kang, "China More important Than US for Korea," *Korea Times*, August 14, 2008.
9. "United Korea 'Could Overtake Japan, Germany,'" *Chosun Ilbo*, September 22, 2009, http://english.chosun.com/site/data/html_dir/2009/09/22/2009092200297.html, accessed on November 3, 2009.

Selected Bibliography

MANUSCRIPTS

Bleiker, Roland. *Divided Korea: Toward a Culture of Reconciliation*. Minneapolis: University of Minnesota Press, 2005.

Ch'oe, Yong-ho, Peter H. Lee, and William Theodore de Bary, editors. *Sources of Korean Tradition*. Vol. 2. New York: Columbia University Press, 2000.

Eckert, Carter J., Ki-baik Lee, Young Ick Lew, Michael Robinson, and Edward W. Wagner. *Korea Old and New: A History*. Cambridge, MA: Harvard University Press, 1990.

Fuqua, Jacques L., Jr. *Nuclear Endgame: The Need for Engagement with North Korea*. Westport, CT: Praeger Security International, 2007.

Grinker, Roy Richard. *Korea and Its Futures: Unification and the Unfinished War*. New York: St. Martin's, 1998.

Kim, Hyung-chan, with Dong-kyu Kim. *Human Remodeling in North Korea: A Social History of Education*. Lanham, MD: University Press of America, 2005.

Kim Il Sung. *Kim Il Sung Selected Works V*. Pyongyang: Foreign Languages Publishing House, 1972.

———. *Kim Il Sung Selected Works II*. Pyongyang: Foreign Languages Publishing House, 1968.

Kim, Sun Joo. *Marginality and Subversion in Korea*. Seattle: University of Washington Press, 2007.

Ko, Sung Ho, Kiseon Chung, and Yoo-seok Oh. *North Korean Defectors: Their Life and Well-Being after Defection*. Ford Foundation, 2002.

Koh, Kelly, and Glenn Baek. "North Korean Defectors: A Window into a Reunified Korea." In *Korea Briefing 2000-2001: First Steps Toward Reconciliation and Reunification*, edited by Kongdan Oh and Ralph C. Hassig, 205-26. Armonk, NY: M.E. Sharpe, 2002.

Lee, Ki-baik. *A New History of Korea*. Translated by Edward W. Wagner with Edward J. Shultz. Cambridge, MA: Harvard University Press, 1984.

Lee, Peter H., and Wm. Theodore de Bary, editors. *Sources of Korean History, Volume One*. New York: Columbia University Press, 1997.

Li, Yong Bok. *Education in the Democratic People's Republic of Korea*. Pyongyang: Foreign Languages Publishing House, 1986.

Nahm, Andrew C. *Korea: Tradition and Transformation*. Elizabeth, NJ, and Seoul: Hollym International Corporation, 1991.

Oh, Kongdan, and Ralph C. Hassig. *North Korea through the Looking Glass*. Washington: Brookings Institution Press, 2000.

Reed, Gay Garland, and Yoon-young Kim. "Schooling in North Korea." In *Going to School in East Asia*, edited by Gerard A. Postiglione and Jason Tan, 233-57. Westport, CT: Greenwood Press, 2007.

Shin, Gi-wook. *Ethnic Nationalism in Korea: Genealogy, Politics, and Legacy*. Stanford, CA: Stanford University Press, 2006.

Thomas, Murray R. "The Democratic People's Republic of Korea (North Korea)." In *Schooling in East Asia*, edited by R. Thomas Murray and T. Neville Postlethwaite, 241-62. Elmsford, NY: Pergamon Press, Ltd., 1983.

Wolf, Charles, Jr. "Managing the Costs of Korean Reunification—If It Occurs." In *Straddling Economic and Politics*, edited by Charles Wolf, Jr., 201-4. Santa Monica, CA: RAND, 2002.

———— and Kamil Akramov. *North Korean Paradoxes: Circumstances, Costs and Consequences of Korean Unification*. Santa Monica, CA: RAND, 2005.

Yang, Sung Chul. *The North and South Korean Political Systems: A Comparative Analysis*. Elizabeth, NJ, and Seoul: Hollym, 1999.

PERIODICALS
Journals

Alderman, Harold, John Hoddinott and Bill Kinsey. "Long-Term Consequences of Early Childhood Malnutrition." *Oxford Economic Papers* 58 (2006): 450–74.

Armacost, Michael, and Kenneth B. Pyle. "Japan and the Unification of Korea: Challenges for U.S. Policy Coordination." *NBR Analysis* (National Bureau of Asian Research) 10, no. 1 (March 1999): 5–38.

Bidet, Eric. "Social Capital and Work Integration of Migrants: The Case of North Korean Defectors in South Korea." *Asian Perspective* 33, no. 2 (2009): 151–79.

Cha, Victor. "Defensive Realism and Japan's Approach toward Korean Unification." *NBR Analysis* (National Bureau of Asian Research) 14, no. 1 (June 2003): 5–32.

Chae, Haesook, and Steven Kim. "Conservatives and Progressives in South Korea." *Washington Quarterly* 31, no. 4 (Autumn 2008): 77–95.

Chamberlin, Paul F. "Cultural Dimensions of Korean Reunification: Building a Unified Society." *International Journal on World Peace* 21, no. 3 (September 2004): 3–42.

Choi, Wan-kyu. "North Korea's New Unification Strategy." *Asian Perspective* 25, no. 2 (2001): 99–122.

Chung, Byung-ho. "Between Defector and Migrant." *Korean Studies* 32 (2008): 1–27.

Eberstadt, Nicholas, and Judith Banister. "Divided Korea: Demographic and Socioeconomic Issues for Reunification." *Population and Development Review* 18, no. 3 (September 1992): 505–31.

Hwang, Kyung Moon. "From the Dirt to Heaven: Northern Koreans in the Choson and Early Modern Eras." *Harvard Journal of Asiatic Studies* 62, no. 1 (July 2002): 135–78.

Jeon, Woo-taek. "Issues and Problems of Adaptation of North Korean Defectors to South Korean Society: An In-depth Interview Study with 32 Defectors." *Yonsei Medical Journal* 41, no. 3 (2000): 362–71.

Jo, Yung-hwan, and Stephen Walker. "Divided Nations and Reunification Strategies." *Journal for Peace Research* 9, no. 3 (1972): 247–59.

Kim, Jane. "North Korean Human Rights and Refugee Resettlement in the United States: A Slow and Quiet Progress." *SAIS U.S.-Korea Yearbook* 2008 (2008): 143–59.

Kim, Jih-Un, and Dong-Jin Jang. "Aliens among Brothers? The Status and Perceptions of North Korean Refugees in South Korea." *Asian Perspective* 31, no. 2 (2007): 5–22.

Kim, Joung-won Alexander. "The 'Peak of Socialism' in North Korea: The Five and Seven Year Plans." *Asian Survey* 5, no. 5 (May 1965): 255–69.

————and Myungshin Hong. "The Koreas, Unification and the Great Powers." *Current History* (April 2006): 186–90.

Kim, Samuel S. "North Korea 1999: Bringing the Grand Chollima March Back In." *Asian Survey* 40, no. 1 (January–February 2000): 151–63.

Ko, Sung Ho, Kiseon Chung, and Yoo-seok Oh. "North Korean Defectors: Their Life and Well-Being after Defection." *Asian Perspective* 28, no. 2 (2004): 65–99.

Lankov, Andrei. "Bitter Taste of Paradise: North Korean Refugees in South Korea." *Journal of East Asian Studies* 6 (2006): 105–37.

————. "Koreas Not Eye-to-Eye on Vision 3000." *Policy Forum Online* (Nautilus Institute) 08-045A (June 6, 2008). (Accessed on August 15, 2008 at http://www.nautilus.org/fora/security/08045Lankov.html.)

Lee, Keum-soon. "Cross-border Movement of North Korean Citizens." *East Asian Review* 16, no. 1 (Spring 2004): 37–54.

Moon, Chung-in. "The Kim Dae Jung Government's Peace Policy toward North Korea." *Asian Perspective* 25, no. 2 (2001): 177–98.

Noland, Marcus, and Stephan Haggard. "North Korea in 2007." *Asian Survey* 48, no. 1 (2008): 107–15.

————. "North Korea in 2008: Twilight of the God?," *Asian Survey* 49, no. 1 (2009): 98–106.

Petrov, Leonid. "Russia's 'Power Politics' and North Korea." *Policy Forum Online* (Nautilus Institute) 08-061A (August 8, 2008). (Accessed on November 2, 2009 at http://www.nautilus.org/fora/security/08061Petrov.html.)

Quanyi, Zhang. "What Korean Unification Means to China." *Policy Forum Online* (Nautilus Institute) 07-077A (October 12, 2007). (Accessed on November 1, 2009 at http://www.nautilus.org/fora/security/07077Zhang.html.)

Rhee, Kang-suk. "Korea's Unification: The Applicability of the German Experience." *Asian Survey* 33, no. 4 (April 1993): 360–75.

Roy, Denny. "China and the Korean Peninsula: Beijing's Pyongyang Problem and Seoul Hope." *Asia-Pacific Security Studies* 8, no. 1 (January 2004): 1–4.

Snyder, Scott. "A Framework for Achieving Reconciliation on the Korean Peninsula: Beyond the Geneva Agreement." *Asian Survey* 35, no. 8 (August 1995): 699–710.

Suh, Jae-jean. "North Korean Defectors: Their Adaptation and Resettlement." *East Asian Review* 14, no. 3 (Autumn 2002): 67–86.

Wang, Fei-Ling. "Joining the Major Powers for the Status Quo: China's Views and Policy on Korean Reunification." *Pacific Affairs* 72, no. 2 (Summer 1999): 167–85.

Wolf, Charles, Jr. "Korean Unification: How It Might Come about and at What Cost." *Defence and Peace Economics* 17, no. 6 (December 2006): 681–90.

Yoon, In-jin. "North Korean Diaspora: North Korean Defectors Abroad and in South Korea." *Development and Society* 30, no. 1 (June 2001): 1–26.

Young, Namkoong. "Similarities and Dissimilarities: The Inter-Korean Summit and Unification Formulae." *East Asian Review* 13, no. 3 (Autumn 2001): 59–80.

Zhang, Quanyi. "What Korean Unification Means to China." *Policy Forum Online* (Nautilus Institute) *07-077A* (October 12, 2007). (Accessed October 1, 2009 at http://www.nautilus.org/fora/security/07077Zhang.html.)

Asia Times

Lankov, Andrei. "Working through Korean Unification Blues." *Asia Times On-line*, November 15, 2007. (Accessed on May 30, 2009 at http://www.atimes.com/atimes/Korea/IK15Dg01.html.)

Lee, Sunny. "Defector Deaths Raising Concerns in S. Korea." *Asia Times On-line*, September 15, 2007. (Acessed on May 17, 2009 at http://www.atimes.com/atimes/Korea/II15Dg03.html.)

"North Korea Opens Up Its Mountain." *Asia Times On-line*, November 9, 2007. (Accessed on June 12, 2009 at http://www.atimes.com/atimes/Korea/IK09Dg01.html.)

BBC

Gluck, Caroline. "Korean Defectors Learn Basics." BBC News.com, May 27, 2002. (Accessed on October 12, 2008 at http://news.bbc.co.uk/2/hi/asia-pacific/2006411.stm).

Bloomberg.com

Lim, Bomi. "South Korea May Punish North's Refugees Who Seek Asylum Abroad." Bloomberg.com, October 5, 2008. (Accessed on October 17, 2009 at http://www.bloomberg.com/apps/news?pid=20670001&sid=aRiU__Y8.lMg.)

China Post

"North Koreans Struggle in New Lives in South Korea." *China Post*, August 1, 2009.

Chosun Ilbo

"Closing Kaesong Industrial Complex Would Hit N. Korea Hard." Digital Chosun Ilbo, May 18, 2009. (Accessed July 12, 2009 at http://english.chosun.com/site/data/html_dir/2009/05/18/2009051800226.html.)

"Korean Unification Cost Growing by the Day: Expert." Digital Chosun Ilbo, 2003. (Accessed on June 20, 2009 at http://english.chosun.com/cgi-bin/printNews?id=200506270020.)

"What Koreans Really Think about Ethnic Homogeneity." Digital Chosun Ilbo, September 6, 2007. (Accessed on March 15, 2009 at http://english.chosun.com/cgi-bin/printNews?id=200709060019.)

Christian Science Monitor

Kirk, Don. "N. Korean Defectors Face New Challenges on Journey South." *Christian Science Monitor*, December 29, 2004.

Korea Herald

Shin, Gi-wook. "Ethnic Pride Source of Prejudice, Discrimination." *Korea Herald*, August 2, 2006.

Korea Times

"Anniversary of Summit." *Korea Times*, October 1, 2008.

"Most N. Koreans Don't Receive Rice Aid from South." *Korea Times*, October 9, 2007.

"NK Fires 2 Scud Missiles toward East Sea." *Korea Times*, July 4, 2009.

"S-N Family Reunions Held at Mt. Geumgang." *Korea Times*, September 27, 2009.

Ha, Michael. "Political Survey Points Out Reforming Welfare System." *Korea Times*, May 18, 2008.

Jung, Sung-ki. "More N. Koreans Defecting to South via 3rd Nations." *Korea Times*, March 19, 2008.

————. "N. Korea Lambasts S. Korean Leader." *Korea Times*, April 1, 2008.

————. "President Linking N. Korea Aid to Denuclearization." *Korea Times*, April 17, 2009.

————. "What Will Be China's Role after Collapse of N. Korea?" *Korea Times*, September 22, 2008.

Kang, Hyun-kyung. "China More Important Than US for Korea." *Korea Times*, August 14, 2008.

————. "Female NK Refugees Undergo Anxiety Disorder." *Korea Times*, November 17, 2009.

————. "Save N. Korean Children with Vaccines." *Korea Times*, February 25, 2009.

Kang, Shin-who. "Is Korea Homogeneous Country?" *Korea Times*, December 12, 2008.

Kim, Se-jeong. "Germany Shares Unification Experience with Korea." *Korea Times*, August 30, 2009.

Kim, Sue-young. "Communication Problem Haunts NK Defectors." *Korea Times*, June 25, 2008.

————. "Gaesong Talks Make Little Progress." *Korea Times*, July 2, 2009.

————. "Job Fair Planned for N. Korean Defectors Tomorrow." *Korea Times*, July 14, 2009.

————. "NK Frees Detained Hyundai Worker." *Korea Times*, August 13, 2009.

————. "N. Korea Making Peace Offensive toward S. Korea." *Korea Times*, August 20, 2009.

————. "N. Korean Defectors Earn Less Than W1 Mil. per Month." *Korea Times*, March 24, 2009.

————. "Plight of NK Women Defectors Deepening." *Korea Times*, July 3, 2009.

————. "South Korea Reassesses N. Korea's Motives." *Korea Times*, August 17, 2009.

————. "Three Centers for N. Korean Defectors to Open." *Korea Times*, March 23, 2009.

Kim, Tae-jong. "Depression Hits 70% of Defectors." *Korea Times*, June 26, 2007.

Lankov, Andrei. "Borderline Issues." *Korea Times*, June 24, 2007.

————. "Gaesong Industrial Complex Faces Serious Threat." *Korea Times*, May, 15, 2009.

————. "North Korea Adopts New Propaganda Tool," *Korea Times*, November 23, 2008.

————. "What Will Become of N. Koreans after Unification?" *Korea Times*, October 31, 2008.

Lee, Jin-woo. "NK Demands Wage Hike in Kaesong." *Korea Times*, April 17, 2007.

Na, Jeong-ju. "Lawmakers Urge NK to Set Free S. Korean Worker." *Korea Times*, July 24, 2009.

————. "NK Fires Short-Range Missiles." *Korea Times*, July 2, 2009.

————. "Seoul has No Plan to Send Envoy to N. Korea." *Korea Times*, August 6, 2009.

Park, Si-soo. "Defectors Struggle in Capitalistic South." *Korea Times*, May 25, 2008.

————. "Textbooks to Take on Conservative Overtone." *Korea Times*, August 4, 2009.

Petrov, Leonid A. "Neo-cons in Pyongyang." *Korea Times*, December 9, 2008.

Rhee, Soo-hyun. "North Korean Defectors in South Korea." *Korea Times*, July 23, 2008.

Seok, Kay. "Human Rights in North Korea." *Korea Times*, February 17, 2009.

The Los Angeles Times

Glionna, John M., and Peter Nicholas. "A 'Grand Bargain' for North Korea." *The Los Angeles Times*, November 19, 2009. http://www.latimes.com/news/nationworld/world/la-fg-obama-korea19-2009nov19,0,5275232.story (accessed November 20, 2009.)

NPR

Kuhn, Anthony. "Magazine's Clandestine Look at Life in North Korea." NPR Online, June 23, 2009. (Accessed November 15, 2009 at http://www.npr.org/templates/story/story.php?storyId=105807899.)

Reuters

Herskovitz, John. "North Korean Teen Defectors Get Capitalist Education." *Reuters*, December 2, 2008.

Thatcher, Jonathan. "North Korea Readies Missile, Makes New Threat." *Reuters*, March 26, 2009.

Spiegel Online

Berg, Stefan, Steffen Winter, and Andreas Wassermann. "The Price of a Failed Reunification." *Spiegel Online*, September 5, 2005. (Accessed on September 12, 2009 at http://www.spiegel.de/international/spiegel/0,1518,druck-373639,00.html.)

Stars and Stripes

Rowland, Ashley, and Hwang Hae-rym. "North Korean Defectors Struggle to Make It Work." *Stars and Stripes*, July 26, 2009.

Time

Powell, Bill. "The Next Great North Korean Famine." *Time Online*, May 6, 2008.

UPI Online

Zhang, Quanyi. "Why China Supports Korean Unification." *UPI Asia Online*, November 6, 2008. (Accessed November 23, 2009 at http://www.upiasia.com/Politics /2008/11/06/why_china_supports_korean_unification/2763/?view=print.)

Voice of America

Achin, Kurt. "S. Korean School Isolates N. Korean Defectors to Better Integrate Them." VOA.com, December 4, 2008. (Accessed September 12, 2009 at http://www .voanews.com/english/archive/2008-12/2008-12-04-voa9.cfm.)

Ramirez, Luis. "China Faces Predicament over North Korean Refugees." VOA.com, April 16, 2008. (Accessed September 12, 2009 at http://www.voanews.com/english /archive/2008-04/2008-04-16-voa38.cfm?renderforprint=1&pageid=448551.)

Wall Street Journal

Kissel, Mary. "South Korea's Bulldozer Heads for the White House." *Wall Street Journal*, June 13, 2009.

Washington Post

Faiola, Anthony. "What Do They Want in South Korea?" *Washington Post*, September 8, 2003.

Harden, Blaine. "At the Heart of North Korea's Troubles, an Intractable Hunger Crisis." *Washington Post*, March 6, 2009.

Xinhua

"S. Korea to Build Nursery at Joint Kaesong Industrial Park." *Xinhua.net*, September 22, 2009. (Accessed on October 12, 2009 at http://news.xinhuanet.com/english /2009-09/22/content_12096106.htm.)

Yonhap News Service

"N. Korean Defectors under Spotlight after Arrest of Woman Spy Suspect." Yonhap News Service, September 4, 2008.

Kim, Hyun. "Hanawon Center, a Litmus Test for How Koreas Can Unite." Yonhap News Service, July 1, 2009.

GOVERNMENT SOURCES

Manyin, Mark E. (2007). "CRS Report for Congress: Japan-North Korea Relations: Selected Issues." Congressional Research Service: Washington. (Accessed on February 14, 2008 at https://www.policyarchive.org/bitstream/handle/10207/1888/RL32161_20031126.pdf.)

Margesson, Rhoda, Emma Chanlett-Avery, and Andorra Bruno (2007). CRS Report to Congress: North Korean Refugees in China and Human Rights Issues: International Repsonse and U.S. Policy Options." Congressional Research Service: Washington. (Accessed on September 5, 2009 at http://www.fas.org/sgp/crs/row/RL34189.pdf.)

Nanto, Dick K. (2003). "CRS Report to Congress: North Korea: Chronology of Provocation, 1950-2003." Congressional Research Service: Washington. (Accessed on August 15, 2009 at http://www.fcnl.org/pdfs/NKprovocations.pdf.)

————, and Mark E. Manyin (2008). "CRS Report to Congress: The Kaesong North-South Korean Industrial Complex." Congressional Research Service: Washington. (Accessed on September 11, 2009 at http://www.nautilus.org/fora/security/07061CRS.pdf.)

Refugee Review Tribunal (Australia). "RRT Research Response (Korea)." January 24, 2005. (Accessed on August 7, 2009 at http://www.mrt-rrt.gov.au/docs/research/KOR/rr/KOR17175.pdf.)

U.S. National Intelligence Council. "Strategic Implications of Global Health (2008)." (Accessed on July 21, 2009 at http://www.dni.gov/nic/PDF_GIF_otherprod/ICA_Global_Health_2008.pdf.)

Index

About the Author

Currently the Assistant Provost for International Affairs and chief international officer at Auburn University at Montgomery, Jacques Fuqua is a retired U.S. Army officer who served the last twelve years of his career as a foreign area officer in Japan and South Korea, involved in various international security negotiations. He is author of *Nuclear Endgame: The Need for Engagement with North Korea* (Praeger Security International, 2007). He has taught Japanese history at the University of Maryland (Asia Division), and "The History of East Asian Diplomacy (1844–Present)" and "The History of Korean Diplomacy (1392–Present)" at Indiana University (Bloomington) and the University of Illinois at Urbana-Champaign.